If you're passionate about i   erful book for fresh ideas t

—C

I love the biblical basis of this powerful book. If you want to saturate your city with the living water of Jesus, I dare you to pray the bold prayer that the leaders of Liquid Church prayed.

—**MARK BATTERSON,** author, *The Circle Maker*;
lead pastor, National Community Church

This book will grip you. In my view, the chapter on preaching is worth the price of the book alone. If you want to reach the next generation of young adults, you've picked the right book.

—**CAREY NIEUWHOF,** host, *The Carey Nieuwhof Leadership Podcast*

Offers practical and inspired strategies for our dried-up and tired ministry models. I highly recommend this resource as a trustworthy guide to innovative ministry for your context.

—**KADI COLE,** leadership consultant; author,
Developing Female Leaders; kadicole.com

Reads like a *Purpose-Driven Church* for today's generation of leaders. This book should be on every church leader's required reading list for making an impact in their community.

—**RICH BIRCH,** host, *unSeminary* podcast;
author, *Church Growth Flywheel*

Offers a rare combination of timeless truth and cultural relevance. Grab your team and work your way through these ideas and insights together. You'll be glad you did.

—**LARRY OSBORNE,** pastor, North Coast
Church; author, *Thriving in Babylon*

Brings practicality and passion together like two rivers converging toward an ocean of possibilities. Read it and realize your church's full potential.

—**WAYNE FRANCIS,** lead pastor, Authentic Church; @waynefrancis

What a gift! Hundreds of thousands are grateful that God inspired Tim to pray, "Open my eyes, Lord," which God did. And so will this beautiful book.

—**MICHAEL J. MANTEL,** president and
CEO, Living Water International

Read this book and you'll be not only reshaping your perspective on reaching people for years to come but also putting its ideas into action this week.

—**MARK JOHNSTON,** lead pastor, The Journey Church

This book is fresh, vivid, and compelling. Read it and get ready to catch an ancient vision made new for today's generation.

—**WILLIAM VANDERBLOEMEN,** founder and
CEO, Vanderbloemen Search Group

Rick Warren's *Purpose Driven Church* changed the landscape for a generation of leaders. I see this book doing the same for this generation and beyond.

—**TOM KANG,** lead pastor, NewStory Church

If soul winning is your focus, let Tim mentor you on how to contextualize the gospel to effectively engage today's culture.

—**DAVID D. IRELAND,** lead pastor; author,
One in Christ; www.DavidIreland.org

The six principles in this book have worked in New Jersey; I've stolen many of them over the years and they have worked on Long Island as well. I'm sure they will work for you too.

—**BRIAN MCMILLAN,** lead pastor, CenterPoint Church

Inspiring and practical! This book will not only give you hope for the future of your church but also equip you to see those hopes come to fruition.

—**JENNI CATRON,** author, *The Four
Dimensions of Extraordinary Leadership*

Not only will this book inspire you but it will also challenge you to go into the deep with the Holy Spirit. It truly renews passion, hope and faith for revival now and for future generations.

—**ANDI ANDREW,** cofounder, Liberty Church;
founder, She Is Free; speaker; author

When you're setting out to learn something, make sure you learn from someone who is winning at it. When it comes to reaching your city, Tim is definitely one of those who is winning at it.

—**DINO RIZZO,** executive director, ARC
(Association of Related Churches)

LIQUID CHURCH

LIQUID CHURCH

6 POWERFUL CURRENTS TO SATURATE YOUR CITY FOR CHRIST

TIM LUCAS

AND WARREN BIRD

ZONDERVAN REFLECTIVE

Liquid Church
Copyright © 2019 by Tim Lucas and Warren Bird

Requests for information should be addressed to:
Zondervan, *3900 Sparks Dr. SE, Grand Rapids, Michigan 49546*

ISBN 978-0-310-10010-2 (softcover)

ISBN 978-0-310-11262-4 (audio)

ISBN 978-0-310-10011-9 (ebook)

Cover design: Tim Green / Faceout Studio
Cover art: Kotoffei / iStockphoto
Interior design: Kait Lamphere

Printed in the United States of America

19 20 21 22 23 24 25 26 27 28 29 /LSC/ 15 14 13 12 11 10 9 8 7 6 5 4 3 2 1

Tim dedicates this book to his wife, Colleen, who helped birth Liquid all those years ago. Who knew the grand adventure God had in store for us, sweet girl?

To our children, Chase and Del, who will one day write new chapters for their generation.

And to our Liquid Church family: it's the thrill of our lives to love, laugh, cry, play, and serve Christ and his kingdom with each of you.

CONTENTS

FOREWORD

Many church leaders tell me the reason their church isn't growing is because of their context. The problem, they say, is that it's just not in the right city or neighborhood. Or their church is in a hard-to-reach state or region of the country.

Plus, many say, young adults are almost impossible to reach. And if you do reach them, they don't give, serve, or really get behind the mission.

At some point, the conversation turns to how people are consumed by travel sports, vacations, time at the lake house, and almost anything other than church. Then when you finally think you're catching a break, the weather turns. "Last month all the Sundays were too cold/hot/sunny/cloudy/snowy/rainy/windy and, as a result, attendance tanked." (Not kidding, I have actually had a church leader tell me the reason their attendance struggled was wind.)

So this is a book about a church in New Jersey that's crushing it with thousands of unchurched people—specifically, millennials, gen zers, and young families.

Did you catch that? *Jersey*. Thousands upon thousands of *millennials* in *Jersey*.

Not to insult New Jersey, but if you were sitting in a board room praying and strategizing about where to plant a church that's going to saturate its state with the gospel and reach the next generation for Christ, the guy who raises his hand and suggests Parsippany, New Jersey, is probably not going to get invited back to the next meeting.

But over the last decade, in Parsippany, New Jersey (and six other Liquid Church locations), thousands of people who had no religion, who called themselves spiritual but not Christian, or who were simply done with the faith their parents (sort of) had, have given their lives to Jesus and leaned hard into the mission of the church.

For the record, I'm taking notes. And that's why I'm so grateful for this book. I've known Tim Lucas and some of the other leaders at Liquid for a number of years and followed the story of Liquid Church almost from the beginning. In this book, Tim tells the story of Liquid Church in his signature funny, quirky, honest way. This book will grip you, just like Tim's teaching and leadership have gripped so many thousands of people in the Northeast and beyond.

This powerful book does more than just tell the Liquid story, though. It can help you rethink yours. Since your community has unique challenges for connecting thirsty people to the living water of Jesus, it requires a saturation strategy all of its own. Good news: many chapters conclude with guidance for how to do just that.

Tim Lucas and Warren Bird weave beautiful threads of narrative, personal stories, and data on our culture to share Liquid's successful strategy for reaching and discipling today's generations.

In my view, the chapter on preaching (chapter 5) is worth the price of the book alone. If that's not enough, Liquid has a fascinating approach to social justice and community outreach that is resonating with young adults at a deep level. How deep? Well, they have a waiting list for volunteers. Yes, people have to go on a waiting list to serve at Liquid. Crazy.

Best of all, Tim brings a refreshing honesty. This book isn't all about wins and miracles. There are many losses and mistakes along the way.

This book is real life, just like your life and mine.

So if you want to reach the next generation of young adults, you've picked up the right book. Amazingly, thousands of people show up at Liquid every weekend whether it's windy or not.

Here's to many more churches reaching the next generation. Including yours.

—*Carey Nieuwhof, author and founding pastor, Connexus Church*

INTRODUCTION

I (Tim) remember the moment the ambulance arrived in the middle of our Sunday service. Liquid Church was only a year old, and we were meeting in a hotel ballroom. Standing behind the pulpit, I watched the paramedics wheel a stretcher down the center aisle and thought, *Our church will never survive this.*

Moments earlier, I had held up a sock that appeared to be soaked in blood. It was part of a sermon illustration about the dangers of overworking and ignoring God's command to rest. I told the story of how baseball pitcher Curt Schilling had played with a torn tendon in his ankle in a key game against the Yankees. Preparing for another game in the series, Schilling told team doctors to staple his torn tendon to his anklebone, stitch him up, and shoot him full of painkillers. They did as they were told, and the Red Sox flamethrower took the mound to face his archrivals. That was the day Schilling became a legend. With every pitch he threw, the sutures in his ankle tore open. The tendon slowly ripped away from his bone. Blood began oozing through his sock—a bright red bull's-eye enlarging with every pitch.

In retrospect, I probably should have run this story by my wife. It was a bit graphic. But I was a sports fan and wanted our congregation to see how our culture celebrates those who push past their breaking point. (Fact: Schilling's bloody sock is today in the Baseball Hall of Fame.)[1]

To illustrate my sermon example, I had a clever idea, or so I thought! The night before my message, I took a white athletic sock from my dresser and stained it with bright red paint from my daughter's finger-painting set. The result looked quite real. Holding it up, I thought, *This prop will make an impact.* Did it ever.

That Sunday as I preached, our church video team projected my bloody sock on the giant screen over the altar. As I held it up—now ten times its normal size thanks to the video magnification—it had a serious impact.

Vividly describing the ghastly torn tendon, I saw a man in the first row sway back and forth in his seat and fall on the floor. Face-plant. Passed out cold.

I figured the Holy Spirit had knocked him over. And I kept right on preaching.

Moments later, a woman in the back screamed. The man sitting behind her had vomited onto her hair. I had wanted my example to touch people, but not that way!

A murmur rippled through the crowd; either the Holy Spirit was moving or something sinister was at work. "They're gassing us!" a woman yelled. "Call 911!"

The paramedics confirmed what none of us had guessed. The man in the first row was overcome by a vasovagal seizure; the sight of blood (bright-red finger paint) on the big screen had caused him to faint. The person in the back who had vomited also had been overcome.

My preaching made him puke.

Such is the start of an inexperienced preacher and a year-old church plant. My Sunday sermon sent two people to the hospital. (They fully recovered and returned the next week, thank God.)

> We boldly failed forward and learned a lot in the process. The entire story of Liquid Church is like that.

Looking back a little more than ten years later, we now laugh and refer to that infamous service as Bloody Sock Sunday. It was also the weekend we discovered the power of show-and-tell communication, video, IMAG (image magnification), and visual preaching. This was the messy birth behind our media ministry, which is a cornerstone of Liquid Church today. (I'll say more in chapter 5, "Ignite the Imagination: Creative Communication.")

Leveraging visual storytelling in our ministry started by accident.

Although folks puked and passed out at first, we boldly failed forward and learned a lot in the process. The entire story of Liquid Church is like that—a series of happy accidents that God somehow redeemed and turned into one of America's 100 Fastest Growing Churches.[2] More important, we believe God used our stumbling efforts to teach us something powerful—and transferrable to other churches—about reaching today's show-and-tell culture. (More on that momentarily.)

HOW DO YOU REACH THIRSTY GENERATIONS?

No doubt, you have your own war stories to tell, ministry moments that made you laugh and some that made you cry. This book is full of both. Whether you serve a brand-new church plant or an aging congregation ready for reinvention, we want to encourage you with inspiring stories of God at work in spite of leadership failures. We want to alert you to fresh and creative ways to communicate the gospel to new generations in a rapidly changing world.

In these pages, we spotlight six ministry currents the Holy Spirit is blessing not just in our region but across America in churches of every shape and size.

These currents include special needs, creative communication, a focused compassionate cause, ministry mergers, guilt-free giving, and untapped leadership talent. More than anything, we want to challenge you to consider whether the currents we highlight are ones the Holy Spirit is leading your church to leverage to saturate your city with the gospel, and if they are not, we will help you identify trickles and currents more fitting to your city and context.

If there's a theme to unite the six currents and to explain why they connect with today's culture, it ties back to something you probably learned (and loved!) in kindergarten: show-and-tell. Remember that? I remember loving as a boy the classroom exercise in which kids first displayed an item (show) and then talked about it (tell). One time, I brought a brand-new toy fire engine to school for show-and-tell. I remember holding up the little red truck in front of the class and dramatically pulling out the long ladder and uncoiling the hose. The class was riveted. When I showed how the hose squirted water, their eyes grew wide in amazement. And I hadn't even spoken a word yet. Then I told them a few facts about firefighters and the hands shot up with questions. Talk about audience engagement; that's the power of show-and-tell. Or should I say show-then-tell?

For the last five hundred years, the bias at most churches has been to tell the gospel first—to declare and explain the truth of God's Word and then to show, to demonstrate its power with action. But to reach today's increasingly postmodern, skeptical (or even cynical) culture, it's critical that leaders learn to show-then-tell—to demonstrate the gospel's truth with our works before we declare it with our words. Each current in this book involves first showing the gospel as a way of earning credibility first—or at least stoking curiosity—then telling the gospel. (And as we introduce each current, we'll show you, and then we'll tell, and perhaps that can become a model for how you introduce these currents to your church as well.)

We're going to dive into the story of Liquid Church, applying it to small, medium, and large churches—any church wanting to reach new generations and impact their city for Christ. Our prayer is that we'll fuel your eagerness to identify and ride one of the waves that God is cresting through his church to impact the city you serve.

We get it: your village, town, suburb, or city is unique. But it's probably full of thirsty people—men and women, young and old—who have given up on church (or religion in general) but haven't given up on God. When Jesus crossed racial, gender, and religious boundaries to interact with the Samaritan woman at the well (John 4), he didn't see merely a notorious sinner in need of saving; he saw a spiritually thirsty person worth loving. Her subsequent salvation had a ripple effect that evangelized an entire town.

> Your village, town, suburb, or city is full of thirsty people—men and women, young and old—who have given up on church (or religion in general) but haven't given up on God.

Ministry momentum is like that. It's like a wave driven by invisible currents that God uses to saturate a city. We believe he wants to use your church in a new way to have more impact than ever before on reaching lost people.

WARNING: THIS BOOK WILL BE WET!

The vision of Liquid Church is to saturate the state of New Jersey with the gospel of Jesus Christ. Our state is both spiritually dry and densely packed—more than nine million people squeezed together into a tiny place where most of them couldn't care less about going to church.[3] If saturate means to soak something thoroughly with liquid, we want every person to be so touched by the living water of Jesus' grace that they have repeated opportunities for their souls to be refreshed by God. Most of us needed many exposures to the gospel before our hearts softened, and that's why we're drawn to the concept of saturation. Our saturation strategy in the Northeast may be unique, but we've followed principles that can apply to a church of any size in any region.

In the opening chapter of this book, we'll share the inspiring vision of Ezekiel (Ezek. 47:1–12) which describes a liquid church. The Old Testament prophet had a vivid vision of water flowing out of God's temple—a tiny trickle that grew into a raging river, a Spirit-empowered force that saturated and infused everything it touched with new life.

Building on that prophetic picture, the liquid metaphor runs wild through the pages of this book. Rivers are powerful and represent the Spirit of God flowing through his church. So buckle up: you're in for a whitewater ride! We'll describe the ways that streams of ministry become powerful currents, how spiritually thirsty people find refreshment, how dry regions become saturated with the living water of Jesus, and more. At numerous points, we'll help you apply our ideas to your ministry.

Charles Finney once likened his experience with the Holy Spirit to being overcome by "waves and waves of liquid love."[4] We like that. Waves of liquid love. Surf's up, friends. Let's ride the Spirit's waves together!

HOW THE BOOK FLOWS

With that setup, here's how the book flows. Part 1, titled "Living Water Running Wild," introduces lead pastor Tim Lucas, our church's story, and the main metaphor for this book. Chapter 1, inspired by Ezekiel's vision, dares you to imagine that God can use your church to take the gospel and spread it to the point of saturation—not a sprinkle or trickle but an unstoppable river of hope in whatever city you serve. Chapter 2 tells the backstory of the "accidental birth" of Liquid Church and how it became one of America's fastest growing churches with more than 2,400 baptisms in its first twelve years. Chapter 3 explains Liquid Church's saturation strategy in an environment where many have given up on church but not on God.

Next comes part 2, the heart of the book. It's titled "Six Currents That Form a Powerful River," and each chapter highlights one ministry idea that started as a trickle but has become a powerful current driving evangelistic impact, compassionate service, and explosive church growth in our community. One way to remember our six currents is by the acronym LIQUID, which quickly summarizes our strategic approach in a post-Christian culture: Love the overlooked (chap. 4), Ignite the imagination (chap. 5), Quench their thirst (chap. 6), Unite the generations (chap. 7), Inspire generosity (chap. 8), and Develop untapped talent (chap. 9). Together, these six LIQUID currents combine to generate tremendous ministry momentum in our rapidly changing, skeptical twenty-first-century culture. Each speaks to the show-then-tell climate that seems to communicate so well today.

Each chapter in part 2 includes a section titled "Every River Starts with a Trickle" to show the baby steps Liquid Church took in faith on a small scale with limited resources. That's the cool thing about Spirit-led momentum—you don't need a ton of cash or sophisticated strategies to make an impact. You just need a willingness to read the cultural currents, take a step of faith out of your boat to follow Jesus, and trust the Spirit for the outcome.

Wanna dive deeper? Each chapter in the book ends with discussion questions for three levels of engagement. We had a handful of people read an early draft, and every single one highlighted this "Dive Deeper" section as one of their favorite features of the book, so plan to think through these questions, either individually or in a discussion group. At the end of each chapter in part 2, we also include sections called "The Broader Current" and "Other Churches Making Waves" with links to inspiring churches that are pioneering best ministry practices and ideas to impact your city.

The third and final part of the book will show you another biblical foundation for the idea of a river that brings spiritual life in Christ (chap. 10). Then chapters 11 and 12 will guide you through some next steps to take as you prayerfully consider which currents God wants you to pursue. There you'll discover some easily accessible launch points in the river to get your journey started.

TOLD FROM TIM'S VOICE

The "we" behind this book are Tim Lucas, founding pastor of Liquid Church, and Warren Bird, a board member there and a national researcher. Every sentence and paragraph in this book is the result of a tag team effort, but from this point forward the "we" voice will change to "I"—Tim's voice. Sticking to one voice, we believe, will make the message of the book clearer. Plus, according to both Tim and Warren, Tim's stories are funnier than Warren's statistics. Don't worry: we'll include both stories and statistics so that you're both inspired and informed by innovative ministry ideas as well as national research.

As long as we've introduced the idea of statistics, here's one to start: your city is packed with reachable people who are thirsty for a taste of living water from Jesus. Specifically, among unchurched US adults, 51 percent say they are seeking something better spiritually than what they have experienced.[5] They may have given up on church (with or without ever trying it), but they haven't given up on God.[6]

> Among unchurched US adults, 51 percent say they are seeking something better spiritually than what they have experienced.

Going one step farther, these reachable family members, friends, neighbors, and business associates are far more ready than most Christians realize to talk about spiritual matters. All they need are people living Spirit-saturated stories: scattering seeds, building trust, and creating curiosity about the Jesus we follow.

No matter how dry your city or region of the country is, we want to see it get wet—saturated, soaked, drenched—with the living water of Jesus Christ. I have been convinced from day one that God was birthing something very special at Liquid Church. Many people say the Northeast is a spiritually dry, burned-over region. They describe it as a graveyard for churches (and maybe you feel that way about your area). But I believe a graveyard is the best place to be if you want to witness a resurrection.

Are you ready to dive in?

Part One

LIVING WATER RUNNING WILD

CHAPTER ONE

I DARE YOU TO DIVE DEEPER

*It was a river that I could not cross, because the
water had risen and was deep enough to swim in.*
—EZEKIEL 47:5

I t started with a trickle. A stream so small, Ezekiel almost didn't see
it at first. The angel pointed, and the aging prophet bent over to get
a closer look. Sure enough, there it was: a small, unmistakable flow of
water leaking from under the threshold of the temple.

That's strange, Ezekiel thought. *Did somebody leave the water running? Have the pipes burst in our house of worship? Or maybe the ritual
bath overflowed?* The angel led Ezekiel to show him where the water
was flowing: from the inner sanctuary, out the door, and down the steps.

Ezekiel had always hoped for a vision of God's temple the way he
knew the Lord would one day restore it. But he hadn't expected to
see what today we might call a liquid church—a church with water
spilling down its stairs and out into the city streets.

Walking away from the temple, the angel led Ezekiel into the
water. As Ezekiel waded in, the trickle became a small stream reaching
his ankles. Shuffling along, Ezekiel hiked up his tunic as the water
rose to his knees. Going farther, Ezekiel found himself waist deep in
the rapidly rising current.

It didn't make sense. Rivers don't flow out of temples, and they
certainly don't start small and grow deeper and wider as they go.

But what began as a tiny trickle was now a raging river saturating everything in its path.

The churning liquid swirled around Ezekiel's body. The prophet began to panic as the powerful current swept him off his feet and threatened to carry him downstream. He had to be thinking, *Lord, help me!*

The angel reached down, plucked Ezekiel from the water, and planted him safely on the riverbank. "Do you see this?" the angel asked (Ezek. 47:6), probing whether the prophet understood God's message in the liquid chaos.

Ezekiel squinted into the distance and was astonished by the sight. The river was transforming everything it encountered. Fruit trees flourished along the riverbanks. Schools of fish swarmed in the waters.

Ezekiel's eyes grew wide. In the distance, the swirling river poured into the Dead Sea—the place where nothing grew or lived. The Dead Sea gurgled and churned, the brackish water transforming into pure, crystal-clear, fresh water teeming with new life!

> What began as a tiny trickle was now a raging river saturating everything in its path.

Ezekiel's heart leapt as he watched the river saturate the city and surrounding countryside. Whatever the liquid touched sprang to life! Wherever the water flowed from the liquid church, God's healing and blessing followed.

IS YOUR CITY SPIRITUALLY DRY?

As a pastor, I had read this powerful Old Testament prophecy before but never grasped the power of Ezekiel's vision for churches in the twenty-first century. The post-Christian Northeast where I serve is considered one of the most spiritually dry regions in America.[1] Our broadcast campus is located about twenty-five miles outside of New York City. Although historic revivals bubbled up here in the 1700s and 1800s, those wells have run dry. Younger generations and busy families in the metro area have drifted far from organized religion or regular church attendance.

Sadly, the Northeast is not alone in its spiritual decline. Here's reality across the United States: Perhaps the most prominent example is the rise of the "nones"—those who say they have no religious affiliation. That group has grown rapidly in recent years to 23 percent of the US population—by some calculations even outnumbering evangelicals or Catholics.[2] While many of the nones are more accurately the "dones" (still into God but done with church), atheists and agnostics account for roughly a quarter (27 percent nationally) of all religiously unaffiliated Americans.[3] The national headquarters of American Atheists is located in Cranford, New Jersey, just ten minutes from one of our church campuses.

A second example is the precipitous drop-off in mainline churches. As recently as the 1960s, more than half of all American adults belonged to just a handful of mainline Protestant denominations— Presbyterian, Methodist, Lutheran, Episcopalian, United Church of Christ, Disciples of Christ, and American Baptist. Presidents, congressional representatives, judges, business leaders, and other members of the elite overwhelmingly came from such backgrounds. But by 2010, fewer than 13 percent of US adults belonged to a mainline Protestant church.[4]

Fortunately, many of those people who have given up on church haven't given up on God yet. Although my home state is a spiritually dry place, I believe church should be refreshing. Energizing. Fresh. Replenishing. Like a cold glass of water on a scorching summer day. That's what the radical grace of Jesus is like. And people are desperate for it.

Our church's core group started super small. A dozen twenty-something friends sat on mismatched folding chairs in a cinder block church basement. But we've seen the Holy Spirit pour fresh life into cities and neighborhoods as we reach out to meet the needs of thirsty people. We offer them the unfiltered gospel—the living water of Jesus Christ—which quenches the thirst in the hearts and minds of hipsters, Wall Streeters, former drug dealers, soccer moms, college kids, and teens with autism, from the up-and-comers to the down-and-outers.

After building a core group of three hundred volunteers, we launched Liquid as an independent, nondenominational Christian church, and in a little more than a decade since our launch, we've seen Ezekiel's vision spring to life in the cities where Liquid has campuses, from a tiny trickle to a raging river of more than five thousand weekly worshipers committed to a singular vision: to saturate our state with the gospel of Jesus Christ!

IS THIS GOD'S VISION FOR YOUR CHURCH? FOR YOUR CITY?

Close your eyes and picture the Dead Sea as Ezekiel first saw it—full of stagnant, brackish water. Now imagine it as a picture of what's lifeless in your community that God has chosen your church to resurrect and restore.

Look around: What is dead or dying in your city that needs to be revitalized? What is broken in your community that needs healing? What is dry that needs a fresh outpouring of the Holy Spirit? Which group of spiritually thirsty people has your church been uniquely positioned and called by God to reach?

New Jersey has the highest rate of autism in the nation. This was a clue that sparked Liquid's cutting-edge ministry to families with special needs (which I'll explain in chapter 4, "Love the Overlooked"). As we've reached out to serve children with autism, Asperger's, ADHD, Down syndrome, and more, families with special needs have poured into our church. Instead of experiencing rejection or misunderstanding, they have found a home filled with rest, hope, acceptance, and the radical grace of Jesus!

> What is dead or dying in your city that needs to be revitalized? Which group of spiritually thirsty people has your church been uniquely positioned and called by God to reach?

Ezekiel 47 is a picture of God's preferred future—today's church in the New Testament era, flowing in the power of the Holy Spirit and saturating communities with the living water of Christ. Would you dare to believe God that Ezekiel 47 is a prophecy about the church *you* serve? Could your church become a liquid church, a church flowing in the powerful currents of God's Spirit, bringing life and hope to a brand-new generation of spiritually thirsty people in your city?

My prayer is that God will use your reading of *Liquid Church* to liquefy the church you serve, unleashing the river of Jesus' love into your local community and cities around your region. Before you read another word, would you ask the Spirit for eyes to see how Ezekiel's vision could become your reality as well?

THREE DEGREES OF SATURATION

Behind my house, there's a small creek where I took my kids to catch crayfish when they were little. On hot summer Saturdays, we would put on our Crocs and wade into the tiny stream. My seven-year-old daughter Chase would grip my hand as we inched slowly downstream together. Younger brother Del was more adventurous. He boldly splashed on ahead into deeper water, in pursuit of what he called "crazy crawdaddies!"

One weekend, I took the kids to the creek after a rainstorm. It had poured all night, as in the days of Noah. When we arrived, the stream was swollen. I could see white froth spinning in the whirlpool pockets downstream. Wading in, we felt the cold currents rippling past our ankles. As we inched forward, the current grew stronger. My son bounded fearlessly ahead as usual and disappeared around the corner.

"Daddy!" he cried. I ran to find my five-year-old boy up to his neck in water. He was sputtering and flailing as the creek's current slowly swept him downstream. For a split second, I thought about how I would explain this to my wife and imagined the headline: "Son Swept Away in Crawdaddy Creek: Careless Dad Should've Known Better."

Fortunately, our crawdaddy net has a long handle, so I plunged into the water up to my waist and extended the net. My son grabbed the pole, and I pulled the little guy to safety.

Back on shore, he sniffled, "The water's too deep, Daddy. I like it on my feet, not over my head!"

Our quaint creek had become a swollen stream—in a five-year-old's mind, a raging river.

If you study Ezekiel 47:1–12 (which I strongly encourage), you'll notice a curious detail: the farther the water flows from the temple, the deeper it becomes! Likewise, the farther God's river of life flows from his church, the deeper and wider it becomes.

Look how the angel reveals the increasing depth of the river to Ezekiel: "Measuring as he went, he took me along the stream for 1,750 feet and then led me across. The water was *up to my ankles.* He measured off another 1,750 feet and led me across again. This time the water was *up to my knees.* After another 1,750 feet, it was *up to my waist.* Then he measured another 1,750 feet, and the river was too deep to walk across. It was *deep enough to swim in,* but too deep to walk through" (Ezek. 47:3–5 NLT, emphasis added).

Notice, God's river of living water has three degrees of saturation.

1. Ankle deep
2. Knee deep
3. Waist deep

Eventually, the river becomes too deep to cross, and Ezekiel has a choice: it's sink, swim, or be swept away! Let's imagine that these three liquid levels represent different degrees of Holy Spirit saturation and gospel impact. Some churches are only ankle deep in their current ministry. They long for more response but perhaps are only making inch-deep inroads in their community. Others are knee deep in the Spirit, alive and flowing in high-impact ministry to the spiritually thirsty and broken in their city. Wading deeper still, other churches are waist deep or even over their heads. Through the resurrection power of Christ, they are pioneering new currents of ministry and even raising dead things back to life.

We want to invite you to take your next step, to get your feet wet and discover the deeper currents of the Spirit already at work in your community. Throughout our journey, we'll take a look at cutting-edge, innovative churches who are leading the way in outreach and transforming the cities, towns, suburbs, and regions where they minister. I hope these examples will inspire you to boldly move deeper in the river where you lead. To help identify your next step, each chapter of *Liquid Church* ends with a section called "Dive Deeper" that will provide practical steps you can take in your ministry.

Springboarding off Ezekiel's vision, we'll suggest three degrees of Spirit saturation for increased impact in your community.

ANKLE DEEP This beginning level is for those just getting their feet wet. You may have no sweet clue how to identify and serve families with special needs (chap. 4) or how to give a cup of cold water in Jesus' name (chap. 6) or how to demonstrate radical generosity to your neighbors (chap. 8). That's okay, neither did we; we'll teach you what we've learned.

KNEE DEEP This intermediate level is for those ready to wade into deeper water. In the example of special needs, we'll teach you how to develop a buddy system at your church, in which children with special needs are paired on Sundays with a trained volunteer caregiver so they can be included in mainstream kids' and students' programming. In our leadership chapter (chap. 9), we'll show you how to tap into a hidden vein of volunteers waiting to be empowered in your ministry.

WAIST DEEP This advanced level is for those ready to take a deeper dive and follow the flow of God's Spirit. If you don't have ongoing overseas partnerships that send teams trained in compassion-based evangelization, let's take a deep dive and dream about what's possible!

START SMALL, THEN INCREASE YOUR IMPACT

At what depth would you describe your faith and ministry today? Are you saturating your city for Christ in fresh, innovative ways? Or are you only repeating programs that are past their expiration date?

Is your church consistently baptizing new believers? Do you have a steady flow of new followers of Jesus? Are they mobilized for ministry or paralyzed in the pews? Is your church healing broken lives at a street level?

Don't be discouraged. In God's economy, powerful movements often start small. Before it grew into a raging river, the stream in Ezekiel's vision was just a tiny trickle. Zechariah encourages us, "Do not despise these small beginnings, for the Lord rejoices to see the work begin" (Zech. 4:10 NLT).

So get your feet wet!

DON'T LET FEAR KEEP YOU AT STATUS QUO

Also, don't be afraid to experiment. Before Liquid began launching campuses to reach thousands of people, we were small and scrapped for survival. Our leaders had so many fears and frequently felt overwhelmed (we still do at times!). Breaking out of the status quo can feel scary, but don't let your fears limit what the Lord can do.

- Before we baptized our 2,416th person,[5] there was my first call for baptism, when I boldly asked people to publicly identify with Jesus, and three people said yes.
- Before we pioneered a cutting-edge ministry for families with special needs, I worried that our one-on-one buddy system would cannibalize our already thin volunteer ranks.
- Before five million dollars' worth of church buildings and properties were donated to us, we barely filled a rented ballroom with mediocre music and a portable sound system full of static.
- Before we developed a dynamic communication plan to visually engage the next generation of screenagers, I stayed up until 2:00 a.m. making crappy PowerPoint slides for my Sunday sermon.
- Before we drilled more than 280 clean water wells for thirsty people in Africa and Central America, I seriously wondered whether we could afford to do just one!
- Before we reached a weekend attendance of five thousand people, I begged five friends to help me set up chairs and brew bad coffee in a church basement.
- Before we unleashed a tidal wave of talented volunteers to serve our city and neighbors, I frantically searched for warm bodies just to greet people walking in the front door.

What's my point? I'm not pushing big size so much as big faith—taking big risks for a big God who loves to use humble beginnings to make a huge impact. Before the floodgates open, God often starts small with just a trickle. In hindsight, I realize this is neither a curse nor a test; rather it is a blessing as our Father increases our dependency on his supernatural provision. When the breakthrough finally comes, we can't help but know it's all him!

Whatever form a church takes, Jesus is always inviting his disciples to go deeper: "Put out into deep water, and let down the nets for a catch" (Luke 5:4). For us, the river of life is fed by one church with multiple campuses. For you, it may be planting new churches, mobilizing urban missionaries, launching an inner-city Dream Center, or enlarging a marketplace ministry that floods your neighborhood with new jobs, fresh hope, and life-changing gospel impact.

Don't despair if your church feels stuck; God can get it flowing again. The current of the Holy Spirit is already flowing powerfully beneath the surface of your ministry as you take increasing risks to saturate your city for Christ. One day, by God's grace, that small stream may grow into a raging river for which only God can get the credit.

THE CURRENT CAN CARRY YOU ALONG

I'm a fan of the Pixar movie *Finding Nemo*, which vividly illustrates the power of ocean currents. When a funny little clown fish named Nemo goes missing, his overprotective dad and a forgetful friend named Dory search the sea to find him. When they hear Nemo was last seen swimming south, they don't know what to do, until they run into a stoner sea turtle named Crush.

Crush has droopy eyes and speaks with a surfer's slang. "Duuuudes!" he says. And then he shares a secret. "You need to hitch a ride on the EAC!" The EAC—or East Australian Current—is like a high-speed superhighway in the ocean. In the movie, sea creatures jump off and on this invisible tube of ocean water that rushes along at warp speed. Even turtles ride the express current super fast.

But the EAC isn't a Hollywood invention.[6] In real life, the East Australian Current runs south of the Great Barrier Reef down the east coast of Australia. The current is massive, running sixty-two miles wide and almost a mile deep. While it's not quite the autobahn for aquatic life that *Finding Nemo* depicts, the EAC can reach speeds up to seven kilometers per hour—pretty fast for a turtle!

Try to get your mind around this: this powerful current moves forty million cubic meters of water every single second. Imagine an

Olympic-size swimming pool. Now try to envision 960,000 of these swimming pools (almost a million) being moved every minute by an invisible current flowing under the surface of the sea.

That's a powerful current! Although you can't see it, the current flows with tremendous power. Just like the Holy Spirit. As Jesus told Nicodemus, "The wind blows wherever it pleases. You hear its sound, but you cannot tell where it comes from or where it is going. So it is with everyone born of the Spirit" (John 3:8).

Just as the wind stirs the ocean up, the Holy Spirit creates momentum in Jesus' church to speed its mission, empower its ministry, and embolden its witness. He generates waves of momentum that can shift the direction of a city or state, preparing an entire region for revival.

The skeptic in you might be doubtful when you see a social media post describing spiritual awakenings that caused a dramatic downturn in crime and a spontaneous uptick in good deeds. I'm delighted to report that some of those accounts are true! One person wrote a doctoral dissertation analyzing American revivals and found that they always positively impact the surrounding culture. "The Second Great Awakening [from about 1790 to 1820] resulted in the abolition of slavery, the end of child labor, the beginning of the feminist movement, the move for universal literacy, and the reformation of prisons."[7] It's also inspiring to consider the number of hospitals, universities, and community service organizations (from Goodwill to the Salvation Army) triggered by Christians whose faith motivated them to do good in their cities. One Harvard scholar compared the amount of volunteering, such as helping a neighbor in need, by professing Christians with that by others. The difference was night and day—yes, with Christians resoundingly leading the way![8] The values you model, the priorities you choose for investing your time, talent, and treasure, and even the words of blessing you speak over others—all fulfill what Jesus told his followers: "Let your light shine before others, that they may see your good deeds and glorify your Father in heaven" (Matt. 5:16).

Sometimes I coach church leaders to go with the flow in their city, and they misinterpret what I'm saying. My intention is not to echo Crush the sea turtle: "Duuude, sit back, relax, and just drift along with what's culturally relevant." Rather I challenge leaders to identify where the Holy Spirit is already working in their city. What are the deep needs of people? What is God already blessing? Where is the current of the Spirit already flowing?

To lead a liquid church that saturates your city requires bold questions and risk taking. It's not for leaders who like to drive twenty mph in the right lane with their hazard lights on. It's a thrilling ride marked with sharp turns and some steep drops. But believe me, it's worth it. Just as Nemo's dad rode the EAC all the way to Sydney and found his lost son, you too will rescue lost people whom the Father loves as you follow the flow of his Spirit!

THE BEST IS YET TO COME

Did you know? When Peter preached at Pentecost (Acts 2:14–41), some believe he may have been standing on the southern stairs of the temple from which the water in Ezekiel's vision flowed. This public area contained the *mikvehs* (ceremonial baths) where three thousand people were baptized that day in Jesus' name. Can you imagine the crazy logistics of that baptism service?

That's how Jesus' church was birthed: the Holy Spirit dropped, the waters broke, and the church was born kicking and screaming into a hostile first-century culture. It started with a tiny trickle of ragtag followers who first boldly shared the gospel in their city. First to hundreds, then to thousands. Their ministry became a rapidly rising current, quickly growing from ankles to knees to waist deep as the message spread out to surrounding cities, countries, and eventually the ends of the earth. Talk about a ripple impact!

Good news, leaders: God has more lives ready to be transformed through the flow of your ministry than you think. Even if you feel stalled or stuck, the Holy Spirit can jump-start your ministry to a brand-new season of service to your town, city, or suburb. You may have to let go of some old practices to follow the Spirit's flow to a deeper level of impact, but believe me, with Christ the best is yet to come!

So I'll ask again: What depth of the river are you currently in? What depth do you believe God is calling your church to? What next small step will you take to go with the flow of the Spirit and saturate your city for Christ?

Dive Deeper

As you jump into this journey to explore the spiritual currents in your community, saturate yourself in God's Word.

 ANKLE DEEP Reread Ezekiel 47:1–12. Write down the parallels you see that seem most relevant to the state of your church and your city. Describe the effect of the living water flowing out of the temple and into the surrounding area. Name three or four blessings that result from the rising river. What promises from God do you see here? Ask two or three others to commit to pray daily with you for God to fulfill these promises in your church.

KNEE DEEP Find a partner to pray with you and read this book together. As you process what you're reading, regularly ask each other, "What is the Spirit saying to you? To me? What is God calling each of us to do about it?" At the end of each chapter, explore the links to example churches and talk through the "Dive Deeper" section as it applies to your unique context.

WAIST DEEP Plan a weekend retreat by a lake or a river with three or more ministry leaders. Ask everyone to read this book, journal honestly about where your ministry may be stagnated, and dream out loud about bold new risks to reach your community for Christ. Take regular breaks to play and pray by the water together and soak in the spirit of Ezekiel 47.

CHAPTER TWO

THE ACCIDENTAL BIRTH OF LIQUID CHURCH

> Jesus stood and said in a loud voice, "Let anyone who is thirsty come to me and drink. Whoever believes in me, as Scripture has said, rivers of living water will flow from within them."
> —JOHN 7:37–38

When people hear the name Liquid Church, they assume we're either a cult or a drinking fraternity. But we named our church Liquid for a simple reason: in the gospel of John, Jesus offered living water to thirsty people. And we believe church should be refreshing.

Unfortunately, refreshing isn't a word people in our region typically associate with church. Dry. Boring. Irrelevant. Many are skeptical at best. Folks up and down the East Coast are fleeing the faith in droves, disillusioned by what they see as outdated rules, hollow rituals, and snoozer sermons. My wife attended a parochial school and was taught by a religious instructor who spoke about hell as if she were born and raised there. Like many of our friends, once my wife became a teenager, she was outta there.

The good news is that Jesus didn't die to start a new religion. That wasn't his goal. Rather Jesus came to invite us into a vibrant, grace-based relationship with God that is personal, authentic, and a whole lot messier than most Christians are willing to admit. But if we're willing to follow Christ out of our comfort zone to engage spiritually thirsty people, amazing things can happen.

MARGARITAS IN CHURCH

Tammy and Vanessa were two twentysomething party girls sitting at the bar in our church. I know what you're thinking: *A bar in a church? Now I see why it's called Liquid!* Lemme explain. At the time, our congregation was meeting in the rented upstairs ballroom of a downtown hotel. The hotel lobby included a lounge where people sipped margaritas and watched football on flat-screen TVs.

It was Sunday, and Tammy and Vanessa were sipping Cinco de Mayo specials. Upstairs in our worship service, our band began rocking. The young women asked the bartender, "Where's that music coming from?"

"The band upstairs at Liquid," replied a church volunteer who was handing out programs nearby.

"What's Liquid?" asked Tammy. "A club?" She stirred her drink with a little pink umbrella.

"Come and see," the volunteer said, smiling.

With margaritas in hand, the girls left their barstools and followed the crowd upstairs. Reaching the top, they looked around at the sea of people. Normal-looking people. People wearing shorts and flip-flops. Some dressed in jeans and sundresses. All who fit the look of people going to a concert.

The band was cranking, and as people flowed into the ballroom, Tammy and Vanessa followed. As the crowd took their seats, the girls squeezed into a back row to watch. The band finished their opening set, and a pastor came onstage to pray. And that's when it dawned on them.

"Wait a minute! Is this a church?" Vanessa whispered, looking panicked. Tammy dropped her straw, but it was too late. We slammed the doors and had them trapped!

Just kidding. A volunteer assured them they were most welcome at our church and to sit back, relax, and enjoy the service. We just wouldn't be providing refills.

As I got up to preach, I noticed their nervous faces in the back row. Twentysomething party girls sipping margaritas in what they assumed was Sunday Mass.

"CHEERS, FATHER"

We don't call our worship services Mass at Liquid. Liquid is a non-denominational Christian church. It includes people from all sorts of religious backgrounds, some kicking the tires of spiritual faith for the first time. It doesn't matter whether people grew up Protestant, Catholic, Jewish, or Jedi Knight; at Liquid, everyone is welcome to encounter Jesus. We believe that Christ alone has the power to offer the purpose and meaning we're all thirsting for.

After the service, I shook hands with Tammy and Vanessa on the way out and thanked them for coming. "Absolutely," Tammy said. "This was amazing!"

I'd been teaching from the Bible on God's design for marriage. Vanessa added, "I wish my boyfriend was the kind of man you're talking about. Pray for me, Father."

I smiled and noted that, while I wasn't a priest, I'd be happy to pray for her, and did so. When we finished, Vanessa wiped tears from her eyes. "This is so strange," she said. "I feel like God was speaking directly to me."

"Me too," Tammy agreed. She hoisted her empty margarita glass into the air. "Cheers, Father! We'll be back!"

I smiled as I watched them return to their barstools downstairs, chattering about the role of God in relationships. *Now, that's refreshing,* I thought. I understand that welcoming bar patrons into a worship service may be a stretch for some, but I think Jesus finds it refreshing too.

LOTS OF VANESSAS AND TAMMYS OUT THERE

It's refreshing to discover how many people like Vanessa and Tammy say they are open to an invitation to a life-giving church. By even conservative estimates, one third of Americans—more than one hundred million people—are not active in a church,[1] but most of those people say they would attend if invited in the right manner. One study found that 67 percent of Americans say a personal invitation from a family member would be very or somewhat effective in getting them to visit a church. A personal invitation from a friend or neighbor would effectively reach 63 percent. Nearly two-thirds (63 percent) are very or somewhat willing to receive information about a local congregation or faith community from a family member, and 56 percent are very or somewhat willing to receive such information from a friend or neighbor.[2]

> Sixty-seven percent of Americans say a personal invitation from a family member would be very or somewhat effective in getting them to visit a church. A personal invitation from a friend or neighbor would effectively reach 63 percent.

Not surprisingly, the more often people go to church, the more likely they are to invite someone to go along. Research tells us that nearly two-thirds of Protestant churchgoers say they've invited at least one person to visit their church in the past six months. Interestingly, the regional variation is wide: 58 percent of churchgoers in the Northeast say they have invited someone, while 63 percent of Midwesterners have. By contrast, 76 percent of Southerners and 74 percent of those in the West say they've recently invited someone.[3]

Bottom line: many people are open to a conversation about your church and the Jesus you represent!

But you'll need to overcome some stereotypes first. The next generation (millennials and generation Z) seem far less receptive to old-school marketing techniques like mailers or flyers left on a car windshield. Those kinds of impersonal invites are seen as inauthentic and flat-out annoying. If you want to build organic connections with young adults, authenticity and relationships are essential. This means that a simple invitation to share dinner or watch a game together can become a natural but highly effective bridge builder that precedes an invitation to visit your church.

WHO'S THIRSTY?

It surprises people to discover that Jesus didn't spend the bulk of his time in a church or temple. Rather he went to places like a local watering hole where thirsty people were sure to gather. Remember the time Jesus dropped by a public water well in Samaria? It was noontime, and Jesus was thirsty from his journey. So he asked a local woman at the well for a drink. "The Samaritan woman said to him, 'You are a Jew and I am a Samaritan woman. How can you ask me for a drink?' (For Jews do not associate with Samaritans)" (John 4:9).

To say that Jews did not associate with Samaritans was putting it politely. Samaritans were considered half-breeds, a mixed race despised by God-fearing Jews. Jews went out of their way to avoid contact with them. But not Jesus. He didn't live by such restrictions. Instead he engaged the woman in a spiritually rich conversation.

> Jesus answered her, "If you knew the gift of God and who it is that asks you for a drink, you would have asked him and he would have given you living water."
>
> "Sir," the woman said, "you have nothing to draw with and the well is deep. Where can you get this living water?" . . .
>
> Jesus answered, "Everyone who drinks this water will be thirsty again, but whoever drinks the water I give them will never thirst. Indeed, the water I give them will become in them a spring of water welling up to eternal life."
>
> —John 4:10–14

Everybody is thirsty for something. I'm not talking about margaritas, just as Jesus wasn't talking about literal water. Call it significance, purpose, acceptance; we are spiritual beings created for a relationship of unconditional love with our heavenly Father. Sadly, most folks attempt to quench this spiritual thirst with physical pursuits. People chase after money, sex, relationships, travel, hobbies—all in an attempt to satisfy their soul's thirst.

Some people even try religion.

FROZEN CHOSEN

Like many of you, I grew up in a church that was dry as a bone. We never would have allowed folks like Tammy and Vanessa through our doors. We had standards and decorum. Men wore suits and ties; women wore long dresses. And the whole show ran on military time. Each service was exactly seventy-five minutes long. The order was as predictable as the fill-in-the-blank notes that accompanied each sermon. As a boy, I discovered that every Bible passage has three main points that always seem to magically rhyme or spell something clever. (How do you spell *joy*? Jesus-Others-You!)

Faith was primarily an intellectual exercise. We memorized verses. We debated dogma. And I hated it. It wasn't just that I dreaded wearing a tie as a teenager (though that was cruel and unusual punishment). It was something else. The environment seemed lifeless. Funeral-like. Although we sang about having the "joy, joy, joy down in our heart," the people in the pews seemed drained of life.

We were the Frozen Chosen. At our conservative church, no one showed emotion or dared raise their hands in worship. It was as if there were an invisible force field at belt level, keeping everyone's arms pinned down. We sat frozen in our seats until closing prayer. After the service, the adults would mill about, speaking in hushed tones in the foyer—everybody calling each other "brother" and using other religious jargon—while we kids ran outside to rip off our ties and play hide-and-seek in the parking lot.

There were exceptions. I remember a young seminarian named Billy who brought a spark of life to the church. One snowy Sunday, Billy took a risk to bring his Sunday school class of middle school boys outside to play in the snow. It was like being born again. Liberated from the bland world of flannelgraphs and sermon notes, we threw snowballs at each other with glee. For a single, shimmering Sunday morning, we tasted freedom!

But a few weeks later, it was announced that we had a new Sunday school teacher. We never saw Billy again.

Looking back, it's no surprise that few people visited our church. We had our own list of Samaritans—people to steer clear of.

- People who drank
- People who cursed
- People who were divorced

- People who lived together
- People who liked secular music
- And pretty much everyone else

Instead of building bridges to spiritually thirsty people, we focused on safeguarding our traditions. By age fourteen, I was a crispy critter. I was bored to tears and developed migraines on Saturday nights in dread of all-day church on Sundays. I vowed I'd never become a pastor.

To be sure, my childhood church wasn't all bad. I was blessed by first-rate Bible teaching and a robust understanding of theology that prepared me to attend Wheaton College, one of the finest Christian schools in the country. However, my church's Frozen Chosen environment had a toxic effect on my soul. It was intellectually precise but relationally sterile. Instead of an open door, our church had a closed gate. Although we loved God with our minds, I didn't catch Jesus' heart for broken people. People like Tammy, Vanessa, and the woman at the well.

HIGH NOON

By rights, Jesus never should have spoken with the woman at the well. To begin with, she was a Samaritan. Strike one. Secondly, she was female. A powerless minority in a patriarchal culture. Strike two. But her biggest flaw was revealed when she accepted Jesus' offer of a drink.

> The woman said to him, "Sir, give me this water so that I won't get thirsty and have to keep coming here to draw water."
>
> He told her, "Go, call your husband and come back."
>
> "I have no husband," she replied.
>
> Jesus said to her, "You are right when you say you have no husband. The fact is, you have had five husbands, and the man you now have is not your husband. What you have just said is quite true."
>
> —John 4:15–18

Strike three, four, and five! In a moment of prophetic insight, Jesus suddenly raises a most awkward topic—the woman's failed relationships. How did he know?

John 4:6 notes that "it was about noon"—the hottest part of the day. Under the Middle Eastern sun, no one ventured out at midday to gather water. Except this woman, which likely meant she was avoiding others. She was probably sick and tired of being labeled a five-time failure and chose to suffer the scorching sun rather than more shame from her neighbors.

Yet Jesus leans in on her vulnerable spot. On her point of greatest need and desire. This is a woman desperate to be loved well by a man. But there's a hole in her bucket. *Is it possible,* Jesus seems to ask, *that you're drawing water from the wrong well?*

The woman tries to change the subject from relationships to religion—a popular smoke screen whenever conversation gets too personal. But it's at this messy level—the point of people's greatest pain, failures, and moral mess-ups—that God does his deeper work in the heart.

HAPPY CLAPPY

Because I'd grown up in the emotionally sterile world of the Frozen Chosen, I pretty much dropped out of church during college. This wasn't as easy as it sounds. Wheaton held weekly chapel services, and it took some special charm to convince the attendance monitor to check off my name each semester.

On Sundays, I'd often sleep till noon. When my parents called and asked if I attended church, I would sometimes lie. I'd say yes while imagining my attendance at Bedside Baptist or Pillow Presbyterian.

Honestly, I didn't miss church. But that was because I hadn't experienced God's deep heart of compassion for broken people.

All that changed when I met my future wife, Colleen. The first time I saw her in freshman writing class, I was smitten. I'd like to tell you my attraction to her was purely spiritual, but when I saw her tan legs and big, blonde, Aqua-Netted hair, this Jersey boy had one thought: *Badda bing—I'm home!*

I mustered the courage to ask her on a date one Friday night, but her response shocked me. "I'd love to go," she explained, "but I can't. I'm going to prison on Friday night."

I'd been given excuses before, but this was a new one! Colleen clarified her conflict. "No, I'm not being locked up," she said, laughing. "I tutor young girls from the inner city who are in juvenile jail."

I was incredulous. "Did you get busted for skipping chapel or something? Is this required for a class? Or community service?"

"No." She laughed again. "The girls struggle with math and reading, and I love to help them."

I'd been a Christian for years, but I'd never known anyone who voluntarily gave up Friday nights to hang out with prisoners—in this case, young women who were incarcerated for auto theft, drug use, and other crimes. I was familiar with the theological concept of social justice. I'd read about it in the Bible, but I didn't know anyone who actually lived it. Colleen's compassion intrigued me, and we began dating. She tutored young girls at that prison every Friday night for four years at Wheaton.

Over Thanksgiving break, Colleen invited me to visit her home church in New York City—a storefront Pentecostal church in the Bronx. It was like walking into an urban street fair. If we were the Frozen Chosen, these folks were the Happy Clappy! As I walked through the glass doors into the modest worship space, I was greeted by a couple of women who had their shoes off. They'd been dancing in the back of the room with tambourines and were waving flags. The church was awash in sound and color and emotion. People were clapping and dancing with hands raised in front of the small stage. Others were lying on the floor, crying and praising Jesus.

Colleen looked at me and smiled. I grinned back weakly. *What are these nuts doing?* I wondered. Everything seemed chaotic and unpredictable.

The guy up front leading worship on his guitar suddenly changed choruses for no apparent reason. I whispered to Colleen, "Is he winging it?"

She smiled and said, "That's called being led by the Spirit."

"In my church," I replied, "we call it unprepared."

All the emotion and spontaneity was waaaaaaay out of my comfort zone. Yet as I looked around, the authenticity and diversity touched me. I saw Latino, Asian, black, and white; street people, drug pushers, executives, and professionals; young and old—side by side, worshiping and praising God together. There was a palpable warmth and sincerity in this mass of humanity as they all worshiped God. I thought of Jesus' words to the Samaritan woman: "God is spirit, and his worshipers must worship in the Spirit and in truth" (John 4:24).

After an hour of singing (an hour!), the pastor finally got up to begin his message. To my shock, there was no three-point outline and no fill-in-the-blank notes in the program. Rather he stitched together a jumble of verses about God's love and forgiveness for people who'd screwed up their life and needed a second chance. He spoke from the heart. "If you need a fresh start, today's your day! We worship the God of second chances!" The congregation shouted, and some raised their hands.

"Not just a second chance," he continued. "God can give you a third, fourth, or even fifth chance!" The congregation nodded, and I realized the Samaritan woman would've felt right at home. "Who wants a second chance?" he asked, eyes searching the room. *Here comes the altar call,* I thought cynically. As a child of the Frozen Chosen, I sat there smugly judging his effort, certain no one would respond to his spontaneous appeal.

Without warning, a half dozen people quickly came down the aisle toward the small stage. The guitar guy started playing, and someone shook a tambourine. "Praise Jesus!" the pastor cried. "Welcome to the family of God!" I couldn't believe it. During two decades at my child-hood church, I couldn't recall a single person shifting pew positions, let alone coming forward to renounce their sins publicly.

The pastor handed his microphone to a man who introduced himself as Louis. Through tears, he described his ten-year battle with drugs, an addiction that cost him his job, his marriage, and his family.

"But I don't want that anymore," Louis said quietly, looking down. "I tried so many times, and it feels kinda hopeless." He paused. "I been coming here for a month, though, and you all been so nice to me. I figure I might as well give Jesus a chance." He looked up and put down the microphone. "Well, God," he said with a catch in his voice, "here I am."

The Happy Clappies exploded. A throng of people mobbed Louis, hugging him and laying hands on him in prayer. Louis wept with his head bowed.

I stood watching and glanced at my watch. The service was now almost two hours long! Yet I had to admit: it was the most beautiful prayer I had ever heard. My heart warmed as I watched a river of God's grace flow down the aisles and wash over Louis.

All the stories I'd heard about Jesus reaching out to people living on the margins—maybe that's how the church today is supposed to be? Maybe all this gospel stuff was really true after all? Maybe today's tax collectors and prostitutes can experience God's love and freedom and forgiveness in a church, without three hymns and a sermon outline?

The experience—while uncomfortable—was thrilling to my heart. I could feel a joy and wonder bubbling up through the desert floor of my soul, which had shriveled up in theological staleness. Before my eyes, I watched the gospel go from black and white to vivid technicolor as I finally saw what was so amazing about God's grace for broken people. Even self-righteous sinners like me.

This was the beginning of the vision for Liquid Church, but we didn't know it at the time.

HOW TIM KELLER TAUGHT ME TO ENGAGE CULTURE

After graduating from Wheaton, Colleen and I each moved back to New Jersey and were married (I wrote about many comic moments of our early marriage in *You Married the Wrong Person*[4]). We became involved in a young church named Redeemer Presbyterian in Manhattan. We were about two hundred people at the time, mostly young adult singles and newly marrieds.

I had one of those aha moments watching senior pastor Tim Keller preach to a culture that finds more relevance in the *New York Times* than in Holy Writ. As the old expression goes, Keller preached with the Bible in one hand and the newspaper in another. Leveraging current events, he built bridges to hardened skeptics without diluting the Scriptures. Here was someone who seemed like he'd be most at home in the Oxford library. He often pulled from the literary greats. But he was just as likely to pull a storyline out of *Sex and the City* and then make a biblical connection to the sexual lives of cosmopolitan New Yorkers, in which anything goes.

I was wowed every week, having discovered the kind of church that's theologically robust and rooted yet also faces outwardly with a burning passion to reach people far from Christ. At Redeemer, I had a refreshing realization: What we learned on Sunday mornings always applied to how we lived and worked on Monday mornings. God's unchanging truth was relevant to an ever-changing culture.

We were at Redeemer Presbyterian for three years, mentored from afar by watching Tim Keller's creative engagement with secular culture. I discovered that you don't have to check your brain at the door to reach today's generation for Christ. Colleen volunteered in a faith-based recovery program to help homeless women (of course!). I talked with many professional people, from investment bankers to creative directors to Broadway actors, who took very seriously the call to carry their faith back into the marketplace.

Colleen's storefront church and our time at Redeemer Presbyterian represented two streams of vibrant faith that merged in my heart. The mixing of these streams eventually led to the birth of Liquid Church.

MILITANT BAPTIST?

After three years at Redeemer, we started attending a suburban church to be closer to home and work. It was a 150-year-old congregation named Millington Baptist Church, which a couple of college friends had recommended. The senior pastor, Dr. Peter Pendell, had a shepherd's heart to help get new folks connected—especially young adults, who were in short supply. Soon enough, he asked us to lead a Sunday school for twentysomethings. We scanned the crowd of senior saints and asked, "There are other twentysomethings here?" He laughed and said we might find eight others—including his daughter—if we looked hard enough.

When Peter asked us to lead that class for twentysomethings, we had no idea what God was planning.

Just to show you what a colossal lack of vision we had, I replied, "It depends. How early do we have to be here?"

Sunday school started at 9:30 a.m., and with Peter's blessing, we set aside the fill-in-the-blank curriculum that was a typical part of the overall Sunday school program. We asked if we could create something more culturally engaging so others would feel comfortable inviting their non-Christian friends and coworkers. Peter agreed, and we made plans to talk about the Bible's perspective on relationships, sex, career, and discovering our purpose in life.

On our first day of class, Colleen and I were nervous. We didn't know if anyone would show. Twelve people did, including Peter's daughter, Aimee. In the church basement, we sat together awkwardly in mismatched chairs, drank stale coffee, and introduced ourselves.

At the time, I was teaching English in a public high school and had learned a few tricks. As a new teacher, I had been tasked with teaching "motorhead English"—a class for at-risk seniors who could care less about Shakespeare. I discovered that when I used visual aids (movies, video clips, digital media, modern illustrations) to teach the text, it came alive and students were highly engaged.

Teaching Hamlet to fifth-year seniors, I discovered a secret of effective communication: if you take a text and marry it to a visual aid that connects emotionally, it burns in people's brains and they remember it forever.

> If you take a text and marry it to a visual aid that connects emotionally, it burns in people's brains and they remember it forever.

I transferred that learning to our little Sunday school class. We started with topics that were on people's minds—sex, money, purpose, dating, marriage, and more. But then we dramatically illustrated how the Bible had something both relevant and life-changing to say about each. Every week, I started with a movie clip or story to engage the heart, and then I carefully led a conversation around God's Word for the day. Young adults loved it. Laughter, conversation, movie clip sound effects, and music spilled from our classroom.

Our tiny gathering of a dozen twentysomethings quickly doubled. Then it grew to forty in number, and then seventy, as folks invited their friends. I invited a colleague in my English department to join us. "I teach a Bible class for twentysomethings on Sundays. Wanna come?"

"Where is it?" he asked.

When I told him Millington Baptist Church, he replied, "Militant Baptist? No thanks, bro. I'm not into politics." I realized we had a long way to go to change people's perceptions of church in our region.

We were meeting in a traditional, white-steepled church, having no idea of the new kind of church God was planning to birth out of this group.

CHURCH IN A TAVERN

Peter was a wonderful mentor to me as our class outgrew its basement meeting room. As we brainstormed ways to make room for others, he asked, "What obstacles can we remove to reach young adults far from God?" Although he was a seasoned senior pastor, he had a huge heart for the next generation.

With his blessing and the elders' permission, we moved the class a mile down the road to a local tavern called the King George Inn. We learned later that it was located right where one of America's earliest revivals had occurred. Although it was a historic tavern, we didn't serve beer; I just taught the Bible, and we had lively conversations about it. People started bringing their non-Christian friends and coworkers who found the "third place" location less intimidating than a Baptist church basement.

In one of my first lessons at the tavern, I shared the story of Jesus' encounter with the Samaritan woman at the well and how God's heart is to meet thirsty, broken people at their point of greatest need. When I opened the floor for table talk, dozens of young adults began speaking openly about their struggles and how thirsty they were for this kind of community and nonreligious connection with God.

Inspired by John 4, we started calling the ministry Liquid and inviting people to come and see. After Jesus revealed to the Samaritan woman that he was the promised Messiah who could forgive her sins and change her life, the Scripture says, "Then, leaving her water jar, the woman went back to the town and said to the people, 'Come, see a man who told me everything I ever did. Could this be the Messiah?' They came out of the town and made their way toward him" (John 4:28–30).

As people continued inviting their non-Christian friends to Liquid, the tavern became the equivalent of a modern well for our generation!

We were drawing thirsty people into dialogue about the broken parts of their lives and introducing the love of Jesus into the middle of the mess. Many visitors were hearing the gospel for the first time and becoming full-fledged followers of Christ.

Our early Liquid meetings were alive and electric, brimming with energy as hundreds of twentysomethings gathered to hear and discuss the message in a way that made sense to their hearts and minds.

> We were drawing thirsty people into dialogue about the broken parts of their lives and introducing the love of Jesus into the middle of the mess.

Unbeknownst to most of them, Colleen and I left the tavern each week at eleven o'clock to drive back to Millington Baptist for "big church." We were still expected to attend the traditional service, and I would even change into a tie and jacket as we drove a mile up the road to do our duty.

But a gap was growing. Increasingly, our pagan friends would stay behind at the tavern and order brunch so they could enjoy community and continue talking about our topic for the morning. Our heart was to stay with them, but we felt conflicted.

One Sunday as we drove the mile back to Millington Baptist, I pulled the car over and asked Colleen, "Are you feeling what I'm feeling?" She smiled and nodded. We turned around, went back to the tavern, and enjoyed brunch with our friends. We never made it to big church that morning.

Later that week, I went to see my pastor. "Peter, we're seeing scores of people encountering Jesus. It's thrilling! The living water is real, and people are thirsty for it. Our generation may have given up on traditional church, but they haven't given up on God."

He again responded with vision and a shepherd's heart. "What's the next obstacle we can remove to reach them?"

I replied that while the tavern location was ideal, the early-morning time slot was not. "Most of our friends are out late on Saturday nights. What if we shift to Sunday night?"

With blessing from Peter and the elders, we moved Liquid back to the church—this time in the main auditorium—and started meeting on Sunday nights. There was just one problem: The sanctuary featured pews, organ pipes, a baptistry—all the trappings of a traditional church environment. It was very un-Liquid-like.

Our team of volunteers worked round the clock to transform the space. We turned the lights down, lit candles, put couches on the stage, and rehearsed a rock band that sounded like Coldplay. Immediately we got complaints from the suit-and-tie crowd who worshiped in the morning. Rumors began to spread: "Liquid looks like a seance at night. They light candles and play weird music." "I drove by and saw motorcycles. People were smoking in the parking lot."

Thank God for Pastor Peter. He had our back and told our critics, "Shouldn't we be praising God that we're finally reaching the next generation?" He helped crack the code for objectors by comparing the leadership team at Liquid to missionaries who travel to another country to reach tribes with the gospel in their native language. "Our church sends missionaries across the ocean," he said. "But we have an unreached tribe right across the street. To reach them, we need to speak in their language, sing their style of music, and dress like part of their culture. That's what Tim's doing, and I rejoice at how God is using his team. Liquid doesn't need our criticism; it needs our celebration and support."

I'm so grateful for Peter's missionary mindset. His confidence was a gift to me as a young leader.

In those early days, we made a ton of mistakes, like spilling candle wax on the carpet. And some of our ideas were controversial, like the time we handed out bottled water to folks at a Gay Pride Parade in a way the *New York Times* spotlighted in an article.[5] I was blessed that Peter always gave me enough rope to innovate but not enough to hang myself. Now that Peter is retired, he remains one of my closest friends and spiritual mentors. I love the man and like to blame him for being the godfather of Liquid Church.

THE ACCIDENTAL CHURCH PLANT

As hundreds of young adults began flocking to Liquid on Sunday nights, we expanded to two services. Peter and I kept pressing the question, "What's the next obstacle we can remove to reach thirsty people for Christ?" Our story is simply one of two generations dreaming together of fresh ways to bring the living water of Jesus to thirsty people.

We didn't have a long-range vision. Nor did we have money to pull off fancy outreaches. But I thank God for Millington Baptist Church; it was the perfect environment for a fledgling ministry like Liquid to incubate. As our team concentrated on reaching broken people with Jesus' radical grace, our parent church covered our back. If we busted a drum skin on Sunday night, the drum fairy came and magically fixed it during the week. I can never repay them for their support and sacrifice.

> Peter and I kept pressing the question, "What's the next obstacle we can remove to reach thirsty people for Christ?"

In many ways, Liquid is an accidental church plant. And I'm an accidental pastor. If you had told me what God had planned for us, I probably would have freaked out and messed up the whole thing. But in his sovereign mercy and grace, God was planning something new. After six years at that 150-year-old church, Liquid was ready to spread its wings and fly.

In 2007, with the blessing of Peter, the elders, and the congregation, Liquid launched out as an independent Christian church. We initially met in a rented ballroom of a downtown hotel thirteen miles away. We launched with a core group of three hundred volunteers and enough money to survive for three months. It was a huge leap of faith to leave the safety of our mother church, and I think some folks assumed we would crash and burn. To be sure, we've made plenty of mistakes (and I'll share many of them in the chapters to come). But our courageous volunteers were faithful, and more important, so was our God! Liquid not only survived our initial launch; our fledgling church exploded with new believers thirsty for God's love and acceptance.

To date, we've baptized more than 2,400 new believers in Jesus' name across our state. Each time I stand in a hot tub to baptize a new follower of Christ, I think of the Samaritan woman at the well and how he washed away her guilt and shame that day with his amazing grace.

Today we're blessed to have a church that reaches people from every age, stage, and spiritual background. Our church has seven locations—what we call campuses—that meet in just about every kind of facility imaginable: school auditoriums, hotel ballrooms, movie theaters, and a Walmart-size warehouse that we've renovated into a state-of-the-art broadcast campus. Our diverse family of five thousand regular attenders includes:

- People who are divorced
- People battling addiction
- People recovering from legalistic religion
- People struggling with sexual desires they don't know what to do with
- People who have messed up morally
- And everyone else

As we like to say, faith is a journey, not a guilt trip. We don't care whether folks grew up Frozen Chosen, Happy Clappy, or with no church experience at all. Skeptics are especially welcome. At Liquid, everyone is invited to come encounter Jesus and drink deep of his amazing grace! With congregations in multiple cities (and more to come), we have a vision to saturate our state with the gospel of Jesus Christ.

And it all started with twelve people in a basement, thirsting for something more.

Dive Deeper

Before we jump into the ministry currents God is using to reach today's generation, reflect on these discussion questions.

ANKLE DEEP What are the parallels between your church experience when you were growing up and mine? Do you relate more to the Frozen Chosen or to the Happy Clappy? What is the greatest spiritual thirst that your relationship with Jesus has quenched, akin to how he identified and met the spiritual needs of the woman at the well (John 4:1–30)?

KNEE DEEP It's been said that faith is spelled R-I-S-K. What's the greatest risk you've ever taken in ministry to reach people who may have given up on church but not on God? How did it go, or how is it going? How did you see God show up in a surprising way? What did God teach you?

WAIST DEEP My mentor Peter Pendell regularly asked me, "What's the next obstacle we can remove to reach people far from God?" What's the answer for your ministry? What obstacles are preventing the living water from reaching thirsty people outside of your church's four walls?

CHAPTER THREE

OUR SATURATION STRATEGY

You, God, are my God,
  earnestly I seek you;
I thirst for you,
  my whole being longs for you,
in a dry and parched land
  where there is no water.
—PSALM 63:1

Have you ever been so thirsty that you thought, *If I don't get a drink soon, I'm going to die?*

That's exactly what Colleen and I thought four hours into our hike to the bottom of the Grand Canyon. It was July, and we had taken a trip to experience America's grandest natural wonder. But we were woefully unprepared for the heat. We were novice hikers from New Jersey, accustomed to walking around air-conditioned shopping malls. We heard Arizona had a "dry heat," and when we arrived, it was 102 degrees in the shade. But being dry means it's not really that hot, right?

On the morning of our hike, we slept in late. Leisurely making our way to the hotel breakfast buffet, we stuffed ourselves full of bacon and pancakes drenched in syrup. Then, wearing cotton shirts and sneakers, we casually hit the South Kaibab Trail around noon. It was a ghost town. "Where are all the other hikers?" Colleen wondered aloud. Like fools, we hadn't realized that experienced hikers leave before the sun comes up, to begin their trek in the coolest part of the morning.

So we began our descent under the blazing midday Arizona sun, two happy kids in love skipping merrily down a red dirt path, blissfully unaware of the danger ahead. An hour into our hike, we walked past amazing layers of red rock and sandstone.

Then we saw a sobering sign. It featured a giant skull and crossbones with the words "Heat kills" stamped in bold red letters. Below it was a thermometer that read 118 degrees. We took a swig from our shared water bottle and noticed it was half empty.

We were three hours into our descent when the water ran out. Colleen was getting shaky. She looked at our empty bottle. "Honey, I'm so thirsty. I feel lightheaded. Are we close to the bottom?"

"It's not far," I replied. "Just a few more steps; we'll be there soon."

She let out a deep huff and we hiked on.

We turned a corner, and the view took our breath away. For miles, the sky stretched like an electric-blue canvas dotted with cotton ball clouds. A large bird circled overhead, and I privately hoped it wasn't a vulture.

The canyon walls were glowing orange, changing colors as the afternoon sun shifted and began setting. And that's when we saw it: the Colorado River, snaking like an emerald ribbon on the canyon floor.

"See, I told you we were close!" I declared with confidence. By this point, I was getting shaky too. We hadn't had a drop of water in two hours and were dangerously dehydrated. Our mouths were filled with dust. I was soaked in sweat (we learned later that our cotton clothes were an especially poor choice), and Colleen's skin was turning red with sunburn.

I had mistakenly assumed there would be a refreshment stand or gift shop midway through our hike. But the Grand Canyon is truly an unspoiled gem—no shops, no shade, no bathrooms, and no water for sale on the trail.

The sight of the Colorado River lifted our spirits. At the bottom, we'd be able to dip our feet and heads in the cold river and rehydrate with fresh drinking water supplied by Navajo guides who lived there.

But that's when I realized my second mistake: the river was beyond our reach.

Looking down, we saw a series of at least a dozen more switchbacks; the trail zigzagged for another couple of miles to the canyon floor. We'd never make it. Out of water, out of energy, and now out of hope. Colleen sat down on a rock and cried. This is what happens when two idiots from New Jersey ignore the basic rule of human survival: water is essential for life.

LIVING WATER

Water is not just essential to life; water is life. Science confirms it: roughly 60 percent of the adult human body is water (infants are about 75 percent). Your brain and heart are composed of 73 percent water, and your lungs are about 83 percent water.[1] That means human beings are basically walking bags full of water plus about two dollars' worth of minerals. Our planet has the same liquidity: about 71 percent of the earth's surface is covered by water.[2]

The spiritual parallel couldn't be clearer: your soul is the same way. If it is not saturated—hydrated properly by a life-giving faith, not rules and regulations—it too will shrivel and die from a lack of living water.

> The spiritual parallel couldn't be clearer. If your soul is not saturated—hydrated properly by a life-giving faith—it too will shrivel and die from a lack of living water.

That's why one of Jesus' favorite metaphors was offering living water to people thirsty for a drink. In John 7, at the festival of Sukkot, when Jewish people prayed and pleaded with God to bless them with rain, Jesus stood up and shouted, "'Let anyone who is thirsty come to me and drink. Whoever believes in me, as Scripture has said, rivers of living water will flow from within them.' By this he meant the Spirit, whom those who believed in him were later to receive" (John 7:37–39).

The ancient Hebrews had a beautiful term for living water; they called it *mayim chaim* (MY-eem KHY-eem), or water from heaven, given as a gift from God to bless, nourish, and sustain his people.[3] In the Middle East, water is scarce. The land is a study in contrasts: where there is no water, the hills are brown and barren, but where rivers flow, lush vegetation grows and blossoms.

According to the apostle John, living water represents the Holy Spirit. As Ezekiel prophesied, "Where the river flows everything will live" (Ezek. 47:9). We are called to be a liquid church, flowing from our sanctuary seats out into the cracked, dry city streets, bringing life to barren places and parched people.

CHARLIE'S ANGEL

I've never met an angel in real life, but Charlie and his wife came close. As Colleen and I sat stranded on the side of the canyon trail, a cheery couple came up the path. "Are you guys okay?" Charlie asked, introducing himself. "You look dehydrated." Colleen nodded and Charlie's wife knelt down. She was wearing one of those hydration backpacks that carries multiple liters of cold water. "Here, take a sip," she said. Colleen did, and her dull eyes began to flicker with life.

Charlie pulled a bottle of ice water out of his backpack, and I thought I might be hallucinating. He handed it to me and said, "Take this; we've got plenty." I guzzled it like a desperate man who'd been stranded in the Sahara for a month. Never in my life had water tasted so good, so utterly refreshing.

As I thanked Charlie and his wife, I began to wonder if these strangers were really angels in disguise sent by God to rescue us.[4] Rehydrated and renewed, Colleen and I dragged ourselves down to the canyon floor by sunset. With wobbly legs and grateful hearts, we stuck our swollen, blistered feet in the Colorado River and thanked God we survived.

A SATURATION STRATEGY

That night, we slept at the Phantom Ranch, a rustic lodge nestled at the bottom of the Grand Canyon. It's the only lodging below the canyon rim and is tucked beside Bright Angel Creek. It felt like an oasis. Before turning in for the night, we purchased multiple bottles of water, salt pills (for water retention), jerky (for protein), and carbs to fuel our hike back up in the morning.

Rangers from the ranch heard about our scary experience on the trail and pulled us aside. "You need a saturation strategy for your return hike," one said. He told us to set our alarm for 4:00 a.m. "Start when it's still dark," he counseled. "And before you start hiking, stick your clothes in the river. Your shirt, your shorts, your hat. Soak it all and make sure your clothes are completely wet."

"Won't that weigh us down?" I asked.

"You'll be dry soon enough," he explained. But the total immersion would keep our skin hydrated and body temperature lower. It was the saturation strategy we needed to survive.

The next morning, Colleen and I did as we were told. We drenched our clothes in the ice-cold creek and began hiking in the predawn darkness. Sure enough, two hours in, as the sun began to rise, our clothes were bone dry. We followed the Bright Angel Trail, which offered shade and a couple of creeks to rehydrate our clothes. Instead of one water bottle, this time we were armed with eight.

It took us five hours to hike to the top. We rationed our water and made sure to keep stopping and drinking the entire way, even when we weren't thirsty. By the time we reached the rim of the canyon, we had one bottle left. And a life lesson we'll never forget: water is vital for survival.

And another lesson: without a saturation strategy, life withers and dies.

WHY OUR GOAL IS TO SATURATE

The vision of Liquid Church today is to saturate our state with the gospel of Jesus Christ. Saturate means to thoroughly soak or utterly immerse something in liquid. By God's grace, we hope to have at least one Liquid campus in every New Jersey county one day so that the nine million people in our densely populated state get the chance to taste the living water of Jesus for themselves. The Northeast is one of the most spiritually dry regions in America,[5] a good focus for us, but we believe God dreams of a day when every city across the globe is saturated with the love and grace of Jesus.

EVERY RIVER
Starts with a Trickle

Note to readers: You'll see this section in each of the six chapters of part 2. It's a way to explain our origins and to encourage you that faith plus God's guidance and blessing can have impact beyond your or my wildest imaginations.

The vision of Ezekiel 47 describes a life-giving river so powerful that it can reanimate the Dead Sea. And it all starts with a trickle.

I didn't have faith that could desalinate the Dead Sea when I led the launch of Liquid Church, but I did have enough to believe that God wanted a trickle to become a stream. So I challenged the core group we had been building to step more deeply into the water.

I vividly remember our final Sunday evening at Millington Baptist as a next gen ministry before morphing the next week into a new church plant. Frankly, we didn't know what to expect for the following Sunday morning. Not only were we moving from a church building to a rented hotel ballroom, but it was a twenty-minute drive away.

Would our people stay with us? Did they really have enough contacts in the new area, and would they actually invite and bring them? We had incubated for six years, having started with twelve mismatched chairs in the church basement (see the full story in chapter 2). In seven days, we'd find out.

My message that night was a rallying cry for folks to go all in with our new church launch. After a scriptural challenge, I told everyone we needed all hands on deck to make church happen. We couldn't afford for anyone to sit on the sidelines and asked every adult to join a team—helping set up equipment, greeting new guests, running media, ministering to children, and a thousand other details.

As if that weren't enough, everyone was given a second job: to bring a friend, coworker, or neighbor with them. This was essential if the gospel was to saturate our city, but it meant our people had to serve at one service and then attend the second service with their guest. Our prayer was that our core of three hundred volunteers wouldn't burn out and that the new people would return.

On opening day, God showed up in a remarkable way as people filled the rented ballroom at the Hyatt Regency Hotel in downtown Morristown, New Jersey. To our surprise, many guests returned the following week and brought their friends with them! The momentum began to build, and two years later we had grown to one thousand people attending on Sundays in a portable environment. Our saturation dream was moving in the right direction.

That's when we hit a new problem: we were running out of seats in our prime-time morning services and had to set up chairs in the hotel lobby, which was a less-than-stellar experience. We wondered, "Where are all these people coming from?" One of our leaders used Google to make a "heat map" that showed us where people were clustered, and we noticed that lots of people were coming from thirty minutes south of our hotel.

We identified 170 people who were driving for half an hour or more. That was a big pool of contacts. My buddy Mike Leahy (more about him later) said, "What if we had a campus there?" That sounded great, but how could it happen? We had no experience with the emerging multisite movement.

So we looked into other churches making waves. Specifically, we traveled down to Atlanta to visit North Point Community Church, where Andy Stanley was pioneering video-based teaching. "That will never work in New Jersey," I predicted. But we felt God nudging us to take a risk and try it.

We launched a second campus in the Hyatt Hotel in New Brunswick, New Jersey, which is home to Rutgers University. Everything about the Sunday service was live—live worship, live on-site pastors, live kids' ministry—except for the sermon, which was projected on a giant movie screen. To our surprise, the video teaching was received well (I share some secrets of "pixelated preaching" in chapter 5). Under Mike's gifted leadership, our second campus grew very quickly to seven hundred people.

But we made a key miscalculation that almost tanked the church: we assumed new people would start engaging, tithing, and serving as quickly and at the same level as those who came before them. News flash: College kids don't tithe. Neither do new Christians, at least not right away.

By our third year as a church, we feared that we had shot a hole in our boat. I remember our leadership team getting on our knees with a desperate prayer: "Lord, what have we done? We stepped out of the boat, but we're about to sink. Please save us!" We made budget adjustments to survive, barely. We regained momentum, and when we launched our third campus, we found a savings: launching in a public school, which was a third of the cost of a downtown hotel.

Our locations now formed a triangle in north central New Jersey. Then, as a total surprise, the Miracle at Mountainside happened, resulting in our first permanent building (see the story in chapter 7). God set this surprise fourth campus smack-dab in the middle of our other three locations. This provided a stable core of volunteers and tithing families to fill our new permanent facility. More important, it gave us hope to keep pressing ahead.

It's amazing to look back and see how God faithfully led us through the first couple of years of a shaky start-up. Somehow we had survived; more than that, we had multiplied—all essential to saturation. In the process, we developed a guerrilla mindset toward ministry: when scrappy people are willing to take risks for Jesus and trust him with the results, anything is possible. To this day, we firmly believe the church isn't about buildings; it's about building people up!

We chose the city of Morristown (population nineteen thousand) for the location of our original church launch because it had a mix of young creative professionals living side by side with immigrant families newly arrived from Central America. This gave us natural opportunities for outreach—saturation on many fronts. As commuters walked to catch the morning train, the volunteers in our newly launched church greeted them with bottled water and granola bars with a handwritten note: "God loves you, and so does Liquid Church!" For the immigrants who worked as dishwashers and landscapers, we hosted a "free market" to bless their families. Everyone knows what a flea market is—people sell their junk to make money. But Liquid's free market was just the opposite. We asked our young congregation to bring their best—lightly used clothes, furniture, baby cribs, bikes, and more—and we lovingly cleaned each donation, carefully repackaged it, and gave it away for free to single moms and families in need.

"Muchas gracias," said a Latino mother with three little children in tow. Her shopping bag was filled with new shoes, coveralls, and snow jackets for the winter. "Dios te bendiga [God bless you]," replied a Liquid volunteer as they exchanged hugs. We worked with local social service agencies to identify families living at or below the poverty line and gave them the dignity of shopping in our free market for essential items they couldn't afford. There was no catch; everything was free, just like God's love!

As our outreach to people in our city grew deeper (more practical examples in chap. 8), our vision grew wider. We added more campuses and came to realize that Liquid was a regional church, not just a local church. Morristown is located in Morris County, and we began seeing the opportunity to broaden our impact. Today our main broadcast campus is located in Parsippany (population fifty thousand), the largest town in Morris County. But as we opened new campuses beyond our original location, we began to refer to each by county name, such as our Essex County campus. At that point, we begin describing Liquid's reach as north central New Jersey.

As Liquid expanded to four campuses in the area, I began to ask God what his BHAG[6] was for our growing church. I think every church needs a Big Hairy Audacious Goal that only God can get the credit for achieving. One day while writing in my prayer journal, I found myself musing, *Wouldn't it be amazing if Liquid had a campus in every county of the state?* I shared the idea with our leadership team, and when we discovered that New Jersey has twenty-one counties, we sat with it for a year, mulling and praying. That would be twenty-one different locations, and perhaps more if we birthed campuses in the most populous or most spread-out counties. Talk about a Big Hairy Audacious Goal (or better yet, a Big *Holy* Audacious Goal!). That's when we first began voicing the notion of saturating the entire state with the gospel of Jesus Christ.

> Our leadership team prayed and made a pivotal decision: let's attempt something so big that it's bound to fail unless God shows up.

It seemed so ridiculous, and yet a disturbing percentage of New Jersey's nine million residents are unchurched. The vast majority of people do not know a growing, authentic follower of Christ who can serve them and share the good news about Jesus. Our state is the most densely populated in the nation, and yet so many communities lack a life-giving church or an adequate number of life-giving churches.

So our leadership team prayed and made a pivotal decision: let's attempt something so big that it's bound to fail unless God shows up.

THE TIPPING POINT

What will it take to saturate your town, your city, your state? Tim Keller says, "It takes a movement to reach a city.... It's the Holy Spirit moving across the whole city and as a result the overall body of Christ is growing faster than the population, and the city is being reached. And there's an impact for Christ made in the whole city."[7]

In his bestselling book *The Tipping Point: How Little Things Can Make a Big Difference*, Malcolm Gladwell defines a tipping point as "the moment of critical mass, the threshold, the boiling point."[8] In the context of evangelizing your city, a tipping point is reached when the message of Jesus begins to spread like a virus, infecting a community so deeply and widely that its impact is undeniable.

Keller notes, "When a gospel movement is underway, it may be that the Body of Christ develops to the point that a whole city tipping point is reached. By that I mean the moment when the number of gospel-shaped Christians in a city reaches critical mass. The Christian influence on the civic and social life of the city—on the very culture—is recognizable and acknowledged. That means between 10 and 20 percent of the population."

What would it look like if 20 percent of your town became followers of Christ? It may help to narrow that down to an image you can see in your mind's eye: what if 20 percent of your neighbors or people living in your apartment complex shared your faith? How would that transform your community, its schools, its businesses, and the wider city?

When I think about saturating our city, I think of spiritually thirsty friends like Linda, Mr. Z, Marie, and Dr. Thomas, who have been drawn to Jesus through the life of our church. Each is a friend of my family and represents hundreds of other people at Liquid who are similarly reaching their neighbors with the good news. Last summer, I realized Liquid was approaching a tipping point in our community when I saw God's impact at our local diner, my daughter's school, a convenience store, and the doctor's office.

- Linda is a waitress at the diner in the center of town. She's quick with a cup of joe and witty banter. A few years ago, when she heard that I was a pastor, she confided that a customer had invited her to "that crazy church of yours." "Will you come visit?" I asked as she filled my coffee mug. "Will hell freeze over anytime soon?" she replied with a laugh and a wink. Linda had led a hard life; her family struggled with addiction issues. But hell froze over one Sunday when I saw Linda nervously clutching a program as she looked for a seat in the sanctuary. She loved the worship band ("They rock!"), began coming to church regularly, and discovered ordinary people just like her, and she and they became quick friends. Counseling helped with her sobriety, and a month later God's free offer of forgiveness and grace for broken people pierced her heart. Linda gave her life to Christ and was baptized. My Samaritan sister still works at the diner, serving pork roll sandwiches (a Jersey delicacy)[9] and high-octane coffee, but now uses her platform to invite everyone she knows to church. "Faith is a journey," she tells them, "not a guilt trip!"
- Imagine my surprise when my daughter came home from her first day of fifth grade sharing how her new teacher, Mr. Z, began class by describing a 9/11 remembrance service he had attended at "some place called Liquid." A friend had invited him, and as he heard about Jesus' sacrifice to save our lives, he connected the dots. "I grew up in an Italian family and went to Mass like everyone else," he recalls. "But I stopped going because it didn't seem relevant to modern life. But the Bible began to make sense at Liquid, and faith was connected to real issues." Mr. Z not only encountered Jesus at our church; that fall he found a wife. I performed their wedding, and together they've dedicated their two children to the Lord's service. Now a fifth-grade classroom has a faith influence too.

- Marie's son committed suicide in his twenties, but you'd never know it from her cheery disposition. She's a clerk at a convenience store who visited our church at the invitation of a friend. A chain-smoker most of her life, Marie was at first worried she might not fit in with "Holy Rollers." Instead she was invited to help roll volunteer T-shirts and found a family in serving with other women in the office. After receiving Christ as Savior, she began opening up about the hurts and heartache in her life. Her circle of fellow volunteers (later we'll tell you why we call them Dream Teamers) pray with her and have become her supportive sisters. Marie is quick to put into practice what she's learning in church. One morning I was in a crowded checkout line, waiting to pay for my coffee. As the clerks were stressing and scrambling to fix a broken register, Marie told them, "Hey, God says don't be anxious about nothing! Isn't that right, Pastor Tim?" I smiled as Marie transferred God's truth about anxiety from our Philippians study into the chaos of a convenience store checkout line!

- Dr. Thomas is a pediatrician who has seen our two kids sprout up from babies into teens. He's one of the warmest, most caring doctors you could meet but wasn't into religion, as his mother raised him more as a humanist. But Dr. Thomas is a movie buff, and my wife went out on a limb and invited him to church for a message series that builds a bridge between Hollywood blockbusters and gospel themes. To our surprise, he showed up with his whole family. They fell in love with the church and began serving at our outreaches to the hungry and homeless. In a heartfelt note, he thanked our team for putting Christ's compassion for the poor into action. We celebrated this man of medicine for serving as the hands of Jesus to help heal broken lives. When Colleen and I visited his office recently to pick up our kids' summer camp forms, Dr. Thomas said, "I wanna show you something." He led us to his exam room and opened a cabinet drawer filled with Liquid Church pens that we give away to new guests. "I've got a confession: I've been stealing your pens," he said with a wink. He explained how as he gets to know the patients and their families, spirituality and family beliefs often come into the conversation. If it feels appropriate, he gives the Liquid pens to those families. I told him his secret was safe with me, and to feel free to steal our Bibles too!

A doctor, a waitress, a schoolteacher, and a clerk—all within five miles of my house—have had their lives radically altered by the living water spilling out of our church. That's saturation. It's not just that they're giving their lives to Christ; they're evangelizing others too! This is a key insight about saturating your city. It's vital to reach unchurched people with the gospel, because new Christians are typically the most passionate witnesses. They've tasted the living water and are excited to tell others what they've experienced. It's organic evangelism at its best.

> It's vital to reach unchurched people with the gospel, because new Christians are typically the most passionate witnesses.

LIQUID BEGINS WITH LOVE

How has the living water rippled out and started saturating our city? The acronym LIQUID represents the six ministry practices we've seen God use to help us reach both the nones and the dones in our spiritually thirsty region: **L**ove the overlooked (chap. 4), **I**gnite the imagination (chap. 5), **Q**uench their thirst (chap. 6), **U**nite the generations (chap. 7), **I**nspire generosity (chap. 8), and **D**evelop untapped talent (chap. 9). As you read each chapter and consider each current—special needs, creative communication, compassionate cause, ministry mergers, guilt-free giving, and leadership culture—ask God's Spirit to reveal how each one might strategically flow through your own area of influence.

These are the practices that started as small trickles but that God has increasingly deepened into a raging river that delivers life to spiritually thirsty people and saturates our city for Christ. Later chapters will help you find your church's trickles and streams, but let's begin at the headwaters of the LIQUID river, which start with Jesus' command to love the overlooked.

Dive Deeper

Before we dive into the ministry currents God is using to reach today's genera-
tion, chew on these discussion questions and think about the spiritually thirsty
people God has positioned you to reach.

ANKLE DEEP Most leaps forward in outreach begin with a sense of biblical imperative. The Bible is brimming with descriptions of God's divine provision of living water. Look up these saturation Scriptures: Isaiah 35:5–7; 44:3–4; Joel 2:23, 27–29; John 4:13–14; 7:37–39. Why do you think God uses water to depict the flow of his Spirit? Write down the names of a few spiritually thirsty friends or neighbors in your sphere of influence. What is currently working right now at your church in terms of reaching people who have given up on church but not on God?

KNEE DEEP Saturation is a compelling image. Imagine a sponge so waterlogged, it can't absorb any more liquid. What would it take for your city to be saturated with the gospel like that? What would it look like if the geographic area surrounding your church was saturated according to that definition? What biblical examples could help you picture how your town might change? What would it look like if your city was filled with the teaching about Jesus? (Acts 5:28).

WAIST DEEP Does your church or ministry have a BHAG—a Big Holy Audacious Goal? Before Liquid had a vision to saturate our entire state, we had a simple goal of surviving for three months, with the hope and prayer that several people would come to Christ during that time. But God enlarged our vision as we took risks to reach thirsty people in our region. Get together with your leadership team and consider this commitment: "Let's try something so big, it's bound to fail unless God shows up." What would you attempt, with God's help, that would change the landscape of your city? Do some dreaming, ideating, and praying!

Part Two

SIX CURRENTS THAT FORM A POWERFUL RIVER

CHAPTER FOUR

LOVE THE OVERLOOKED: SPECIAL NEEDS

Speak up for those who cannot speak for themselves.
—PROVERBS 31:8

Ethan was so excited for his birthday. He had just turned seven years old, and his parents let him invite a few of his classmates over for a party. Like every boy dreaming of his birthday, Ethan envisioned the fun he would have eating ice cream cake, blowing out candles, and playing Nerf guns with his friends. He couldn't wait for the day to arrive.

But the night before the party, his parents had to cancel it. There was a problem: only one child RSVP'd. What was the cause? Maybe a scheduling conflict? An email snafu?

Ethan's dad explained, "We were sad but not surprised. It's been this way ever since our son was diagnosed with autism." Like one in fifty-nine children in America, Ethan has a neurobiological disorder that makes it difficult for him to communicate clearly and interact socially with his peers. When you're seven years old and words are hard to come by, so are friends. His parents had no choice and, with deflated spirits, canceled the party. "It felt like a knife to the heart," his father recalled. Ethan had suffered rejection at school, but this pain felt even more personal.

But that's when God stepped in. And Ethan's church stepped up.

Ethan's parents had called our church office to share the disappointing news of the party's cancellation because one of our special needs volunteers was planning to stop by. "When I heard no one wanted to come to Ethan's party, my heart just broke," said Suzi Soares, who oversees our church's special needs inclusion ministry. "I spoke with our volunteers, and we decided that is totally unacceptable. Every seven-year-old boy deserves a birthday party to celebrate the unique way God made him."

That afternoon, the church flew into action. Volunteers ran to the store to buy balloons and streamers; they decorated the church and planned fanfare, knowing that Ethan loved attention. One of our small groups heard the news, and the members quickly texted each other. A group of young moms descended on the mall for a spontaneous shopping spree, filling a cart full of toys, games, trucks, and stuff Ethan loves. They hand-wrapped each birthday gift and delivered it to the church.

That Friday night, Ethan walked quietly into our church with his parents and was greeted by the smiling faces of dozens of friends clapping and cheering his name. Horns blew and confetti fell as Ethan smiled like the rock star VIP he is. Volunteers sang songs, played Nerf wars on their knees, and devoured cupcakes with one extremely happy boy. For one shining evening, the social challenges that autism creates melted away like leftover ice cream cake. As he watched his seven-year-old son being celebrated with pride, Ethan's dad teared up and posted on Facebook, "I have to say something and let the world know what church really is . . . It's truly unbelievable. Can the love of Jesus be any more evident here? Ethan was supposed to have a party on his birthday, and sadly we had to cancel. But then our church decided to have a special party for him. We are so blessed to be part of this amazing family! Ethan had bags and bags of gifts . . . Look at that smile! Thanks to the entire team, all the volunteers that love the kids with special needs, and his buddy Gaby for always taking care of our boy on Sundays. May God return what you have sown and shown! #TrulyBlessed #Overwhelmed #LiquidChurch"

C'mon. Who doesn't want to be part of a church that throws birthday parties for kids like Ethan?

A PRIVILEGE AND A PASSION

At Liquid, we believe it's our privilege and passion to serve children with a wide variety of special needs, including autism, Asperger's, Down syndrome, and ADHD. We don't see these children as disabled or dysfunctional; rather we believe each one is uniquely crafted in the image of a loving God and should be celebrated for their God-given gifts and abilities, not defined by their limitations.

And what an opportunity we have. In New Jersey, the rate of children identified with autism spectrum disorder is not the national average of one in fifty-nine but one in thirty-four—the highest rate in the nation, according to the Centers for Disease Control and Prevention (CDC).[1] What a chance for our church to demonstrate the compassion of Christ! People with autism can have difficulty interacting with others, building relationships, and using language. Often, it's hard for them to regulate their emotions or understand others' points of view.

For families facing these challenges, not only are school and social situations difficult, but church can be a nightmare to navigate. A recent study found that "the odds of a child with autism never attending religious services were nearly twice as high as compared to children with no chronic health conditions. The odds of never attending also were significantly higher for children with developmental delays, ADD/ADHD, learning disabilities and behavior disorders."[2]

Does someone in your family have trouble learning or fitting in? Overall, one in six children in the US is reported to have at least one developmental disability,[3] and we feel blessed to minister to these special kiddos.

> "The odds of a child with autism never attending religious services were nearly twice as high as compared to children with no chronic health conditions."

Would it surprise you to know that 68 percent of Jesus' miracles involved people with special needs—what some used to call handicaps or disabilities?[4] On your next read through the gospel of Mark, underline all the chronic health challenges that Jesus welcomed, from paralysis (2:1–12) to shriveled hands (3:1–6) to blood disorders (5:25–34) to blindness (10:46–52). As Jesus embraced and touched each person,

"News about him spread all over Syria, and people brought to him all who were ill with various diseases, those suffering severe pain, the demon-possessed, those having seizures, and the paralyzed; and he healed them" (Matt. 4:24).

Jesus didn't merely help ailing adults; he had a special heart for children. Think about the boy who suffered epileptic seizures (Luke 9:37–43). We know of at least two children that Jesus raised from the dead! One of Jesus' most repeated sayings? "Let the little children come to me" (Luke 18:16, more on that incident later).

> If God has such a huge heart for people with special needs, shouldn't we?

If God has such a huge heart for people with special needs, shouldn't we?

Part of Jesus' vision for his church was creating a beloved community that champions the unique beauty of those with physical, emotional, and intellectual limitations, providing perhaps the one place in the world where they are completely loved and accepted, are befriended, and are celebrated as glorious people with sacred worth.

A PLACE AT THE TABLE

God's compassion for hurting people who are routinely overlooked by the world didn't begin with the ministry of Jesus. We see a beautiful glimpse of the Father's heart in the story of David and Mephibosheth in 2 Samuel 9:1–11.

King David ruled during Israel's glory days, and his reign was marked by "doing what was just and right for all his people" (2 Sam. 8:15). The Lord had given David "victory wherever he went" (v. 14). After conquering Israel's enemies, David became the most powerful monarch in the Mideast. But once he sat down on Israel's throne, he had an unusual request.

King David didn't ask his servants to throw a feast celebrating his power or to guild his palace with gold. Rather he asked, "Is there no one still alive from the house of Saul to whom I can show God's kindness?" (2 Sam. 9:3).

I'm sure the royal court was shocked by the king's question. Remember that Saul was Israel's previous king, who'd been insanely jealous of

David because God had anointed David to replace him. Saul had chucked spears at David's head and hunted him like a dog in the desert.

But in an act of lavish grace, King David asked if there were any relatives of Saul left to whom he could show kindness. One of the servants spoke up. "There is still a son of Jonathan; he is lame in both feet" (2 Sam. 9:3).

The young man's name was Mephibosheth. His father, Jonathan, had been David's BFF, and now Jonathan's son had a special need. Mephibosheth was crippled in both feet—a disability he had lived with since age five, when his caretaker dropped him (2 Sam. 4:4). Had he been born into twenty-first-century royalty, perhaps Mephibosheth would have wheeled around in a motorized wheelchair.

Understand: David had every reason not to treat Mephibosheth kindly, since he was a grandson of his enemy Saul. On top of that, Mephibosheth was—as he called himself—a "dead dog" (2 Sam. 9:8) because of his disability. In David's day, there was a spiritual stigma associated with physical disability. If you were crippled or blind or had any other kind of physical deficit, you were forbidden to "approach the altar" in the temple with an offering to the Lord (Lev. 21:19–21). You faced not only social rejection but spiritual isolation as well.

In Old Testament times, there were no wheelchairs, no handicap-accessible ramps, no special aides, and no gadgets to help with the toilet or bath. Those with health and wealth were seen as blessed by God. If you had a disability, you were seen as spiritually cursed. So when Mephibosheth appeared before David, he may well have assumed David was about to settle old scores and put him out of his misery.

But this is where we see why God called David "a man after his own heart" (1 Sam. 13:14). The gracious king didn't return evil for evil; rather he announced the opposite of what Mephibosheth was expecting. "'Don't be afraid,' David said to him, 'for I will surely show you kindness for the sake of your father Jonathan. I will restore to you all the land that belonged to your grandfather Saul, and you will always eat at my table'" (2 Sam. 9:7).

> Mephibosheth, whom society rejected at every level, had just been invited to a privileged seat at the king's table! What a beautiful picture of the father heart of God.

The royal court must have been shocked again. Mephibosheth, whom society rejected at every level, had just been invited to a privileged seat at the king's table! In essence, David said, "Mephibosheth, you may be the last in the world's eyes, but in my house you'll receive the royal treatment. You're under the king's protection now. I will treat you like one of my sons and provide for your needs. As long as I'm king, you will always have a place at my table."

What a beautiful picture of the father heart of God. Scripture reports David followed through on that promise: "So Mephibosheth ate at David's table like one of the king's sons" (2 Sam. 9:11).

THE ROYAL TREATMENT

When this poignant passage first touched my heart, I was in Panera Bread, enjoying a lunchtime devotional. Tears welled up in my eyes as the Spirit impressed a picture on me: King David—the most powerful warrior, king, and anointed ruler in antiquity—wielding his royal power to lavish favor on the overlooked. It was like Almighty God had dropped a hand grenade into my heart. In the middle of Panera, I started weeping in my tomato soup. Right then and there, I vowed to use my position and power as lead pastor to give kids with disabilities the royal treatment.

I felt God saying, *In my house, I always want there to be a privileged place at the table for people with special needs. Especially the children. Give them the royal treatment, Tim, and my favor will follow you all the days of your life.*

That was eight years ago. Today nothing thrills me more than when I see our church lavishing the love of the Father on his special children. Liquid has become a place of refuge, rest, and healing for entire families—parents, siblings, and all those involved in caring for loved ones with special needs.

WELCOME HOME, ANDY

José and Kayra never planned on moving to New Jersey. Born and raised in Puerto Rico, they loved their island home, where they both enjoyed successful careers as lawyers. But when their son Andy was born with

Down syndrome—a genetic disorder affecting roughly one in every seven hundred babies born in the United States[5]—everything changed. At first, they were devastated. "All the dreams you have for your child suddenly change," Kayra explained, recalling Andy's diagnosis. "We were so happy to have our son but also felt such grief and heartache. We realized God's plan for his life would be way different than we had dreamed."

Most people can't understand the daily pressures of parenting a child with special needs.

- The extra costs to families for medical care, special equipment, and occupational therapy. Kayra and José are saving for two lifetimes—theirs and Andy's, as he may be dependent on his parents as an adult.
- The school battles over IEPs (Individualized Education Programs) and classroom support.
- The impact on the child's siblings, as extra attention is often channeled to the one with special needs.
- The sense of social isolation that surrounds the family; normal activities like shopping or eating out are logistically complex, if not impossible.
- The long-term questions that generate parental anxiety: *Will our child outlive us? Who will take care of our child then? What about college? Is marriage in our child's future? Will they be capable of working a job? And can we find one that suits their strengths?*

It's impossible to overstate the impact of a child with special needs on a family's life.

In the case of Andy, Kayra says he was a happy baby and grew into a fun-loving, affectionate toddler who loved food and dancing to music. At the same time, Kayra and José quickly realized the school system in Puerto Rico had limited resources to support his special needs. They feared their son might not reach his full potential if they stayed there.

So they left it all behind. Everything. They left their home, legal careers, friends, family, church, and even Spanish as a primary language to move to the States. They relocated to New Jersey, which offers some of the most robust educational and social services in the nation

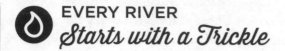

EVERY RIVER
Starts with a Trickle

Dave and Lois Brooks were one of the first households with a family member with special needs who got involved with Liquid Church. Their son Robby was the greeter with Down syndrome who first welcomed Kayra, José, and their young son Andy.

The Brooks' oldest daughter had attended Liquid during her summer break from college, and the rest of the family tested the waters a few months later. "The first time I visited," Dave says, "we sat in the balcony. We didn't know how we'd fit in; there didn't seem to be many gray-haired people like me nor any other kids like our teenage son."

Soon, when the church relocated to a hotel and formed new volunteer teams, Dave, Lois, and son Robby stepped forward. Initially, Dave and Robby helped set up the Liquid Family area each week, but after a few months Dave was out of a job. One of the other volunteers began staying with Robby all morning on Sundays for both setup and takedown, as well as a few bagels in between. Dave and Lois were a bit concerned about giving anyone else the responsibility of their son, but Robby loved the independence and the friendship that had grown. The other volunteer assured them, "Doing this with Robby makes my day."

Meanwhile Robby's high school was encouraging its students with special needs to volunteer with area companies, so a staff pastor made the connection for Liquid to become one of those places, even though our church rented a very small office to work in. Soon Robby and a bunch of his school friends were working on the worship programs each week, pulling out reusable pieces from previous bulletins and preparing new ones for the weekend to come.

Then Robby shifted to the Sunday greeting team, in which his mom was already serving. This would set a precedent; was it okay? "Pastor Tim and other leaders have always been incredibly supportive of having our volunteers with special needs on the front lines," Dave says. "It's actually become our preferred approach to greeting today."

I am so thankful that God brought the Brooks family to courageously lead our church. Robby has helped people learn to feel comfortable serving alongside and hanging out with someone who has special needs. Having Robby and his family as an integral part of Liquid has been a huge blessing for our church and the Brooks family, truly a win-win. He has found a place other than his home where he belongs, and people other than his family who love him.

It's important to note: People with special needs want our compassion, not our pity. As a character in *Speechless*, the ABC sitcom about a teen with cerebral palsy, explained, people with disabilities "are not one-dimensional saints who exist to warm the hearts and open the minds of able-bodied people."[6] We believe each person is uniquely made in God's image and has one-of-a-kind gifts to contribute to the body of Christ. One child with Down syndrome does not represent all children. Their diagnosis is not their identity. That's why we always prioritize people before their condition and train folks to use "people first" language ("child with autism" rather than "autistic child").

> People with special needs want our compassion, not our pity. Their diagnosis is not their identity.

When Robby first came to Liquid, our total attendance was around three hundred people. After Robby began serving, our special needs ministry grew naturally and organically. Today we have more than three hundred families with special needs involved in the daily life of our church!

The next growth spurt happened when the Soares family got involved in the church.

Suzi and Alex Soares were active volunteers in their church before having their first and second child. That all changed when their third-born, Ethan, was diagnosed with autism and epilepsy. One of the many adjustments the family had to make was finding a new church. Before visiting Liquid for the first time, Suzi emailed, but unfortunately we dropped the ball and didn't reply. "We were about to give up on Liquid as an option, but my husband said, 'No, let's give it a try' and convinced me to go," Suzi recalls.

They showed up, got their older kids checked into Liquid Family, and then found the class for Ethan, who was four. Suzi remembers giving the team a quick rundown, saying, "He will try to escape if you're not right on him, he can't communicate, he loves trains, and call me if he's too much!"

Suzi recalls her feelings after the service as if it were yesterday. "I was afraid they were going to tell me that they couldn't take Ethan again." Instead the children's pastor asked if they could meet to learn how Liquid could best serve Ethan. When they got together, Suzi described her dream of creating a safe place for kids like Ethan to have a meaningful church experience and of creating a place of rest for parents and siblings.

Several months later, Suzi began volunteering in the children's ministry and soon had opportunity—first as a volunteer, and later as a staff member—to start a ministry that now offers one-on-one buddy support for children with special needs, training for volunteers, plus support groups and monthly respite nights for parents.

Suzi observed, "All the people in Ethan's life have been paid to be there—therapists, aides, and others. Liquid has been the exception. Besides relatives, it's the only place in our world where people show up for him just because they love him. One of Ethan's former buddies is still very much a part of his life and spends time with him on weekends. The church has an incredible witness because of this reality."

I couldn't have asked God to send a better leader than Suzi to be the architect and champion for our thriving special needs ministry. Today she says, "Our son Ethan feels like a rock star here. He knows everyone loves him. And that's how we want others to feel too."

to families with special needs. "We knew the move would be painful, but we were determined to help our son," Kayra says.

As soon as they arrived, the young family began searching for a new church home, and one of their first visits was to Liquid. Our church was meeting in a rented hotel at the time, and the two of them entered with a sense of trepidation. José recalls, "We didn't know what to expect. Would the experience be overwhelming for Andy? Would the church welcome us?"

Their question was answered before they even entered the auditorium. The first person they met was Robby Brooks, a young adult with Down syndrome who serves as a front door greeter. José and Kayra marveled as they watched Robby hand out programs and greet guests with a crooked smile. "José and I were holding hands when we saw him," Kayra reports. "I squeezed my husband's hand and whispered, 'What kind of a place puts a person with Down syndrome as their first impression?'" A flicker of hope lit up their hearts.

Andy was immediately welcomed in the kids' ministry and paired with a trained volunteer buddy, who leveraged Andy's love for music and dancing to teach him Bible stories. "When we picked him up, he didn't want to leave!" Kayra recalls. "Several months later, Pastor Tim did a Christmas series where he shared Liquid's vision for serving families with special needs. He said he wanted Liquid to be known as the one place in the world where people with special needs would have a privileged place at the King's table," Kayra says. "That's when we knew we were home."

Liquid Church has been their spiritual family ever since. "We are all in," Kayra says. "We can't wait for Liquid to be known as the best place in the Northeast for ministry to families with special needs."

SOME CHURCHES MISS IT—BADLY

I'm the first to sadly acknowledge that churches haven't always sent the right signals to families with special needs who are looking for acceptance and inclusion. Often, this comes from simple ignorance and lack of experience; many adults don't know how to relate to or interact with someone with autism or cerebral palsy who lacks social or verbal skills.

Before any church even considers starting a special needs ministry, it must have excellent safety procedures for its existing children's ministry. These procedures are essential and need to be outlined and taught, tested and practiced. If not, the result can be potential abuse of children, followed by devastating damage to the church's reputation with those they hope to reach.

But safety is only the starting point. Parents quickly notice how churches treat (or mistreat) their children, and so does the media. One national ministry recently made headlines across the US when they escorted a twelve-year-old boy with cerebral palsy out of the Sunday service for making noises during worship.

It was Easter. "The boy's mother said, 'Easter Sunday he got all dressed up, got ready to go, no small feat with a kiddo like him.' But . . .

after the opening prayer inside the sanctuary the boy voiced his own kind of 'Amen.'"[7] His sound of praise was louder than others', and it didn't end on cue with everyone else's.

"'We were very abruptly escorted out,' the mother said. Following the incident, the boy's mother contacted church leaders with an offer to start a ministry for special needs children. She told reporters that the idea was 'rejected.'"

Tragically, instead of apologizing for their insensitivity, the church leaders explained they had a high value on creating a "distraction-free environment" in worship—words that, I fear, only confirm that they're tone-deaf to families with special needs.

Honestly, the report made me livid. I couldn't help but think of the four men who loved their crippled friend so much that they ripped the roof off the place where Jesus was preaching (Mark 2:1–12). I wonder if Jesus found that distracting? Instead of calling for security, Jesus stopped his sermon and healed the man on the spot, and the place erupted in praise. That was an object lesson if there ever was one!

To put this boy's experience in national perspective, 32 percent of families who have a member with special needs have changed their place of worship because their child "was not included or welcomed." Overall, only 45 percent of Americans who identify as having a severe disability say they attend a place of worship each month—compared to 57 percent of all Americans.[8]

> Thirty-two percent of families who have a member with special needs have changed their place of worship because their child "was not included or welcomed."

As one researcher, who did a study on health conditions that hinder children and their families from attending church, said, "In many ways, this population is unseen because they never show up, or when they do, they have a negative experience and never return."[9]

It may be easy to blame the church that responded so poorly to the little boy's unique amen, but remember that even Jesus' disciples had to be trained how to demonstrate mercy before they saw the light. When people brought children to Jesus, the disciples shooed them off at first. In response, Jesus became irate, saying, "Don't push these children away" (Mark 10:14 MSG). "Then, gathering the children up in his arms, he laid his hands of blessing on them" (v. 16 MSG).

At Liquid, the way we bless families best is through our training and preparation. On Sundays, each child with special needs is paired with a trained volunteer called a "buddy," who is specially equipped to work with their particular learning style. The goal is for each child to be included in mainstream classroom activities. Our children's areas are equipped with "chill spaces" where kids can cool down if overstimulated or play with sensory "fidgets" that improve focus and help with redirection. We train our volunteers to use tools like visual schedules and timers to facilitate transitions, and headphones to muffle auditory overload. Through their tithes, our congregation even paid to build a multisensory gym room that allows families the chance to enjoy kinetic play and develop their child's motor skills in a safe environment free of charge on weekends. One mom says that similar for-profit kinetic gyms in the community used to cost their family more than one hundred dollars per visit. But our church's gym is open free to the public during the summer months to bless families in our community.

Interestingly enough, two-thirds of our special needs coordinators are young adults. We find that younger generations instinctively gravitate toward this specialized kind of mercy ministry and are eager to invest in the next generation coming up. Even the culture around us today is pro-inclusion. Companies like Target and some clothing brands now feature models with disabilities. For the first time ever, in 2018, Gerber named a child with Down syndrome as its baby of the year.[10] Right now, there is a cultural awakening that champions the inclusion and celebration of people with special needs. What an opportunity for churches of every shape and size! With hundreds of thousands of underserved families with special needs all across our country, we have a chance to lead the way and fulfill our Savior's mandate to love the overlooked.

GRADY GOES TO CHURCH

Recently, I received an email from a mom and dad about their son Grady. Grady is a playful eight-year-old boy with Down syndrome who loves to wrestle and to run around any room he's in. In previous church situations, his high level of energy was treated by teachers as a behavioral problem. After suffering the sting of rejection from several churches, his family stopped going to church altogether for about three years. When they heard from a friend about Liquid's inclusive environment, they drove more than an hour to visit. They've been coming to our church ever since and tell us the long drive is "absolutely worth it for our family."

Grady's mom shared how Grady also has verbal apraxia, which means he has trouble connecting speech messages from his brain to his mouth. As a result, Grady cannot form full sentences, even though he may know what he wants to communicate. However, his mother was proud to report a major breakthrough. Over dinner one Saturday night, Grady declared to his family, "I wanna go to church tomorrow!" She practically gushed:

It's the first real sentence he has ever spoken in his whole seven years! Isn't that a miracle and testament to God's goodness? Every morning he wakes up and says eagerly, "I wanna go to church!" Our other children see how happy Grady is and are excited to go somewhere they all feel welcomed. My husband and I have needed a Sunday morning service so much. Without a faith community, I felt our walk stumble and our marriage start cracking. These past few months have given us restorative time to begin again and worship together once more.

Thank you . . . for being our safe place to land at the end of the week, for your patience and open arms, and your warm presence with our boy. We thank God that our long struggle to find a place for a family like ours led us to a church like yours. As we always say, "A church alive is worth the drive!"

DESPERATE FOR RESPITE

Parents of children with special needs are often desperate for respite, a place to rest from the daily rigors of constantly caring for their child or children. This is where your church has an incredible opportunity to give families a gift each Sunday. While their child is being loved and cared for by a specialized volunteer, Mom and Dad are able to sit in a service together—perhaps the only alone time of their entire week—and simply worship, hold hands, soak in God's Word, and be spiritually refreshed.

This is a priceless gift to exhausted parents—to rest, be still, and be replenished knowing their child is being loved, is being taught about the Father's love, and is receiving the royal treatment. The response of parents has been so enthusiastic that each month, our church now hosts a respite night called Parents' Night Out. On that Friday night, we open our building and provide free childcare and respite for families in our community with kids with special needs.

Parents drop off all their children (the child with special needs plus his or her siblings) at 6:30 p.m., so Mom and Dad can go out for a quiet dinner, go shopping, or see a movie. Some parents have even reported going home to enjoy a three-hour nap before returning to pick up their kids at 10:00 p.m. Bless them! At Liquid, we believe moms and dads are better parents when they're physically rested and emotionally replenished, not constantly running on fumes. Families with special needs are so thirsty for this kind of personal care, and it's a powerful way to refresh them with God's love and mercy.

KINGS AND QUEENS

When I say that it's our joy to give people with special needs the royal treatment, I mean that in a literal way. As word rippled out about our inclusive environment at Liquid Church, we discovered a creative way to reach out beyond our church walls to the special needs community in our city.

I was reading Luke 14, where Jesus commands his followers (not once but twice!) to avoid giving preferential treatment to the powerful and influential. He tells them to instead lavish it on those with limitations. Jesus says, "When you give a banquet, invite the poor, the crippled, the lame, the blind, and you will be blessed. Although they cannot repay you, you will be repaid at the resurrection of the righteous" (vv. 13–14). Then he shares a parable about a king throwing a party, who instructs his servants, "Go out quickly into the streets and alleys of the town and bring in the poor, the crippled, the blind and the lame" (v. 21).

These parties for the poor paint a striking picture of the kingdom of God. The Father's heart is clear: we're to treat those with special needs as his treasured sons and daughters. They are the King's kids, precious in his sight, kings and queens in waiting. Why not throw a lavish party for them?

As we began plotting how to do this for the outside community, we heard about an event called Night to Shine—a prom for people with special needs, created by the Tim Tebow Foundation. Its vision is to partner with churches around the world to provide an unforgettable prom night experience, centered on God's love for people with special needs, ages fourteen and older. As the foundation's website explains, "Night to Shine is a night for the churches to shine, the volunteers to shine, our honored guests to shine, and most importantly, God to shine!"[11]

After launching in 2015, the movement grew in its first three years by 1,150 percent. This means that by 2018, 537 churches around the world hosted Night to Shine, serving approximately 90,000 guests with special needs and being supported by 175,000 volunteers. The events are funded by each host church, but the Tim Tebow Foundation awards funding to some churches, especially first-time sponsoring churches.

We hosted our first Night to Shine prom at Liquid in 2015, and it was a blast! Talk about the royal treatment—we rolled out an actual red carpet to welcome our kings and queens as volunteers cheered for our guests with special needs while they proudly walked down the runway. We set up beauty bars for the young ladies, where cosmetologists donated their time to do the girls' hair and makeup for free. For the guys, we had stations where the pastors shined their shoes—a modern-day version of washing feet!

We even rented stretch limos to drive our guests around the church parking lot. Each guest with a special need was paired up with a host buddy, whose goal was to make sure their guest enjoyed a delicious dinner, danced the night away, and received the royal treatment all evening long.

We catered a special meal for parents, who watched their son or daughter having the time of their life. Many wept as they watched their child—who may never have been invited to a playdate, sleepover, scouting trip, school dance, or other typical rites of passage—be celebrated for the precious child of God they truly are. Caregivers were also invited to enjoy this special meal and witness this wonderful event.

> Many wept as they watched their child—who may never have been invited to a playdate, school dance, or other typical rites of passage— be celebrated for the precious child of God they truly are.

For one glorious night, the kingdom of God touched down on earth as it is in heaven! Those who are often last in line by the world's standard came first. Wheelchairs rolled down that red carpet while hundreds cheered and clapped wildly for them. It was magical for every person present—guests, volunteers, and parents—and there wasn't a dry eye in the house.

The partygoers danced long into the evening. Then came time for the crowning moment. Parents and caregivers were called into the ballroom to watch as each guest took the stage to be individually spotlighted and crowned as a king or queen of the prom. A tiara was placed on the head of each girl, a golden crown on the head of each boy.

Parents and leaders wept openly as we saw the compassionate heart of God in full display. To this day, Night to Shine remains the best night of the year in our church.

We've hosted Night to Shine every year since, and we love to help other churches take their first steps into special needs ministry.[12] "Seeing Christ's compassion on display leaves you feeling energized, and your heart is full by the end of the night," Suzi Soares says. "Our church has grown to be a more radically inclusive community because of the impact of Night to Shine each year."

BIGGER WAVE OF MOMENTUM

Even more exciting: the current of special needs has created a wave of momentum in our community. In 2017, we hosted five special needs proms in the cities where we have campuses, involving more than one thousand guests and volunteers. What's even more remarkable is that hundreds of volunteer roles were "sold out" within twenty-four hours. In 2018, we had to send people from our church to serve at other Night to Shine locations in the tri-state area because ours were full. Catch this: there is now a waiting list for volunteers eager to serve!

In 2017, Tim Tebow came to visit our church in person to share the gospel and celebrate those with special needs. The two-time national champion, first round NFL draft pick, Heisman Trophy winner, and now professional baseball player is a global celebrity. But on Sunday morning, "Timmy" was down to earth and displayed a huge heart for the King's kids.

Between services, Timmy invited anyone with special needs to visit him backstage. We weren't prepared for the crowds; kids with walkers and wheelchairs flooded into the green room. Kids with autism and Down syndrome rushed the former quarterback and tackled him with hugs. It was pandemonium. In the middle of the chaos, somebody spilled a strawberry milkshake on Timmy's brand-new white sneakers.

"No worries," the sports superstar declared. He pulled off his sneakers and got down on his hands and knees to play with the kids in stocking feet. That's the humble, self-giving spirit of Jesus, and it's inspiring.

THE BROADER CURRENT

Special needs ministry has become a powerful ministry current for us at Liquid. And it could be a huge opportunity for you too. Right now, four million to six million children and adults in the United States have developmental disabilities, whether involving mobility, self-care, language, socialization, learning, or independent living.[13] But don't read into that a lack of spiritual interest: in one study, 84 percent of adults with disabilities and 84 percent of adults without disabilities (equal percentages) considered their religious faith to be important; so clearly, a lack of interest is not what is preventing many people with special needs from participating in congregational life.[14]

Since New Jersey has the highest rate of autism in the country, special needs ministry has become a key part of our strategy to saturate our state. Certainly, we still have plenty of room to grow and learn. We are making long-term plans to incorporate teens and adults with special needs into our small group system and to use their one-of-a-kind gifts on our serving teams.[15] One day, we even hope to provide on-the-job training to adults with special needs by turning our Sunday café into a coffeehouse staffed by adults with special needs.

But your church's calling may be different. What overlooked group in your region may God be calling you to love and serve? Homeless veterans? Senior citizens? At-risk teens? Victims of sex trafficking? Those on the foster care rolls?

Search the Scriptures and then search your heart.

Tears are often a clue. I believe the best ministry is born out of personal pain in a leader's life. What breaks your heart that also breaks the heart of God? Look around: who do you see that's overlooked and needs the tender touch of God's grace? The Lord will often put you, as a leader, in close contact with the people he plans for you to serve. Don't be afraid to start small and do it well. That's how a trickle of compassion can turn into a raging river that spills out of your church into the city streets, flooding your community with Christ's love and with rich opportunities to proclaim the gospel in both words and deeds.

Dive Deeper

Stonebriar Community Church (stonebriar.org) is one of many ministries that have influenced Liquid's special needs ministry. Beyond inclusive weekend services, they offer art classes, home skills training, and fitness classes to build the faith and real-world functioning of people with special needs. Thanks to other mentors, we're still going deeper.

What about you? If your church has a heart to serve families with special needs, consider the following steps.

 ANKLE DEEP Start first with the families with special needs who are already attending your church, plus anyone else interested. As a baby step, invite them to a "listening lunch" with yummy food and childcare. Share one of the Scriptures in this chapter that touched your heart with Jesus' care for those with special needs. Ask for honest feedback about their family's current experience on Sundays. What's working? What's frustrating? How can you better support them? Be slow to speak and quick to listen. Don't overpromise (this is only a fact-finding step), and be prepared to take notes. If you ask, people will tell you!

As a next step, consider signing up to volunteer at another church hosting a Night to Shine prom through the Tim Tebow Foundation, as a way to expose your congregation to the power of ministry to people with special needs. Or partner with another church to host one of these events together.

 KNEE DEEP To cast vision to the wider church, pastors can consider preaching a sermon series from the gospel of Mark on Jesus' ministry of compassion to those with disabilities.

As a next step toward holistic family ministry (not just ministry to the individual), consider piloting a Parents' Night Out—onetime, quarterly, or even monthly—that offers free childcare and respite for parents in your community who have children with special needs. Open your church on a Friday night so parents can drop off their kids (the child with special needs and his or her siblings), so Mom and Dad can go out for dinner, go shopping, see a movie, or grab a nap. Be prepared for new guests from your community; word of safe, free, trained childcare travels quickly!

WAIST DEEP Develop a buddy system at your church, in which children with special needs are paired on Sundays with a trained caregiver so they can be included in mainstream classrooms. Offer customized special needs training for volunteers who feel called to lead this ministry.

For those moving into the deeper waters of special needs ministry, take your team to an accessibility summit hosted by a church in your area, or one listed in the next section. While there, ask God to reveal innovative ways your church can lavish love on families with special needs.

Other Churches Making Waves

Woodmen Valley Chapel *(woodmenvalley.org)* lists its Access Ministry for people with special needs directly on its home page, as one of the choices under "care." It highlights what to expect for new families and invites parents to provide a profile of their child to help facilitate a smooth first visit. Woodmen looks to provide individualized classes, one-on-one buddies, sensory support, and behavior strategies to kids, students, and adults through various church-life programs in order to lead them into a growing relationship with Jesus Christ. Access Ministry also provides respite care throughout the year to give caregivers a moment to regroup, siblings a time to feel extra loved, and participants with special needs a time to feel and be seen.

Prestonwood Baptist Church *(prestonwood.org)* regards special needs as different abilities rather than disabilities. The church offers a support group for families with special needs and provides a suite of specially designed rooms devoted to children and adults with special needs, from ages fifteen months to sixty-nine! Offerings include a weekly Bible fellowship, Awana Special Edition, respite nights every other month, a special friends retreat every October for special friends youth and adults, Night to Shine Prom with the Tim Tebow Foundation, and a special Christmas dinner for the special needs community in their region.

McLean Bible Church *(mcleanbible.org)* has an incredibly robust program that yearly serves more than seven hundred families of children with special needs in the Washington, D.C., area. In addition to Sunday inclusion programming (Access), McLean hosts a summer day camp specially designed for kids and teens with special needs (Soaring Over Seven). The church also founded Jill's House *(jillshouse.org)*, which provides overnight respite care for families of children with intellectual disabilities.

Lakewood Church *(lakewood.cc)* launched its Champions Club *(championsclub.org)* in 2009. This developmental program offers spiritual, intellectual, mental, and physical tools for children, youth, and adults with special needs. Champions Club offers a Bible-based curriculum for purchase, as well as step-by-step plans for starting a program in your area. Champions Club also offers multiple free family events such as a yearly banquet, respite nights, and a resource fair for individuals of all ages with special needs.

Rock Church *(sdrock.com)* named its program Miracle 139, based on Psalm 139's "fearfully and wonderfully made" statement in verse 14. The mission of Miracle 139 is to provide a safe and loving environment where every child has the opportunity to learn about Jesus. In addition to providing supports in the children's ministry environments on Sundays, Miracle 139 also hosts a biweekly parents' Bible study and support group (with childcare provided). Various events are held throughout the year, including respite/date nights, pet encounter therapy, educational seminars, and larger community events such as their annual Summer Sports Spectacular and Day at the Beach. Miracle 139 also offers customized consultation and training to churches (both local and international) that want to launch their own special needs ministry.

CHAPTER FIVE

IGNITE THE IMAGINATION: CREATIVE COMMUNICATION

> Jesus always used stories and illustrations like these
> when speaking to the crowds.
> —MATTHEW 13:34 NLT

The house lights dim, and a giant movie screen flickers to life. The audience settles back in their seats as a throbbing techno soundtrack signals the start of a sixty-second movie trailer. Up on the big screen, a man in a slick, black motorcycle helmet and racing jacket roars down a crowded city street. His engine revs as the sound of police sirens grows louder. A high-speed chase is on.

Quick cut to an overhead drone shot of skyscrapers and a clock tower that looks vaguely European. Is the setting Istanbul, Turkey? Too soon to tell.

Jump cut to a close-up of fingers feverishly typing code into a computer laptop. Some kind of secret message is being transmitted. The cryptic words "7 letters" appear onscreen. The message is uploaded, and the mysterious man takes off running down a hallway, his pursuers not far behind.

The next few seconds of this heart-pounding movie trailer could have been lifted straight out of *Mission: Impossible* or the latest Jason Bourne thriller. The speeding motorcycle races down a labyrinth of city streets while "7 cities"—another ominous clue—flashes onscreen. Clearly, someone is trying to deliver a top-secret message. The tension builds, tires skid, the music crescendos, and the trailer resolves to the title of this riveting thriller: *Se7en Churches of Revelation.*

Turns out, it's not a Bourne movie after all. It's a sermon trailer introducing a seven-week message series at Liquid Church.

Let me state my bias up front: I believe it's a sin to be boring in church. At Liquid, we think the greatest story ever told deserves the most dynamic communication we can imagine. We believe our show-then-tell approach to service programming is vital to effectively communicating God's timeless truth to a new generation raised on digital devices.

> It's a sin to be boring in church. The greatest story ever told deserves the most dynamic communication we can imagine.

When I told our creative team that we were going to teach for seven straight weeks from the book of Revelation, there were some eye rolls. A few recalled the Christian broadcaster who had issued multiple predictions for the end of the world, followed by multiple fails. Others envisioned a hallucinogenic mix of strange symbols and weird images that resembled a Quentin Tarantino movie on acid.

But when the apostle John set pen to paper and wrote the last book of the Bible, he was on the island of Patmos, a prison colony for enemies of Rome. Huddled in a cave, John was visited by the Lord himself and received a divine download foretelling the future of the world. With trembling hands, the aging apostle wrote down what he saw and heard and sent seven letters to seven churches located in seven cities—Ephesus, Smyrna, Pergamum, Thyatira, Sardis, Philadelphia, and Laodicea. These cities were situated along an ancient mail route in Asia Minor and are located in modern-day Turkey.

As the lights came up after the sermon trailer, I stood onstage with a big iron mailbox. Slowly opening the lid, I took out the first letter. It was to Ephesus. I dramatically read it out loud and then explained to the congregation how each week, we'd read one of John's letters from Revelation and ask, "What was Jesus saying to this ancient church?" But then we'd ask a scarier question: "What is Jesus saying to our church today?"

People were hooked. The combination of edge-of-your-seat sermon video and creative staging—which included the iron mailbox and seven giant glowing stars from John's vision—was compelling. For seven weeks, we went line by line through Revelation chapters 2–3, some of the most challenging passages in Scripture.

And catch this: our attendance grew. People invited their friends, using postcard-size invites we provided to share with coworkers and neighbors. In New Jersey! We had record attendance of new guests, who each received a custom-designed study guide on Revelation, with high-resolution photography and discussion questions for small groups.

WHAT IF WE HAD BEEN (YAWN) BORING AND UNCREATIVE?

Now imagine for a moment that we had promoted this sermon series the old-fashioned way, with a verbal tell-only announcement from the pulpit: "Next Sunday, Pastor Tim will begin a seven-week study on ancient apocalyptic literature. Please invite a friend." Nobody would have come. At least, I wouldn't have.

Biblical illiteracy in our country is higher than it's been in more than a century,[1] especially among unchurched people. Just ask your neighbor or coworker to distinguish between Jonah and Noah. (And don't snicker when someone tells you that Noah's wife was Joan of Arc.) That's why creative images, dramatic storytelling, and dynamic video are powerful tools to draw in people to encounter God's Word in a fresh way and experience a life-changing message—to show them and then tell them.

For *Se7en Churches of Revelation,* we posted the sermon trailer on YouTube, and people shared the video with friends across Facebook and Instagram. For two months, we tackled tough topics like cultural compromise, sexual idolatry, the persecuted church, and lukewarm Christian living. And people kept coming back for more. We learned afresh: video, creative staging, and memorable props don't dilute God's Word; they amplify its power!

Biblical illiteracy in our country is higher than it's been in more than a century, especially among unchurched people.

Video, creative staging, and memorable props don't dilute God's Word; they amplify its power!

KILLER CONTENT IS KING

A recent Gallup poll confirmed that "Sermon Content Is What Appeals Most to Churchgoers."[2] Ask the typical American who attends church at least once a month what motivates their attendance, and 75 percent will say, "Sermons that teach about Scripture and connect faith to everyday life," according to Gallup. That's more than double the percentage who say having good music, a choir, or praise band is a major reason they attend.

If you want to reach unchurched people—and get part-timers to become Sunday regulars—killer content is king. At Liquid, dynamic, relevant teaching is our primary engine for growth. It's what brings people through the front door. (What keeps them here is a combination of family ministry, small groups, volunteer teams, and community outreach. We want every guest to have a role and a relationship within their first four visits; that's what closes our back door.) But make no mistake: the greatest thing you can do to bring spiritually thirsty people through your front door week after week is to create killer content every single weekend.

> The greatest thing you can do to bring spiritually thirsty people through your front door week after week is to create killer content every single weekend.

At Liquid, teaching leads. It's our caramel macchiato. Just like Starbucks organizes the entire menu around their cornerstone drink, we organize our entire ministry around a twelve-month preaching calendar designed to feed our flock a balanced diet of culturally relevant Bible teaching that tackles both felt needs and deep discipleship.

You may wonder, *What's the difference between teaching and preaching, anyway?* My friend Carey Nieuwhof (who wrote the foreword to this book) makes a helpful distinction: "It's always hard to define the exact difference between the two, but simply put, preaching speaks more to the heart, teaching speaks more to the head. Preachers facilitate an experience. Teachers convey information. I think the best pastors do both well. . . . Preaching leads people to say 'That's right. I need to change.' Teaching can lead people to say 'He's right. That's a good point.'"[3]

Before I was a preacher, I was a high school English teacher, so I have a little bit of both in me. I love to teach people new things and show them insights into God's Word. But if push comes to shove, I'd rather have people leave responding, "That's right; I need to change" than "He's right; that's a good point." Life change is the ultimate goal of Spirit-filled preaching that transforms the whole person—heart, soul, and mind.

TGIF WORLD

Here's the challenge: We live in a TGIF world dominated by Twitter, Google, Instagram, and Facebook. People live on their screens and are constantly pulled in every direction by tweets, texts, snaps, song downloads, games, memes, and YouTube videos. This has had a profound impact on communication, eroding our ability to concentrate for longer periods and absorb complex information. On the plus side, the next generation is adept at multitasking and fluent in visual literacy (the world of images, photos, and videos). The old analog world was word based, but our digital world is image driven. The first instinct of many young adults is to communicate through texts, emojis, photos, videos, and social media (and many don't even bother with email).

Today's highly visual communication style sounds a lot like how Jesus communicated in the first century. Take his Sermon on the Mount (Matthew 5–7). It takes about twelve minutes to read aloud (113 verses, or 1,997 Greek words). Nineteen different times, he asked a question as a way of engaging his audience ("Why do you worry about clothes?" [6:28]). More than fifty times, he commanded a specific action ("Do not worry" [6:25]; "Go and be reconciled" [5:24]).

> We live in a TGIF world dominated by Twitter, Google, Instagram, and Facebook.

He continually uses word pictures or figures of speech ("See how the flowers of the field grow" [6:28]). And it's hard to imagine any listener not finding immediate relevance in his words about forgiveness, hypocrisy, anger, lust, love for enemies, and more.

Yet today's Western sermon format traces less to the Sermon on the Mount than to the sixteenth-century Protestant Reformation, and it remains little changed since then as an art form. Back in eighteenth-century colonial New England, sermons went so long (two hours was not unusual) that parishioners often dozed off. Some took "day of rest" quite literally! No one considered making the sermon more engaging to help people stay awake. Instead, a church official called a tithingman patrolled the aisles, armed with a long stick. One end was a hard knob or point, the other a feather or bit of fur. When this tithingman (yup, he also made sure people kept up their financial contributions) caught men nodding off, he gave them a rap on the head. Women who dozed got a tickle with the feather or fur.[4]

Sermons may have gotten shorter over the years, but the traditional Protestant sermon has remained more like a college lecture, expounding a scriptural topic before a passive audience who is expected to pay attention. The significant graying of today's church tells me yesterday's format ain't gonna work for this generation.

People today have the attention span of a bumblebee. That means they won't sit still for a forty-minute, one-way monologue; a generation raised on social media expects a multilayered experience that engages them verbally, visually, emotionally, and kinetically. It's like the difference between a megaphone and a telephone. The traditional sermon is like a megaphone: one-way communication aimed at people. But social media is like a telephone: it's two-way conversation between people, including hyperlinks to related content. I post a picture and you comment. You text a video and I tweet it to others.

> The traditional sermon that lacks word pictures and application to modern life is dying; in its place, a new generation of right-brained communicators is rising.

The traditional sermon that lacks word pictures and application to modern life seems to be dying; in its place, a new generation of right-brained communicators is rising. What I see gives me great hope for a new future of relevant preaching.

GRAY MATTERS

Today's digital revolution is rewiring the collective brain of today's rising generations. Their likely preference is to process this chapter as video content, or at least to see the information accented by multimedia. Maybe you too feel that way. That's because of the way your brain is wired.

It's common knowledge that the brain is divided into right and left hemispheres. They process information at the same time but in different ways. Your right brain, the creative half, fires up when you walk on the beach and feel the sand between your toes. It's your passion and creativity that inspires you to spill paint on a blank canvas or write a poem for your spouse. On the other side, your left brain is more linear and analytical, orderly and logical. The left hemisphere fires up when you pay bills or straighten your sock drawer.

Both right and left hemispheres work together to balance creativity and logic. As my friend Mark Batterson, a pastor and author, explains,

> Think of the two hemispheres of the brain as parallel processors. They overlap in function. . . . Now juxtapose brain topography with Matthew 22:37: "You must love the LORD your God with all your heart, all your soul, and *all* your mind" (NLT).
>
> Loving God with half your mind does not cut it. Half-minded is no better than half-hearted. Many preachers, nevertheless, are trying to preach with half their brain tied behind their back, which is about as effective as running on one leg, clapping with one hand, or twiddling one thumb.[5]

I'm calling for a whole-brained revolution in the next generation of communicators. For the last four hundred years of Western church history, there was a disproportionate focus on left-brain logic in preaching. Seminaries taught systematic theology and how to write a three-point sermon, which is no doubt a helpful framework for young preachers who need to learn order, structure, and logical development of a scriptural idea or theme. Ain't nothing wrong with that. Every beginning classical pianist needs to practice scales. But if you wanna play EDM (electronic

If you wanna play EDM for gen Z, you've got to pair right-brain creativity with left-brain logic.

dance music) for gen Z, you've got to pair right-brain creativity with left-brain logic.

As an English major at Wheaton College, I was required to read all sorts of novels, plays, and poetry that fired up my right brain. But to graduate, I had to write well-organized, expository essays that analyzed each text and were supported by scholarly sources. I remember guzzling coffee late at night in the library so I could keep my left brain awake to finish term papers. But I had a secret weapon: the British writer C. S. Lewis. True fact: Wheaton houses a major research collection of Lewis's books and papers, including his family wardrobe that inspired the Oxford don's writing of *The Lion, the Witch and the Wardrobe*.

Because of this historical connection, C. S. Lewis was pretty much the patron saint of the English department. If you got stuck writing an essay and couldn't think of anything else to say, I learned as an undergrad, land with a C. S. Lewis quote, and you wouldn't get less than a B+. (Okay, that may not be completely accurate, but that's how my right brain remembers it.)

Lewis is a great example of a whole-brained communicator. If you read one of Lewis's theological classics, such as *Mere Christianity*, you'll immediately notice he was left-brain logical. But Lewis combined that left-brain logic with right-brain creativity to produce his Christian masterwork the Chronicles of Narnia. Like his close friend and writing buddy J. R. R. Tolkien (another whole-brained communicator), Lewis used his imagination to create a fanciful realm of enchanted creatures that continues to capture imaginations today.

> The church should be the most creative place on the planet, because we serve the Creator of the planets!

I believe God wants to baptize the imaginations of a brand-new generation of whole-brained preachers to reach our TGIF world. The church should be the most creative place on the planet, because we serve the Creator of the planets! Multisensory sermons should spill forth with stories, metaphors, art, video, lyrics, and colorful graphics. This is not just a little sugar to help the medicine go down; right-brain creativity is vital to engage the hearts and minds of this TGIF generation and inspire them to make their faith their own.

THE CREATIVE PROCESS

Recent research suggests that the connection between the brain's two hemispheres is stronger than previously imagined,[6] which to me further validates Liquid's creative process. Also, the widespread idea that people are either visual learners or auditory learners seems to be losing support,[7] giving way to a view that the way people learn is far more complex than we tend to think. Variety seems to be the best and simplest solution, adjusted by audience, context, and the content of the message.

That said, creating sticky sermons that resonate with the next generation does not happen spontaneously! It requires careful planning. At Liquid, we follow a ten-step process.

 1. Plan the Sermon Series

We preach in sermon series and typically spend four to five weeks unpacking a single theme or topic. Some address felt needs such as marriage and relationships, handling anxiety, managing money, or parenting. Others drill down on deeper discipleship topics such as prayer and fasting, spiritual warfare, the end times, or racial reconciliation.

Why teach topically in a series? Because you're preaching to a Netflix generation. I still remember the days when Netflix movies arrived by mail in red envelopes. (Anybody remember renting videos at Blockbuster?[8]) But today's generation watches their favorite shows like *Stranger Things*, *This Is Us*, or *The Crown* on demand. They carry a screen in their pocket and binge-watch entire seasons in a single sitting. Ask your young adults, "What season are you watching?" and they'll tell you. Our minds are being hardwired to think in terms of series, seasons, and episodes. A four- or five-week sermon series is instantly understandable to this audience and, more important, "invitable"— something that will appeal to their friends.

We typically plan twelve sermon series each year on our preaching calendar, anchored by two six-week small group campaigns, one in the spring and one in the fall (seasons when people are most likely to attend consecutive weeks in a row). We publish in-house curriculum for these campaigns, which increases traction with our small groups.

Where do sermon ideas come from? Most come straight from the Bible, but others are triggered by a wide variety of sources—movies, music, news reports, and cultural trends, each begging for God's perspective in Scripture. I call it our magpie process (named after the bird famous for building its nests from random bits of string, foil, and other found objects), and I keep an open file full of potential sermon ideas for future use. Each fall, our teaching team goes on a planning retreat, in which we pray and share our teaching ideas that we've been gathering throughout the year.

2. Write the Creative Brief

For each series, the teaching team writes a two-page creative brief that explains what the series is about from a thirty-thousand-foot level. It includes a blurb, or brief description (similar to an Amazon book summary), an outline of topics or Scriptures to be covered, as well as suggestions for staging and props. What makes the creative brief unique, however, is that we also include a page of photos and pictures, like an advertising lookbook, to immediately begin generating visual ideas for branding.

In January 2018, we did a series called *Divine Direction*, which was based on the missionary journeys of Paul in the book of Acts. We branded it using giant GPS pins to create the look of a Google map and promoted it as a series about personal direction (notice the emphasis on real-life application). Description: "Wouldn't it be great if there were a GPS for life? Directions for which school to attend, who to date or marry, where to live, what career path to follow? Join us this January for *Divine Direction* and learn to discern God's will for key areas of your life! When you know who to trust, it's easier to know what to do with the blank pages of your story. This year, discover your divine direction!"

This was a highly attractional series to kick off the new year, as it touched on people's felt need to begin their year with clear direction and purpose. The application was easy to make while we charted the travels and challenges of Paul as he overcame obstacles and followed the Spirit's leading from Asia Minor to Rome.

3. Choose a Wineskin

Next, we come up with a "skin" to brand each sermon series. The word skin is sometimes used in marketing to refer to the wrapper that a product is packaged in. However, our inspiration comes from Jesus' analogy about wineskins. Referring to his revolutionary message of grace, Jesus said, "No one puts new wine into old wineskins. For the old skins would burst from the pressure, spilling the wine and ruining the skins. New wine is stored in new wineskins so that both are preserved" (Matt. 9:17 NLT). He was speaking of the need for the new wine of the gospel to have fresh containers to carry it to thirsty people.

Think of message content as the wine. While each series contains timeless biblical truth that never changes, we frequently update the container to make that truth culturally relevant. We'll often leverage popular TV shows, movies, and music to skin a sermon series and tackle spiritual issues. We used the skin of *Fixer Upper* (a popular home renovation show starring Chip and Joanna Gaines) to brand a sermon series on Nehemiah (rebuilding the city walls). In the same way, we leveraged the NBC family drama *This Is Us* to skin a series on relationships. Fans of the show invited coworkers and friends, and we delivered some hard-hitting biblical truth on touchy topics including family dysfunction, addiction and secrecy, adoption, and forgiveness, complete with video clips from poignant moments in the show. That's the creative power of skinning a series. New wineskins allow us to earn a fresh hearing for the gospel in a way that connects with our culture and modern minds.

> New wineskins allow us to earn a fresh hearing for the gospel in a way that connects with our culture and modern minds.

At Liquid, music and media are a big part of the way we communicate, and we're not shy about leveraging secular songs and movies for redemptive purposes. I've found that most churches take one of three approaches to our surrounding culture: rejection, reception, or redemption. Some reject secular culture (with judgment). Others receive it with open arms (but without discernment). At Liquid, we choose a third option: we redeem the culture for gospel purposes.

Every summer, we do a special series called *At the Movies*, which explores the biblical truth behind Hollywood's biggest hits. Three weeks prior to this series, we challenge and equip people to invite their unsaved friends and neighbors to church. It's an easy ask. Who doesn't love summer movies and free popcorn in church? (Yes, seriously, we do that.)

But don't let our shiny wrapper fool you. This is a powerful gospel series that disarms listeners and tackles tough scriptural topics. In recent years, we screened clips from *Hacksaw Ridge* (forgiving your enemies), *Wonder Woman* (developing women as leaders), *The Shack* (why does God allow unspeakable evil?), and *The Greatest Showman* (how the church is God's collection of misfits).

> Some reject secular culture (with judgment). Others receive it with open arms (but without discernment). At Liquid, we redeem the culture for gospel purposes.

We regularly have dozens of salvations during our *At the Movies* series as people see glimpses of the gospel reflected on the big screen. Although we don't endorse every film we examine, we mine each one to locate clips that powerfully dramatize the brokenness of our world and the desperate need for hope outside ourselves. As people watch and listen, the soil of their hearts is tilled by a well-told story, and gospel seeds can be planted there.

We do the same thing with music in a series called *Pop God*, which looks at the lyrics of popular songs by artists like Bruno Mars, Maroon 5, and Adele. We've found that modern song lyrics provide a powerful soundtrack to preaching chapter by chapter through the minor prophets of the Old Testament.

I realize some might object to playing secular music or movie clips in church, but the reality is, our culture is deeply influenced by the stories we tell and the music we listen to. Although they may not reflect biblical values at first glance, they are often unflinching in their portrayal of humanity's brokenness and set the stage for God's solution of salvation. Just as preachers exegete Scripture, whole-brain communicators need to exegete culture so they can redeem it.

In the Middle Ages, churches used stained glass to visually communicate the gospel story in images to a preliterate people. Now that we are preaching to a postliterate world of screenagers, as Mark Batterson often says, movie screens are the new stained glass of the church. Each Liquid campus is equipped with a theater-size movie screen so that a livestream of the Sunday sermon can be broadcast to our satellite locations.

At first, some folks are skeptical about experiencing a message via a video screen, but the high definition is so sharp, they often forget about the screen after the first few minutes. Even at our broadcast campus, starting with the third or fourth row, more people watch the teaching on the large side screens rather than looking directly at the stage. Who knew? The Holy Spirit travels through pixels!

> Just as preachers exegete Scripture, whole-brain communicators need to exegete culture so they can redeem it.

4. Design a Look and Logo

After skinning a series, our graphic team designs the look and logo for the series. Increasingly, our culture communicates in icons and easy-to-remember brand names like Apple, Starbucks, or Google. For this reason, we tend to favor short, easy-to-remember sermon brands and logos such as:

- *FAST:* a forty-day sermon series on the power of fasting and prayer. The bright, colorful logo featured fresh fruit and vegetables that looked like they belonged on the cover of a Whole Foods cookbook. We took our cue from the "Daniel Fast" featured in Daniel 1:8–14.
- *SWAT:* a six-week series on spiritual warfare and tactics (SWAT), based on the armor of God passage in Ephesians. For this series, we took high-res photographs of replica pieces of shiny Roman armor, from a red-bristled helmet (salvation) to an abs-of-steel breastplate (righteousness). Then we taught systematically through each theological concept of Ephesians 6:11–18.
- *LIT:* a special Christmas series on how Jesus became the shimmering light of a sin-darkened world through the incarnation (Matt. 4:16). We used thousands of dazzling lights to frame a glittering black-and-gold logo which gave Christmas a fresh, modern look.

Again, the logo and look of a sermon are not window dressing, as some think. It's honoring your brain's bias for processing visual information quickly. People often say, "A picture is worth a thousand words." A single visual can communicate more powerfully than a written description. But the reality is, a good logo is worth way more than a thousand words. As Doug Oss and Mark Batterson point out,

> According to neurological research, the brain is able to process print on a page at a rate of approximately 100 bits per second. But the brain can process a picture at approximately 1 billion bits per second. Mathematically speaking, a picture is worth 10 million words.
>
> Logos are important because of the way the brain processes information. The brain recognizes and remembers shapes first, colors second, and content third. This is the sequence of cognition. If you want people to listen to the content of what you say, you need to think about shapes and colors. If choosing color schemes seems to be void of spiritual significance, read the Book of Exodus. A dozen chapters are devoted to design. God gives specific instructions about colors and scents.
>
> Aesthetics are important.[9]

Liquid's creative team today consists of graphic designers, video producers, and photographers. Some are on staff, and many are volunteer. Some of our most creative artists are teenagers and young adults who naturally think visually.

I often remind them about Bezalel, the chief artisan of the tabernacle, who was in charge of building the ark of the covenant. In Exodus 31, the Lord told Moses, "See, I have chosen Bezalel . . . and I have filled him with the Spirit of God, with wisdom, with understanding, with knowledge and with all kinds of skills—to make artistic designs for work in gold, silver and bronze, to cut and set stones, to work in wood, and to engage in all kinds of crafts" (vv. 2–5). Bezalel was a multimedia designer. God had an artistic vision for visually communicating his glory via color, texture, and design, so he divinely gifted a group of artists led by Bezalel. What an honor!

EVERY RIVER
Starts with a Trickle

When I first started preaching, I didn't have a clue how to structure a sermon. Yes, I was taking seminary classes at night, but my teaching outlines were unimaginative and full of lame alliteration and boring acrostics. Plus I was insecure, so I made a mistake that many young preachers make: I tried to imitate my idol, who at the time was Tim Keller. Big mistake. I'm not nearly as smart as Tim. I sound downright foolish when I try to imitate him. Also, I took far too long to explain my point. If a Bible passage had two main points, I'd preach ten, throwing in every jot and tittle of biblical trivia to prove I had done my homework. Recently, I looked back at some of my early manuscripts—sermons that ran more than twenty typed pages and were more than an hour long. (Forgive me, Father.) I would preach people into the kingdom and out again, all in the same very long breath!

But I was doing one thing right. From day one, I sought to make connections to our contemporary culture as I showed how Scripture applies to life today. I used movie clips during our first weeks as a Sunday school for young adults. And fortunately, our fledgling congregation was patient as I grew and matured along with them. Over time, I began applying what I'd learned as an English major and film student in college.

Namely, less is more.

At Wheaton, I spent part of my senior year studying at the Los Angeles Film Studies Center in Southern California. I was lucky to land an internship at a Hollywood studio, and because of my background in English literature, they placed me in the story development department to read screenplays. They sat me at a little desk in the corner, and on the first day, my supervisor plopped down a stack of unread scripts. "Here you go," he said. "Read the first twenty pages of each one." I looked at the stack of stories that aspired to become motion pictures and thought about the hours that writers had invested in each full-length screenplay. My supervisor held one up and leafed through the first few pages. "If you don't laugh or feel something in ten minutes, file it here." He dropped it in the garbage can next to my desk.

Welcome to Hollywood.

I quickly learned the importance of grabbing attention and evoking emotion within the first ten minutes. So when I began preaching, I used film clips from old-school movies like *The Matrix* and *Braveheart* to capture attention and immediately engage the heart. That first Sunday school class had an old-fashioned flannelgraph, but I replaced it with a TV and used DVDs to begin each Bible lesson. Over time, I found that the power was not in the movies or videos themselves; it was in the power of story and my use of symbols to make connections to contemporary life. Story and symbolism can help bring Scripture to life and would often inspire my audience to take action. So I began to structure my sermons using those elements, which we still use today at Liquid.

SCRIPTURE, SYMBOL, STORY

I have a cherry-red step stool in my office that I use to coach aspiring communicators and pastors. The step stool has three legs, and I ask them to imagine it represents their sermon. I believe an effective sermon is supported by a structure of three legs: Scripture, symbol, and story.

Scripture

As a Christian church that is based on the teachings of the Bible as the Word of God, we start with Scripture as the first foundational leg for every message. The first step is to select the primary biblical text we will be teaching from.

Symbol

The second leg of the stool represents a symbol. Often, the biblical passage will suggest a symbol to illustrate the truth we're trying to convey. In the sermon series *Se7en Churches of Revelation*, we featured a memorable prop or visual hook each week to help the audience see what I was verbally communicating.

For week one, we looked at Ephesus (the forgetful church), and we featured a red plastic heart that was frozen in a block of ice. This visually represented Christians whose love for the Lord had grown cold. As I preached the message, I chipped away at the ice with an ice pick and taught people how to regain their passion for God.

For week two, we looked at Smyrna (the suffering church), and I brought a juice press and a bowl of oranges onto the stage. The believers in Smyrna were being persecuted by the Roman emperor Domitian for refusing to worship Caesar, and Jesus said to them, "I know your afflictions" (Rev. 2:9). In the original language, the word affliction meant to be crushed or squeezed between two plates. As I described how these early Christians were being afflicted in Smyrna, I put the oranges into the juice press and squeezed the life out of each one, wringing out the juice until there was nothing left but a flattened peel. People in the audience quickly understood the symbolism, and they identified some of the ways they were feeling the squeeze in their finances, faith, health, and relationships. The message led us into a time of passionate prayer for persecuted Christians living in North Korea, China, Iraq, and Syria.

Week seven was on Laodicea, the lukewarm church, and we featured a fun moment that no one will forget. In this confrontational letter to the lukewarm Christians of Laodicea, Jesus tells them, "I know your deeds, that you are neither cold nor hot. I wish you were either one or the other! So, because you are lukewarm—neither hot nor cold—I am about to spit you out of my mouth" (Rev. 3:15-16). The word of judgment from Jesus is very strong here. He tells the Laodiceans that their lukewarm faith makes him want to puke! To illustrate the point Jesus was making, I asked for a volunteer from the audience. A teenager in the front row waved his hand wildly, and I pulled him up onstage. I gave him a rain poncho and ski goggles to put on, and then, after taking a long swig of lukewarm tap water and holding it in my mouth, I had the congregation read Jesus' words out loud again. When they got to the words "spit you out of my mouth," I let loose and sprayed the young man from head to toe! The audience was shocked, but the teenage volunteer loved it. Returning to his seat, he high-fived his friends. "I got spit on by the pastor!"

These symbols, illustrations, visual aids, and live demonstrations all bring the Bible to life by creating memorable moments that engage the heart and lead to a clear call for response. Jesus loved to pull ordinary objects from everyday life into his teaching. He'd point to the birds of the air, the lilies of the field, a handful of seeds, a flock of sheep, a net full of fish, using these objects as symbols to illuminate deep spiritual truths.

Story

After we locate a secondary symbol, derived from the primary image or idea in Scripture, we figure out how to incorporate a story. A compelling story will connect the spiritual truth of the Bible to the world of the listeners' emotions and feelings. Personal stories are very powerful and invite the audience to identify with the truth of what's being taught, evoking a range of emotion—compassion, sadness, laughter, or anger. In a sermon series on relationships, I will often tell stories about my early mistakes as a husband, bumbling attempts at romance, or moments of frustration or conflict gone awry, for the audience to identify with. And here's a secret: people would rather learn from your mistakes than be impressed with your success. For younger generations, authenticity is the currency of relational trust. When you come clean about your boneheaded mistakes and share how God responded with grace, you go up a notch in their eyes.

Some of my best anecdotes use humor to make a point. Do you remember my crazy story in the preface about the bloody sock? I used a symbol and a funny memory to make a point and to make you laugh. I believe laughter is one of the hallmarks of a healthy church (echoing Proverbs 17:22: "A cheerful heart is good medicine"). Humor is a great way to build a bridge of connection with newcomers as well. During key outreach seasons like Easter and Christmas, we'll have scores of new guests, and I'll open the message with a funny story to break the ice and put visitors at ease. Laughter truly is the shortest distance between two strangers.

Stories that illustrate scriptural truth can be found anywhere and everywhere. In the early days of our church, I used to record voice memos on my iPhone whenever I heard a story on the news or at the mall, gym, or office. I'm a serial collector of stories, and today we have a team of story curators at our church who assist in this by combing the congregation for stories of life change—a healed marriage, a recovery from addiction, a dig-out from debt, a testimony to the power of prayer. Today we frequently send a video team to record these stories through interviews of the people God touched. Then I incorporate these stories into the sermon.

For a message on God's power to heal the sick, we shared the powerful story of a nine-year-old girl named Leah in our church family who was suddenly paralyzed by a spinal stroke in March 2018. Her parents, Peter and Abby, were devastated and our entire church hit our knees in prayer on behalf of little Leah. We prayed and fasted and begged God to do a miracle. At a special night of worship and healing prayer, we laid hands on the family and asked Jesus to speak the words "Talitha koum!" (which means "Little girl, I say to you, get up!") as recorded in Mark 5:41. Incredibly, over the course of the following weeks, Leah regained movement in her toes. Then her fingers. Then she was able to sit up. Doctors were encouraged and took her off the respirator. Eventually, Leah returned home and began rehabilitation to regain the use of her limbs. It was a miracle in the making.

The following spring, our video team visited the family's home and captured beautiful footage of Leah walking and happily climbing all over playground equipment, well on the road to recovery. We interviewed Peter and Abby, who tearfully told the story of God's miraculous provision in healing their daughter. We showed the family's powerful testimony video in a Sunday sermon called "God of Miracles," and our congregation erupted in claps, tears, laughter, and shouts of praise. It's one thing to talk about a miracle; it's another to show one! Exactly one year later in March 2019, Leah walked across the stage of our broadcast campus and our church family nearly ripped the roof off cheering and praising Jesus for his mercy and goodness. That's the power of story. And the story of a powerful God.

> Our church family nearly ripped the roof off cheering and praising Jesus for his mercy and goodness. That's the power of story. And the story of a powerful God.

So there you have it. Our preaching at Liquid is composed of three elements: Scripture, symbol, and story. They are the three legs of the step stool. Or you can think of them as the ingredients in our secret sauce, like a combination of tomatoes, garlic, and olive oil—the three things that are essential to spicing up a good meal. These three ingredients can make any topic taste good (sorry, but I married an Italian). They make our communication style at Liquid memorable and help us motivate hearts and engage minds, especially for a visual, story-driven generation. We employ this recipe in every teaching environment in our church, from kids to students to adults.

None of this is original to us. We ripped it off from the master teacher himself—Jesus! Our Lord was, unsurprisingly, the most compelling communicator in human history. And when he preached and taught, his audience could hear, see, and feel his teaching. Jesus quoted Scripture as his source material. He told memorable short stories (parables like that of the prodigal son, the good Samaritan, the ten virgins, the lost sheep). And he used striking symbols to illustrate deeper spiritual truth (seed and soil, bread and wine). To follow Jesus' teaching style, the savvy communicator combines all three ingredients—Scripture, symbol, and story—to challenge listeners to take their next step toward Christ.

WHAT'S YOUR NEXT STEP?

Don't forget that none of this means anything if it doesn't help people take their next step toward Jesus. That's what a step stool is for, right? We want people to step up and take hold of something that was previously out of reach. From the very beginning, we've made it the goal of every message to inspire people to take their next step closer to Jesus.

What do these action steps look like? In a sermon, we may ask people to pray to receive Christ as Savior, confess sin or a secret struggle, receive Communion, get baptized, join a small group, volunteer to serve, feed the hungry, forgive an enemy, go on a clean water trip, give tithes and offerings to God, pray for healing, go for counseling, or invite a friend to church. Some of the most powerful moments in our services have been spontaneous, Spirit-led responses when people have come forward in prayer and repentance. I remember one service in which a girl came forward to confess her drug addiction and surrendered a bag full of pills on the Communion table. We not only prayed for her but helped her join a rehab program.

Spiritual steps are how people progress in their journey of faith. A lifetime of small steps, week after week, can result in dramatic life change. Our church is filled with people who have taken their first step in a weekend service in response to a Spirit-filled, convicting message that applied to their life. They took a step closer to Jesus, took a step into community, went for counseling, or released their anger, fear, or addiction to God and are now walking in freedom. Over time, these steps have resulted in changed lives, changed families, changed marriages, and changed hearts that are surrendered to Christ.

Now that you know our secret sauce, let me ask: what's your next step in your teaching ministry?

But notice something important: Bezalel is the first person mentioned in Scripture as being "filled . . . with the Spirit of God." And he was an artist, not a priest. Creativity is a divinely inspired gift, and I guarantee there are Spirit-filled creatives in your church just waiting to be tapped into.

5. Shoot a Series Trailer

After the look and logo for a sermon series is designed, our video team storyboards and shoots a trailer for promotion. A trailer is a short video, typically sixty to ninety seconds long, used to promote the series. Some trailers are action-packed (like the opening video for *Se7en*), while others are poignant, if the subject matter calls for it (marriage or parenting). Others are funny and super shareable on social media. If the trailer requires actors, we feature people from our congregation so the audience sees someone like them on the screen.

If you're thinking, *We can't afford the money or time to shoot our own videos!* try asking a couple of your young adults to create one. They can probably do it on their smartphone. Or visit Life Church's website (*life.church*) and join their Open Network, through which you can download sermon series trailers and graphics, all for free.

6. Create a Buzz

In today's TGIF world, ideas spread best via word of mouse. To promote each sermon series, we create digital assets that can be shared and spread. We make social media graphics and sometimes videos for our people to post on Instagram and Facebook. We also create electronic and printed invite-a-friend cards to support our people's in-person relationships. This combination of word-of-mouth testimony with word-of-mouse technology is the best way to generate buzz about your ministry in the crowded and noisy digital marketplace of ideas.

7. Add Props and Staging

Jesus didn't simply tell stories to make his sermons stick; he plucked props from everyday life to powerfully illustrate his preaching. Whether holding up one of Caesar's coins, scattering seeds on the ground, or pointing to fishing nets, Jesus often used visual aids to drive his message home—an effective show-then-tell approach to teaching.

Over the years, our teaching team has frequently leveraged ordinary objects to communicate scriptural truth. An early Easter message on the resurrection featured a real coffin onstage (spoiler alert: it was empty!). For a sermon on hypocrisy, the teaching pastor held up emoji masks as he preached. One was a yellow smiley face, another featured crying eyes, and the third was the infamous poop emoji to illustrate the toxic effect of hypocrisy.

In a discipleship series designed to teach our people about the power of fasting, we wheeled a grocery cart from a Kings supermarket onstage to represent the choice food of the Babylonian king, which the prophet Daniel rejected. We filled it full of cheeseburgers, fried chicken, pepperoni pizza, carrot cake, chocolate chip cookies, salty chips, sugary soda, and even a six-pack of Budweiser! The point was clear to everyone: this is how the world invites us to feed our flesh.

In contrast, we spotlighted a small table with a simple bowl of fruits and vegetables, as well as a glass of clear water, to represent the Daniel Fast—the restricted diet that Daniel employed to strengthen himself spiritually (Dan. 1:5–16). That weekend, more than three thousand people signed up to take part in a forty-day Daniel Fast, abstaining from breads, meats, sweets, caffeine, and alcohol for six weeks and instead "eating clean" (fruits, vegetables, nuts, and water only) and supplementing their diet with Bible reading and prayer. To make the fast experiential, we served lemon water and fruit cups at our church café instead of the typical Sunday morning coffee and bagels. *FAST* was a mouthwatering series that engaged sight, sound, smell, even taste! Remember, if you want people to remember your message, you need to make it multisensory.

> If you want people to remember your message, make it multisensory.

⋅\|⁄⋅ —WOW— ⁄⋅\|⋅ 8. Surprise People

To shake things up, we like to add an element of surprise at least once every series. Routine is the enemy of engagement. If people walk into church always knowing what to expect—three songs, the announcements, a forty-minute sermon with three teaching points, and an offering—they are likely to grow bored and disengage from active worship. Even worse, they might begin to view their faith as a formulaic ritual.

So throw them a curveball! One weekend I preached on the well-known parable of the prodigal son (Luke 15:11–32). It's a story that even casual churchgoers are familiar with. As our teaching team studied the text, we were struck by how over-the-top the father's response was when his lost son returned home. He forgives his wild child for taking Daddy's money, driving to Vegas, and blowing it all on strippers and partying. But that's not even the best part. In a lavish display of grace, the father orders his servants to throw a party for his broken boy: "The father said to his servants, 'Quick! . . . Bring the fattened calf and kill it. Let's have a feast and celebrate. For this son of mine was dead and is alive again; he was lost and is found.' So they began to celebrate" (vv. 22–24). The spontaneous party was such a shocking, outrageous display of God's heart to welcome home those who've blown it, and my fear is that we read right past it because we all know the punch line to the story.

To recapture the shock and surprise Jesus' original hearers must have felt, we did something over-the-top to illustrate the Father's lavish love for the lost. No, we didn't bring a fattened calf onstage and kill it. But we did the next best thing. In the middle of the sermon, we stopped the service and threw a party. The sanctuary doors burst open, and volunteers fanned out with party platters filled with Krispy Kreme donuts—about as close to a fattened calf as we could get. Party music blared over our sound system—not worship music but Kool and the Gang's party anthem "Celebration."

Half the crowd was startled. The other half jumped right in and began singing along: "Celebrate good times, come on! There's a party going on right here, a celebration to last throughout the years!" I snagged a jelly-filled glazed donut and did a little shimmy onstage as the worship team threw confetti into the crowd.

"That's when I knew this church would become my family," said a seventy-year-old guest after the service. "I've heard a hundred sermons on that Scripture, but I never really understood how happy God feels when one of his lost children returns home." She teared up at the Father's lavish heart and said, "I hope there's a party in heaven for every person saved at this church! Do we have enough donuts?"

As creative communicators, it's our job to tell an old, old story in a fresh new way for each generation and for those who have heard the story so many times, they've forgotten its power. So plan an element of surprise every now and then in your services. Live elements such as drama, dance, compelling music, or an onstage interview can breathe new life into a familiar text so that both the lost and the found can taste God's amazing grace in a fresh way.

9. Lead a Live Rehearsal

Too many preachers settle for a "Saturday night special." They finalize their sermon content the night before it is due to be delivered, but by then many of these creative options are impossible to pull off. It's just too late—too late to get outside feedback, too late to sharpen fuzzy ideas, too late to tweak the sermon length or outline, too late to brainstorm props and creative elements to bring the message to life.

By year two of our new church, I realized I had fallen into a rut. My sermon prep had become predictable, and my preaching was starting to feel stale. I knew I needed fresh eyes and outside feedback to sharpen my craft. So we began something that has now become a game changer. As lead pastor, I instituted a false deadline of Thursday night for the sermon and the supporting elements. Everything had to be complete—the manuscript, graphics, videos, props—and we scheduled a live rehearsal with a team of hand-selected listeners to critique the sermon.

We dubbed it Thursday Night Gospel, and we ran it like *American Idol.* A team of four to five judges (a mix of staff members and trusted congregants) sat behind a table with a manuscript of my message while I preached it live to them from start to finish. I pretended the room was full, and as I spoke, they listened and made notes in the margins, highlighting the good, flagging the bad, and redlining the ugly. We ran through the entire message live, with graphics, videos, and all of the other creative elements firing. We also ran a stopwatch so we knew the length of the message in draft form.

This little innovation—Thursday Night Gospel—has transformed my preaching (and that of others on our teaching team). Once the sermon was over, the knives came out. I wanted honest feedback, so I instructed the team to avoid being nice to me. They quickly learned that I wasn't there for compliments; I wanted their suggestions for improvement. They highlighted ideas that worked, of course, but they also pointed out things that were unclear or fuzzy. They mentioned the illustrations that were effective and the jokes that fell flat.

Page by page, we went through each section of the sermon, with each member giving the gift of candid feedback. Each member of the feedback team had been chosen for the unique perspective they represented as a listener. We included:

- A female counselor who lent insight and real-world expertise to a message on marriage
- An Indian pastor who helped add cultural nuance when speaking on issues of racial reconciliation
- A brand-new, baby Christian who challenged me on religious jargon ("What the heck is substitutionary atonement?") and forced me to put theological concepts into everyday language
- A tattooed twentysomething who offered examples from the world of hip-hop music to help connect with younger congregants
- A single woman in her thirties who provided a window into the victories and struggles of single adults

The message delivery may have taken forty-five minutes, but the feedback session took a full ninety! Still, it quickly became the most valuable part of our preaching process. It was incredibly helpful to learn how my audience heard certain sections, often much differently from how I had written it. I became more aware of ideas that needed improving, sections that needed trimming, stories that lacked nuance, and most important, scriptural truths that needed underlining.

Every communicator needs a coach. Better yet, we need a team of coaches who can lend their ear and provide feedback and constructive critique. The Bible affirms that wisdom comes from multiple counselors (Prov. 15:22), yet most pastors create their sermon in isolation each week. They go off to their study and spend hours squirreled away there, writing alone. They hear the message one way in their head and never bounce it off others for feedback until it is delivered on Sunday morning.

And what's the result? In churches with multiple services, the first service serves as the guinea pig as the preacher discovers whether the sermon is clear, effective, and on point. One pastor I was coaching who preached multiple services on Sunday admitted to me, "The message in my first service is like a warm-up, things make more sense in the second service, and by the third, I finally figure out what I was trying to say!" And if your church has a single service, your people end up getting your unrefined, rough drafts week after week. Imagine the difference it could make if you solicited feedback before the Sunday service to tweak, nuance, and refine your message. I can guarantee your preaching would improve, and your people would bless you for it.

Why treat your congregation like crash test dummies? Find yourself a team of trusted critics and put in the hard work before Sunday. You may need to change your routines and develop a new set of rhythms and patterns to the week. But if you do this and create a midweek feedback loop, I know your entire church will thank you.

To summarize, the benefits of a weekly live rehearsal include:

- Muscle memory improves your weekend message (Sunday ain't your first rodeo).
- You can practice tone and inflection in advance for voice variation.
- Precision with props and other creative elements requires practice, practice, and more practice.
- Big ideas and teaching points that need sharpening are flagged for revision. Often, team members can help you find a shorter, crisper way of saying something.
- The sermon is given a chance to simmer—as in a crock-pot, not a microwave—deepening in texture and flavor.

- If your sermon is broadcast via video (as in many multisite churches with many locations), the communicator gets to practice preaching for the camera, which requires extra eye contact and stage dynamics to liberate you from your manuscript or outline. Little known secret: video preaching requires a much more kinetic, rather than stationary, teaching style to translate through a big screen and keep audiences awake and engaged.
- By rehearsing, you eliminate the guesswork and know exactly how long the sermon will be (and can trim or expand accordingly). Your volunteers will thank you!
- Most important, by rehearsing your message well in advance of Sunday, you give yourself the gift of margin. Now you have that extra time to revise and reflect, without rushing to pull it all together at the last minute.

My family has received the biggest blessing from this. Before we began this practice, on most weekends I was stressed and preoccupied, thinking about church services to come. After we began our Thursday Night Gospel rehearsal, I was able to fully engage with my wife and children, because I knew everything had already been test-driven and tweaked and was much better because of my trusted friends and critics. With this confidence, I could rest on Saturdays and let the Spirit flow freely on Sunday.

10. Perform a Hotwash

Finally, I encourage you to conduct a postservice "hotwash" with your team.[10] Every Monday morning, our programming team meets for thirty minutes to share "God sightings" and verbally review the service from top to bottom—songs, sermon, everything—before starting the planning process for next weekend.

We answer these questions:

- What went right? (Celebrate the wins.)
- Where did God show up? (Identify God sightings.)
- What went wrong? (Why did it happen? And what will we change to fix it for the future?)

- Was anything confusing or surprising?
- What was the pulse of our people following the service?

Our live debrief covers the lessons learned and reveals where we need improvement; then we decide which leader or team is responsible for corrections and assign a timeline for those improvements to be completed. Our creative team has found these Monday morning hot-washes to be one of the most life-giving moments of the week as we see the Spirit at work in our congregation. This is the capstone of the creative process and a vital part of creating a culture of accountability and continuous improvement.

THE BROADER CURRENT

What creative language has God gifted you, your team, and your congregation to speak to your community? The answer will be different depending on your context. Crossover Church in Tampa, Florida, reaches a diverse, multiethnic crowd by featuring hip-hop music. Tommy "Urban D." Kyllonen, the lead pastor, is an internationally known hip-hop artist who has released eight albums and several remix projects. Crossover's weekend worship experience features a wide range of music and artistic expression that includes R&B, gospel, hip-hop, reggae, spoken word, film, dance, and more.

While churches like Crossover and Liquid embody a more modern ministry style, other leading churches are using an ancient-future approach. Christ Presbyterian Church in Nashville is a flourishing community that incorporates expository preaching, liturgy, creeds, confessions, and sacraments in their weekly worship gatherings. More and more young adults are resonating with a longing for historic rootedness, and that is offered by this more traditional approach.

I say this to emphasize that being creative is not primarily about being slick and modern or adopting a super-trendy style. Leaders who wish to engage hearts and minds must thoughtfully discern how the Spirit has uniquely wired the community God has called them to serve. And then, with courage and creativity, they need to prayerfully paint outside the lines to tell the old, old story in a fresh new way.

Dive Deeper

Ready to transform your preaching and teaching into whole-brain communication? I've learned a lot by listening to other creative communicators, such as Craig Groeschel, Tony Evans, Jentezen Franklin, and Priscilla Shirer. Thanks to mentors like them, I'm still going deeper. Here are some steps to increase the way both hemispheres in your own head are communicating.

ANKLE DEEP Choose one of the Gospels and, as you read, trace the development of the number one theme of Jesus' sermons—the kingdom of God. On paper, make a list of all the visual symbols, metaphors, similes, stories, and analogies he uses to describe it ("The kingdom is like . . ."). Following Jesus' style of preaching, how can you incorporate more storytelling and visual communication in your Bible engagement?

Leaders are readers. As you consider ways to transform your preaching and teaching for a visual generation, consider the book *Talk Like TED: The Nine Public-Speaking Secrets of the World's Top Minds* by Carmine Gallo. Also, brothers Chip and Dan Heath offer outstanding insights for communicators in their bestseller *Made to Stick: Why Some Ideas Survive and Others Die*. Get together with one or more communicators from your church to do a chapter-by-chapter discussion of either book.

KNEE DEEP The secret to creativity is collaboration. And the more diverse the gifts of your collaboration partners, the more creativity happens. For an upcoming special season (like Advent or Lent) or sermon series, spend a day with a team you assemble: pray, brainstorm, and plan as specifically as you can. Include both left-brained and right-brained people. Other voices to consider: a graphic designer or artist, a counselor, a business entrepreneur, an addict in recovery, and a life-of-the-party storyteller. Finally, if you're older, be sure to include younger adults; if you're younger, include someone older. Same with male and female, married and single, and those of a different race, ethnicity, or social class.

WAIST DEEP Implement the "gospel hour" idea expressed in this chapter as a dress rehearsal of an upcoming message. Do it enough days in advance that everyone involved has time to make changes based on improvements suggested. Also, be sure to do a hotwash after the message. Where did God particularly show up? What worked well, and why? What should you modify or improve going forward?

Plan a three- to six-month preaching calendar, one that starts about three months from now. Go through the ten-step model in this chapter, applying as many of the steps as are appropriate for your context.

Other Churches Making Waves

The current of creativity is flowing powerfully through many fast-growing churches that are reaching the lost and helping disciples grow. Here are five creative churches that excel at redeeming culture for Christ.

LCBC *(lcbcchurch.com)* is a multisite church with fourteen locations across Pennsylvania. Each summer, it does a movie-themed series that looks at scriptural truths behind Hollywood's biggest hits. Volunteers from the congregation spend weeks building beautiful, life-size movie sets and transforming their church lobbies to immersive movie scenes. When new guests arrive, they can sit in a replica X-wing fighter from *Star Wars*, tumble down the enchanted rabbit hole from *Alice in Wonderland*, or snap a picture with volunteers dressed as the Incredibles or the Avengers. Church members serve free popcorn and movie candy to new guests. People are encouraged to post pictures to social media to take the buzz beyond church walls. LCBC found that the more people are involved in creating these environments, the more they share and invite others to church. The July attendance has gone from being LCBC's lowest attended month of the year to its highest attended month of the year.

Passion Church *(passionchurch.com)* has a passion for taking creative risks to reach people far from Christ in the Twin Cities, Minnesota. Taking advantage of the holidays and pop-culture trends, Passion develops unique outreaches to draw unchurched people in. From their annual egg hunt with more than one hundred thousand candy-filled eggs, to theatrical productions impersonating some of pop culture's biggest names in music, to free giveaways for first-time guests to Minnesota's State Fair each summer, Passion pushes the limits. Although the church has drawn controversy for redeeming culture this way, the resurrection messages that they preach produce a harvest of souls. In 2018, the church saw more than 40 percent growth, earning them twenty-fourth place on the list of America's fastest growing churches by *Outreach* magazine.

Life.Church (*life.church*) has a heart to equip local churches by giving away creative resources for free through a platform called the Open Network. The Open Network is home to tens of thousands of resources, including sermons, graphics, videos, kids' curriculum, songs, and training. Life.Church is also the innovator behind the popular YouVersion Bible App, which has been installed on more than 365 million devices and is also available online at *Bible.com*. Users can read the Bible in more than twelve hundred languages, subscribe to daily devotionals called Bible Plans, and pair their personal photos with Bible verses to create shareable verse images for social media.

Substance Church (*substancechurch.com*) has multiple campuses around the Twin Cities in Minnesota and reaches scores of young adults by featuring electronic dance music (EDM). Peter Haas, the founding and lead pastor, gave his life to Christ in a nightclub while working as an EDM turntablist DJ. "Ever since then, I've always had a heart to reclaim club culture and the dance music that made me come alive," he says. "For years, Substance has always had an easy time attracting artists, performers, and filmmakers." In 2017, Substance launched its first national worship band, Substance Input / Output—a congregational worship project that made it as high as number 24 on the mainstream iTunes charts. In 2018, the church launched a DJ-led dance and rap music experience called Substance Variant. It is led entirely by turntablists, rappers, and controllerism DJs who use video walls cued by turntables and midi controllers to sing a "new song" with Scripture-inspired lyrics. The church has filmed four music videos to show people what DJ-led worship can look like and is leveraging EDM culture to reach a global tribe of young people.

Sherwood Baptist *(sherwoodbaptist.net)* is reaching the world from Albany, Georgia, through the power of film. Senior pastor Michael Catt empowered two young creatives in the church (Alex and Stephen Kendrick) who had a passion to make movies. He challenged the budding filmmakers, "Bring me a script and a budget, and let's see if God is in it." Starting with a largely volunteer cast and crew from the congregation, the church has now produced four feature films—*Flywheel*, *Facing the Giants*, *Fireproof*, and *Courageous*—that have been distributed globally and have become some of the most successful faith-based movies in history. Sherwood Baptist is not just redeeming culture; it's creating it! The church's movie ministry, Sherwood Pictures *(sherwoodpictures.com)*, tells cinematic stories that inspire audiences of all ages to a closer walk with Christ.

CHAPTER SIX

QUENCH THEIR THIRST: COMPASSIONATE CAUSE

> If you give even a cup of cold water to one of the
> least of my followers, you will surely be rewarded.
> —MATTHEW 10:42 NLT

When I first saw Margarita, she was scooping dirty water out of a big mud puddle. I was in the hills of rural Rwanda, in Central East Africa, and I couldn't believe what I was witnessing. A beautiful, short, slender eleven-year-old girl carefully took down a yellow plastic can that she had carried on her head. Quietly she knelt down and began filling the can with the brown, murky water. Mosquitos and water bugs skimmed across the surface as she collected the water for her family.

This is Margarita's daily job. Every morning, she walks several miles to fetch water for her parents and brothers to use for drinking, cooking, cleaning, and bathing. As I watched her scoop the contaminated water into the can, I found myself wondering, *What else is in that dirty puddle besides water? Cholera? Typhoid? Diarrhea? Or worse?*

Back home in the States, when we want a drink, we have unlimited choices. We can take a sip from a water fountain, buy a bottle of Poland Spring or Aquafina, or fill a glass with tap water that runs crystal clear in our homes.

So why was Margarita drinking from a mud puddle? I found out this is her only option. The traditional water source in her village is a swampy runoff from a local mountain. And unfortunately, farmers use the same source to water their cows and goats, whose germs and defecation turn the water toxic.

Sure enough, as I watched, a cow leisurely wandered up and began lapping water from the puddle—and simultaneously urinating—as Margarita filled her can. My stomach turned and I thought of my own son, who was eleven at the time. It was heartbreaking to realize this is Margarita's daily reality. This toxic water source is her family's only option. The people from her village in the Ruhango district have been coming here for decades.

I walked over and our translator introduced us. Margarita smiled shyly and took off her blue and yellow checkered scarf. She carefully wound the scarf around her hand into a tight circle and put this fabric disc on the top of her head. Balancing carefully, she then hoisted the yellow can onto her cushioned head and began walking up the dirt road like a barefoot beauty queen.

Our translator called to her, asking if she'd like some help. Margarita turned around, smiled, and took the can off her head for me to carry. I tried balancing it on my head, but water sloshed out and spilled all over. I tried again, but the can kept falling off. A crowd of local women stopped to watch my futile attempts. They pointed and shouted, "Mzungu!" I assumed they were encouraging me, saying, "Balance!" But our translator told me it meant "White man!"

We may chuckle, but the reality is no laughing matter. In Africa alone, people spend nearly ten billion hours a year collecting water.[1] It's a burden borne mostly by women and young girls, and that's one reason why Margarita doesn't attend school. She cannot get an education, because her days are filled with fetching water five times a day—dirty water that, in a cruel twist, will make her family continually sick.

> Right now as you read this book, 2,300 children will die within twenty-four hours from drinking unsafe water.

Would it surprise you to know that half the world's hospital beds are filled with people suffering from water-related disease? And children are especially vulnerable. Where Margarita lives, normal life includes chronic diarrhea, dysentery, cholera, worms, and parasites.

Right now as you read this book, statistics say, 2,300 children will die within twenty-four hours from drinking unsafe water. That's the equivalent of five jumbo jets full of children crashing every day. Forty-three percent of those deaths will be children under the age of five.[2]

To put the clean water crisis in perspective: diseases from dirty water kill more people every year than wars and terrorism combined. So it is no exaggeration to say this is a global epidemic.[3] And here's the real tragedy: it's entirely preventable. Where Margarita lives, there is an aquifer of pure, potable water three hundred to six hundred feet underground, but the families in her village who exist on subsistence farming lack the finances, equipment, and ability to access that water.

> Diseases from dirty water kill more people every year than wars and terrorism combined.

Our church began to dream and ask what we could do to come alongside children like Margarita, her family, her local church, and other Rwandans. The Rwandan government has set a goal to have 100 percent access to clean drinking water,[4] which would make Rwanda the first country in Africa to meet this goal. We wanted to play a small part in making that dream a reality. Our dream was to give a simple gift—the gift of water for life, in Jesus' name.

WALK A MILE IN HER SHOES

As Margarita and I walked hand in hand up and down the hilly terrain to her home, I realized why Rwanda is nicknamed the Land of a Thousand Hills. My calves began burning as the forty pounds of water sloshed around its plastic container.

We can all agree: where you live shouldn't determine whether you live. But it does, doesn't it? I was blessed to be born and raised in a metropolitan area along the East Coast. I've never given a second of thought to where drinking water comes from. But for girls like Margarita, obtaining water is a daily challenge.

When Margarita and I arrived at her family's farm, her father greeted us, and we handed him the yellow can.

"Murakoze [thank you]," he said.

"You're welcome," I replied through our translator. "And we'll be back," I promised. "We want to bring a clean water well to your village. A gift from Jesus."

"Amen," he replied, nodding in joy. "Thank you, God."

Where you live shouldn't determine whether you live. But it does, doesn't it?

Exactly one year later, we did. Through Liquid's partnership with Living Water International, we funded and drilled a clean water well in the center of Margarita's village.[5] It was one of more than 280 wells we've been privileged to provide to thirsty families in both Africa and Central America as we help saturate developing nations in Jesus' name.[6]

"GOD, OPEN MY EYES"

On my flight into Rwanda, I had prayed a dangerous prayer: "Lord, open my eyes. Break my heart with what breaks yours. Help me see what you see." Before we landed, God led me to Genesis 21. God had promised Abraham a big family with many descendants, but his wife, Sarah, couldn't conceive. So Sarah gave her servant girl, Hagar, to Abraham as a surrogate. Hagar gave birth to a boy named Ishmael. But when Sarah gave birth to her own son, Isaac, she became jealous and tried to kick Hagar and Ishmael out of the tribe.

That's where this story powerfully spoke to my heart. The little boy and his mom are being sent away to go live in the desert on their own. Scripture says, "Early the next morning Abraham took some food and a skin of water and gave them to Hagar. He set them on her shoulders and then sent her off with the boy. She went on her way and wandered in the Desert of Beersheba. When the water in the skin was gone, she put the boy under one of the bushes. Then she went off and sat down about a bowshot away, for she thought, 'I cannot watch the boy die.' And as she sat there, she began to sob" (Gen. 21:14–16).

Can you envision this desperate situation? A mother and little boy, living in a dry and barren country, run out of water to drink. When dehydration happens, children are the first ones affected. She can't bear to watch her son die of thirst. She knows he will go first. Can you feel her mother's heartbeat?

Now imagine your own son or daughter dying because they're the one in ten in the world today who don't have access to clean drinking water.[7] It may break our heart, as it broke Hagar's heart, but I had never noticed that this breaks God's heart too! "God heard the boy crying, and the angel of God called to Hagar from heaven and said to her, 'What is the matter, Hagar? Do not be afraid; God has heard the boy crying as he lies there. Lift the boy up and take him by the hand, for I will make him into a great nation'" (vv. 17–18).

The God of the Bible is a God of unlimited compassion, love, mercy, and grace. When he sees people suffering—particularly children—he is moved to action. Many people today picture God as cold and distant, unmoved and emotionless. But God sees this little boy dying of thirst in the desert and says not only, "I see your tears and I will provide" but also, "I'll give you a future, a destiny!"

God is in the business of blessing afflicted people, of providing for those suffering in abject poverty. As our plane prepared to land in Rwanda, God opened my eyes as he opened Hagar's: "Then God opened her eyes and she saw a well of water. So she went and filled the skin with water and gave the boy a drink. God was with the boy as he grew up" (vv. 19–20).

What was the sign of God's blessing? In his great mercy and fierce love, God provided a well so a thirsty little boy could have clean water. Ishmael not only survived but thrived and became ancestor to many Middle Eastern nations still flourishing today. I believe God handpicked this story to open my eyes on my flight into Rwanda. It was an answer to my prayer, "Lord, open my eyes. Break my heart with what breaks yours. Help me see what you see."

> God is in the business of blessing afflicted people, of providing for those suffering in abject poverty.

The world's most precious commodity is not silver, gold, or oil. It is drinking water. Clean drinking water. Water is life. In Africa, it's a matter of life and death. And just like the setting in Genesis 21, sub-Saharan Rwanda is a dry place. The locals there told us with a smile, "We have three seasons: rainy season, dry season, and very dry season." Currently, 25 percent of Rwanda lacks access to safe, clean drinking water.[8] Especially the rural regions. So I prayed, "God, while I'm here, would you open my eyes like you did for Hagar? Help me see the face of a single child who is thirsty. One little kid like Ishmael who needs a drink of water. A child you created, loved, and want to save." Three days later, we met Margarita.

God opened my eyes and I saw her. But more important, I know God saw her. He also sees each of the 663 million people on the planet who lack access to clean drinking water.[9]

Every. Single. One.

JERRYCAN CHALLENGE

The global water crisis may seem overwhelming, but it's a problem our generation can solve. The challenge is to help people grasp the problem and then take action. The weekend I returned from Rwanda, I taught our congregation from Genesis 21 and told them about Margarita. But it's not enough to say something; often, people need to experience a cause in order to fully embrace it, a powerful variation on the show-then-tell idea.

So we tried something kind of crazy. We ordered some bright yellow, rectangular plastic containers similar to what Margarita carries every day. You've probably seen them before. In Africa, they are called jerrycans.[10] These five-gallon liquid containers were designed by Germans in the 1930s to transport fuel for their military campaigns. During World War II, the Germans littered the African countryside with discarded cans, so they got the nickname jerrycan (the name Jerry was wartime slang for German). Today jerrycans are rarely made of metal or painted army green; they're manufactured of plastic. But they maintain that same classic shape: a flat-sided rectangle with indentations that increase the structural rigidity and allow for expansion and contraction as temperatures change. In Africa, you'll see women and children like Margarita carrying jerrycans full of water everywhere, balancing them on their heads, strapping them to their backs, or attaching them to their bicycles.

As people entered Liquid Church that weekend, our greeters didn't hand them a worship program. Instead they handed them a five-gallon jerrycan filled with water. That's the same forty pounds that I tried to carry for Margarita.

Our ushers said, "Can you please carry this to the row where you'll be sitting?"

People had a quizzical look on their face. "My hands are kind of full," many replied.

"Give it a try," the greeters responded. "And if you want a challenge, try carrying it on your head."

I watched as people entered the auditorium, young women struggling to balance the can in one hand with their purse in the other, and grown men pausing to catch their breath as they found their seat.

We wanted people to have the experience of walking a mile in Margarita's shoes. Actually, they had to walk only about fifty feet to their seat—not even close to a mile. Yet most still struggled. Understand: Margarita does this five times every day, uphill.

As I began teaching about the global water crisis, I challenged folks to imagine the daily burden of having to manually transport their household's water more than three miles every day. Lightbulbs came on as people quickly connected the dots and empathized with Margarita's plight. At the end of the service, we challenged everyone to get involved in one of three ways: pray, give, or go on a clean water trip with our church. Over the last decade, our prayers have unleashed a river of generosity for the global poor. To date, Liquid families have donated more than $3.1 million to the clean water cause in Jesus' name. (Each year, our church tithes 10 percent of its income to missions of mercy that bless the poor.) And we've sent out more than four hundred short-term missionaries—volunteers we call Water Warriors—who raise their own funds and use their vacation time to travel to Africa and Central America on weeklong missions trips to drill wells and bring clean water to thirsty kids like Margarita.

GETTING DIRTY FOR JESUS

Focusing on a single cause—rather than a long menu of mission options—can be extremely powerful for any local church. A focused cause allows the church to mobilize an army of compassion and drill down on a single mission to have a deeper impact. When our team of Water Warriors arrives at a village, they roll up their sleeves and get down and dirty for Jesus. Typically, half of the team members put on hard hats and go to work with the drill rig, drilling deep through mud, rock, and shale. They insert yard after yard of skinny steel pipe, like a giant drinking straw, into the ground. After two days of drilling, they're covered in the red African earth.

But when the drill hits water, watch out! It's a glorious geyser shooting into the air. The entire village often comes out to celebrate and dance in the shower. They shout, "Honey water!" because the fresh water is sweet to their taste—so different from the toxic, brackish water they were once forced to drink. At one village, when our drill rig struck the aquifer, the pastor of a nearby church came running out of his classroom with a group of wide-eyed schoolchildren. After praising God for the new stream of clean water, the kids stripped off their shirts to slip and slide around the river of red mud pooling all around the drill site. I jumped in and joined them.

While all this is happening—and equally as important—the other half of our team is busy teaching the village about sanitation and hygiene. Over the years, we've learned it's not enough to simply provide clean water. To truly elevate the health of a village, a more holistic approach is needed; everyone needs to be trained to practice sanitation and hygiene habits such as handwashing.

To illustrate how invisible germs are transmitted, we pour glitter on the hands of the village kids. We tell them to shake the hand of the person next to them, to hug the person on their other side, and to give their siblings a high five. In short order, the village is full of glittering people laughing and nodding, with firsthand knowledge about germ transmission and handwashing. Through our partnership with Living Water International, we've sponsored several WASH areas. WASH stands for water access, sanitation, and hygiene, each of which contributes to long-term community development.

So what happens when a village like Margarita's gets a clean water well? Life changes dramatically in at least five ways.

1. *Gospel saturation.* Water is now safe to drink, disease levels plummet, and doors open for people to hear about Jesus, the water of life.

2. *Sanitation.* Hygiene workers teach the village about sanitation. The community builds latrines and handwashing stations. Disease rates fall further. In 2018, when our team returned to Margarita's village, a mother with three kids stopped to thank us. "Before the well, my children and I were always sick with parasites, stomach pains, and diarrhea," she said with piercing eyes. "But now we are healthy!"

3. *Elevation of women.* Local women join the committee responsible for protecting and caring for the new water source. For many women in developing nations, this is the first local leadership position they've ever held.

4. *Education.* Instead of walking miles to fetch water, children are now free to spend more time in school. And they have fewer sick days. They graduate to become teachers, nurses, or business owners.

5. *Replication.* Frequently a neighboring village hears how water changed the one next to them. They request a water project too, and the cycle begins again.

Since we funded our first well ten years ago, our church has completed more than 280 water projects in nine nations, bringing a cup of cold water to an estimated one hundred thousand thirsty people!

WATER AND THE WORD

Our dream is for every man, woman, and child in Rwanda to have clean water for life, and this dream always includes the phrase "in Jesus' name." These words are important because they explain the why behind what we do: it's Christ who inspires us to act. This isn't a generic sense of social justice or basic humanitarian motives. We don't do this because we're good people; we do it because we're God's people. As Christ promised his disciples when he sent them out, "If anyone gives even a cup of cold water to one of these little ones who is my disciple, truly I tell you, that person will certainly not lose their reward" (Matt. 10:42).

> The words "in Jesus' name" are important because they explain the why behind what we do: it's Christ who inspires us to act.

Our goal is to bring thirsty people both water and the Word. Whenever possible, we try to partner with a local church to locate the well near their house of worship, which is often in the center of the village. Our goal is to honor the local pastors and draw a direct connection between the water (clean water that saves bodies) and the Word (living water that saves souls). It's a double-barreled approach—both demonstrating and proclaiming the good news, in deed and word.

The well is open equally to everyone in the community and serves as a tangible, visible expression of God's great love and compassion for each person who lives there. With the help of local pastors, we teach the people Bible stories using props and costumes to bring Scripture to life. Living Water International also offers orality training—teaching leaders how to communicate the gospel as story in an oral culture.

Our teams try to stay in the background as much as possible. It's important we are not seen as noble knights from America riding in to save the day. Rather we hold up the pastors and church leaders as heroes because they are the local leaders who will be there to shepherd and care for the people long after we've gone home. We'd rather they know the pastor in their community, whose vision is to bring his people clean water as well as the living water of the gospel. In every project, we do all we can to make this direct connection between a physical thirst and a spiritual need.

> It's a double-barreled approach—both demonstrating and proclaiming the good news, in deed and word.

In the New Testament, Jesus proclaimed the good news about God's grace and then demonstrated it by healing the sick. We aim to do the same. As followers of Christ, we imitate our Savior's example by join-ing Jesus on his mission to save a broken planet in need of rescue.

To cast the vision for this work before our congregation, we host an annual Water Sunday to spotlight our signature cause. We show videos from the field of drill teams in action, interviews with local pastors, and short documentaries about thirsty people like Margarita. But we also have a strategy to share our passion with those new to our faith community.

> As followers of Christ, we imitate our Savior's example by joining Jesus on his mission to save a broken planet in need of rescue.

SERVICE IS THE NEW EVANGELISM

"Welcome to Liquid," Craig said as he poured a cup of coffee for a new guest. Craig Massey is a barista at Liquid Church. He's not on staff; rather he volunteers in our Clean Water Café.

"How much do I owe you?" asked the man, fishing around for his wallet.

"Nothing! The coffee is free," Craig replied. "Because you came to church this morning, we'll make a one-dollar donation in your name to bring clean drinking water to kids like Margarita." He motioned to her picture on the café wall.

"Who's she?" the man asked as he stirred creamer into his free coffee.

Craig shared Margarita's story and pointed to other photos, of water wells we've completed in countries around the world.

"That's amazing," the man said.

"It's coffee with a cause," Craig replied. "Thanks for helping Liquid provide clean water by drinking free coffee!"

We opened our first Clean Water Café in 2017, and it's been a run-away hit. At every campus, we have a coffee area branded with bright yellow jerrycans and large-scale photos from our global water trips.

At our broadcast campus, we even have a forty-foot "water walk" on the floor, printed with statistics about the global crisis (see p. 136). First-time guests are given the chance to carry a full jerrycan down the water walk as they approach the counter for their coffee. It's a

SERVE THE **WORLD WITH US.**

JESUS SAID IF ANYONE **GIVES A CUP OF WATER TO A CHILD,** THEY WILL BE REWARDED.
MATTHEW 10:42

LIQUID CHURCH HAS FUNDED & DRILLED **OVER 280 WELLS IN NINE NATIONS.**

CLEAN WATER ELEVATES **HEALTH & EDUCATION** –ESPECIALLY FOR GIRLS.

A NEW WELL CAN PROVIDE CLEAN DRINKING WATER FOR **450 PEOPLE.**

IN SUB-SAHARAN AFRICA ALONE, WOMEN SPEND NEARLY **6 BILLION HOURS** A YEAR COLLECTING WATER.

EVERY 90 SECONDS **A CHILD DIES** FROM A WATER-RELATED DISEASE.

HALF OF THE WORLD'S **HOSPITAL BEDS** ARE FILLED WITH PEOPLE MADE SICK BY **DIRTY WATER.**

THAT'S **1 IN 10** OF US.

663 MILLION PEOPLE ON OUR PLANET LACK ACCESS TO CLEAN WATER.

powerful way to raise awareness about our cause while making a strong impression on new guests.

Young adults are especially responsive to this approach, as it highlights our heart of compassion for the poor. The café is the front door of our church and a winsome way to engage new guests in our mission from the moment they walk into our church. We've even had guests ask about going on a water trip before they've stepped foot into our worship service!

For the next generation, compassionate service is the most effective on-ramp to evangelism. We've found that before skeptical young adults embrace the faith, they first want to know that it makes a difference (a show-then-tell logic). That's why we consider people like Craig our frontline evangelists. Craig has been on three clean water trips to El Salvador, and as he serves new guests coffee, he loves to tell them how we're changing the world.

"What my wife and I like best about Liquid is the many opportunities for outreach and missions trips like this," Craig says. "They recalibrate my perspective on what's really important in the world. It's a joy to invite others to get involved and make a difference too."

In 2018, our Clean Water Cafés served about sixty-six thousand cups of free coffee. Five thousand of those cups were served to first-time guests, representing fifty thousand dollars donated toward providing clean water in Jesus' name. There are no strings attached for these newcomers. We're simply a blessed and highly caffeinated church that loves to make a difference, even during our times of fellowship!

HEALING NATIONS

Drilling wells in Jesus' name for the world's poorest is fitting for a church named Liquid. In Ezekiel 47, the river of God's love flowing out of the temple had a healing effect. Ezekiel prophesied that the trees growing along the banks grew fruit for food and "leaves for healing" (Ezek. 47:12). Healing broken nations is part of God's dream for redeeming the world (see Rev. 22:2, unpacked in chapter 10), and that's what we're seeing God do in every country in which we work.

In Rwanda, our brothers and sisters are bravely rebuilding their nation as they recover from the horrific 1994 genocide that killed roughly one million people in one hundred days. So in 2015, we purchased a heavy-duty, all-terrain drill rig and gifted it to the Living Water team in Rwanda. It cost more than $250,000, but our people felt blessed to sacrificially donate this powerful tool to the next generation of resilient Rwandans, who are courageously carving a new path of peace and reconciliation.

Our new rig is a beast. It can reach remote regions in the mountainous country and drill down six hundred feet into the earth—the length of two football fields—where freshwater aquifers are waiting to be tapped. Living Water's lead drill operator, a dignified man named Moses, was ecstatic about the new equipment. Moses said, "With this rig, we'll be able to reach more communities throughout Rwanda, which means more people will have access to clean water. That is life-changing for local families. Clean water has a ripple effect; people become healthier, and children are more likely to have an education. It improves livelihoods and transforms communities. Together, we can saturate Rwanda!"

So far, our new rig has drilled 153 wells in Rwanda, and it will continue to drill hundreds of wells, saturating the nation for years to come. That's thousands of children like Margarita who will receive clean water in Jesus' name.

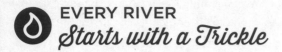

EVERY RIVER
Starts with a Trickle

From the very start of Liquid Church, I was aware that we live in a bit of a bubble in New Jersey. It's a fast-paced culture with suburban parents zipping around in SUVs to school, sports, and shopping. Most towns are designed to provide comfort and convenience, and our proximity to New York City and retail megamalls makes it easy to forget about the plight of the global poor living thousands of miles away.

Right before Liquid launched, I was introduced to Scott Harrison, who would go on to create charity: water, a highly successful nonprofit that has now brought clean water to more than eight million people.[11] Scott was a photographer who had just finished working with Mercy Ships and had been incredibly moved by impoverished children in Africa with terrible facial tumors, many of which were caused by water-borne diseases.

Scott and I became fast friends, and I invited him to display some of his emotionally gripping photos from the field one weekend at Liquid's services in show-then-tell style. After he told our fledgling congregation about the water crisis and the solution that a five-thousand-dollar well could provide, I challenged folks. "Wouldn't it be awesome if Liquid could fund one well this year? Pray about it, guys, and do what God tells you."

That Monday, a man came into our ramshackle church office and plunked down a check on the reception desk. "Here you go," he said bluntly. "This was my down payment for a new Harley-Davidson Softail." He paused and choked up. "I just can't imagine riding a new bike while kids are drinking that dirty water." His five-thousand-dollar gift funded one well.

With his permission, I shared the story the following Sunday, explaining that because of him, an entire village of children would get clean water every day for the next twenty years—the average life of a well at the time. People were visibly moved by his generosity, and the Holy Spirit continued to shake things up. A couple stepped forward, noting that they'd been saving to remodel their basement for a home theater.

"We can't buy a flat-screen TV and Bose system in good conscience," they said. "Our family all voted, and we'd rather help with a second well. Here's twenty-five hundred dollars."

Another man offered to liquidate his baseball memorabilia collection for the cause. He sold off his New York Yankee jerseys, collector cards, and autographed baseballs and donated the proceeds for a third well. The spontaneous outpouring of generosity kept going; week after week, our people donated gifts over and above their normal tithes and offerings to the cause of clean water.

I love when compassion goes viral. These sacrificial donations were clearly Spirit-inspired, and it reminded me of the early church in the book of Acts. "All the believers were together and had everything in common. They sold property and possessions to give to anyone who had need" (Acts 2:44–45). I don't know about where you live, but in New Jersey, when a guy sells his sports collection or donates money earmarked for a Harley, we call that revival. In a matter of six weeks, our young church had enough money to fund not one but ten wells!

At the time, we were an entirely portable church with a skeleton staff. We barely had enough money to survive Sunday to Sunday. Yet love for the Lord began spilling out of our small church. Like the stream of living water in Ezekiel 47, it flowed out, deepening as it traveled thousands of miles to Ethiopia, where our first ten wells were located.

The following year, Colleen and I flew with Scott and his wife, Viktoria, to see the Liquid wells firsthand. In Land Cruisers, we bounced up and down, visiting remote villages in the Tigray region of the country, and we saw the impact of our gifts up close and in person. At each well, villagers sang, danced joyfully, and played homemade instruments in ecstatic celebration over the freshwater source.

It's one thing when you choose a cause, but it's another when the cause chooses you.

That was the moment we knew that clean water would forever be the signature cause of our church. The entire experience was so Spirit-led, we realized God's hand was clearly at work. It's one thing when you choose a cause, but it's another when the cause chooses you.

As our passion for clean water increased, our people had a heart not just to give financially but to go and serve the people in person.

At that point, I was introduced to Living Water International, a Christian nonprofit that took our involvement in clean water one step farther.[12] They offered short-term missions trips for volunteer teams to drill wells, so we organized our first trip to Central America, and it immediately sold out. Volunteers raised their own prayer and financial support and came back from the trip on fire about putting their faith into action. They excitedly shared stories about the beautiful families and thirsty children they served and realized that as we brought the global poor clean water, we were really serving Jesus in disguise. As Jesus commends his followers in Matthew 25, "I was thirsty and you gave me something to drink" (Matt. 25:35).

As our commitment to the cause deepened, we came up with creative ways to raise awareness with outsiders. One of our largest outreaches was a 5K fun run that our church hosted in the center of our city. All the proceeds from registrations and sponsorships went directly to drill new wells in Africa. Our first run started and ended in the city park just down the street from the hotel where we rented the ballroom on Sundays. I was floored by the number of people participating who had no prior involvement with our church. Many hadn't even heard of us. But our people had spread the word virally, inviting coworkers, neighbors, and anyone they knew to help change the world with them.

People who'd never been to Liquid Church suddenly found themselves running more than three miles to serve the thirsty. One couple was Monika and her husband, Greg. They lived right in the city and shared a passion for running. Someone from our church who worked at Monika's office told them about our 5K, and they immediately responded to the cause. "Sure, we'd love our running to have a purpose. What is Liquid, anyway? A club?" Their friend told them about our church and our cause. (What a powerful model of show-then-tell evangelism!)

"I had no idea there was scarcity of water in the world," Monika recalls. "I knew nothing about thirsty people in Africa dying from disease." After the 5K, her friend also invited them to the church. "If some church is going to all this trouble to sponsor a 5K to help strangers thousands of miles away, there has to be something to it," Monika told her friend. Plus she and Greg liked the sense of humor of the pastors, who were emcees at the finish line. So they agreed to visit Liquid the following week.

"On our first Sunday at church, they said that bringing clean water to kids in Africa wasn't just a good thing but a God thing. We were hooked and couldn't stop coming. It was like the Holy Spirit was pulling us in," Monika says. Although they had grown up Christian, the two of them gave their lives to Jesus afresh at Liquid Church and started serving.

A year later, we asked Monika if she'd lead the Clean Water Café at the newest campus we were opening. "Are you kidding?" she replied. "I've been praying for that kind of opportunity!" Together, Monika and Greg went on a clean water mission to Nicaragua. "It was the most amazing trip we've ever taken as husband and wife," she says. "It completely transformed our hearts. We experienced how Jesus came as a human to live as we did, walk in the dirt, serve and thirst as we did, and lead us to true living water. Now our job is to follow the example of Jesus and share the living water with others."

> People who'd never been to church suddenly found themselves running more than three miles to serve the thirsty.

Monika and Greg represent thousands of people who have encountered the heart of Jesus through serving the thirsty. We've found that compassionate cause is a powerful entry point for outsiders, who discover not just a cause to believe in but a God to believe in too.

But it's not just Africa. We work in Central America too and have strategically designed trips so that people of all abilities can have a global impact. Each year, we offer three levels of water trips for people to engage with.

- *Beginner.* These include water trips to accessible countries like El Salvador that we schedule around school breaks and work holidays so people can more easily take a week away to serve in the field.
- *Intermediate.* We schedule trips to Nicaragua and Guatemala in the summer so parents and teens have the chance to experience serving the global poor together. My wife and I took our teen daughter on this trip, and experiencing how the majority of the world lives had a powerful impact on her worldview. This is an

intermediate-level trip because villages are a bit more remote, and volunteers need to be in good physical shape (it's akin to running a 5K).

- *Advanced.* Advanced trips to Rwanda are for experienced volunteers and travelers only. The travel to East Africa is strenuous (more than fifteen hours in a plane), and several hours each day are spent traversing mountain terrain in trucks. Helping operate our drill rig in remote villages requires both strength and stamina (think Ironman or CrossFit competition).

Wherever our Water Warriors are deployed, we offer training and preparation (logistically, spiritually, emotionally, cross-culturally) before they hit the field to bring clean water in Jesus' name.

WHAT'S YOUR COMPASSIONATE CAUSE?

It's been said, "If you ask people to care about everything, they will care about nothing." There are an infinite number of causes your church may care about, but I challenge you to choose one, as we have. In today's world, compassion fatigue is a very real danger. We've discovered tremendous power in focusing on one cause and drilling down deep to make an impact. When a church directs all its energies—money and manpower—on a focused cause, it can change nations. But if you spend your missional muscle trying to advance multiple causes at the same time, your impact is significantly weakened.

Clearly, the calling of Liquid Church is clean water. Like my friend Scott Harrison, we're just crazy enough to believe that we can solve this global crisis in our lifetime. Can you imagine the day when every person on the planet has clean water to drink? Heaven will rejoice!

> We've discovered tremendous power in focusing on one cause and drilling down deep to make an impact.

So what is your cause? Where will you spend your strength to see lives transformed in Jesus' name? Think carefully: Where is God directing your church's path and passion? What global needs are being overlooked? For us, this means staying laser focused on clean water.

Focusing this way means we can do more rather than less. What started with one well has now expanded into hundreds and is having a sustained and lasting impact. But your cause may be different. Where is God calling you to invest your energies?

THE BROADER CURRENT

There are a wide variety of ways in which God can use you and your church to turn a trickle into a stream and ultimately into a river bringing life to the spiritually parched of your world. Maybe there's a need in your city to serve veterans, widows, or single parents. Maybe God wants you to come alongside victims of human trafficking or minister to people with opioid addictions. Perhaps the need is local. Or maybe it's overseas.

Read through Scripture and ask God to open your eyes and your heart. That's what he did for Alex Himaya, senior pastor of The Church At *(thechurch.at)*, a multisite church in Oklahoma with a huge heart for orphan care. Alex spent three months reading the Bible through, cover to cover, noting each time the Scriptures refer to orphan care. "I realized that I had neglected a major aspect of God's Word, one that I believe is the clearest picture of our salvation in Jesus," said Himaya, referring to adoption.[13] Pricked to the heart, Alex and his wife adopted a five-year-old from overseas and encouraged other parents to explore foster care and adoption. The church has since mobilized hundreds of families to both foster and adopt children, with the goal of emptying out the foster care shelter system in their city. The Church At has an orphan care ministry called ADOPT(ED) to guide prospective parents through the challenging pathway of adoption and foster care.

Open God's Word and ask him to open your heart. Whatever compassionate cause God calls you to, may it be said of you, "'He defended the cause of the poor and needy, and so all went well. Is that not what it means to know me?' declares the Lord" (Jer. 22:16).

Dive Deeper

Want to engage emerging generations through the experiential power of cause? I've personally been encouraged by the 10 Days (10days.cc), a nationwide movement challenging college students to make water their only beverage for ten days in the fall and to use the money they save to provide clean drinking water to communities in Africa. The annual campaign raises awareness about the global water crisis and demonstrates how simple choices lead to complex change. Christian and non-Christian students alike learn who their neighbors really are and sacrifice accordingly.

Here are some other ideas to wake up your heart to a compassionate cause.

ANKLE DEEP Read Matthew 25:31–46 and make a list of the physical needs that Jesus mentions. In a mysterious way, Christ indicates, he is present when we compassionately meet the needs of the poor in our midst. Where have you seen Jesus in disguise in your city or town?

Fill a water bottle with muddy water and position it prominently by your sink. Keep it there for a week as you wash your hands, brush your teeth, or grab a drink. Each time you see the cloudy liquid, pause and pray, asking God what role he wants your family or church to play in serving those who lack adequate water, food, or shelter. Try to land on one specific area or need you feel called to address.

Or find a community partner and take your leaders or staff there to serve for an afternoon. Debrief afterward: What moved your hearts? What might God be leading you to do to make a difference?

KNEE DEEP Put a face to the need that God has put on your heart. Identify an organization for your church to partner with, either through your denomination or through one of the many high-quality nonprofits dedicated to various causes.[14] Find a powerful video or story that communicates the need in a way that touches the hearts of God's people at your church. Dedicate a weekend worship service to give laser focus to the compassionate cause. Teach on it from the Bible. Challenge people to pray and sacrificially give toward it, the way Liquid Church initially tried to fund a five-thousand-dollar well. Set a specific date to report back with progress and publicly celebrate the outcome. What gets rewarded gets repeated!

WAIST DEEP Plan an immersion trip, taking key leaders or volunteers with you. The trip should immerse you in the world of need and let you rub up alongside the ordinary lives of those you're serving. If your cause is global, hop on a plane. If it's local, think of a creative way to immerse yourself in the world of those around you in need.

At Liquid, clean water is our global cause, which means flying to Central America or Africa on a short-term water trip. But locally, we have a heart to help the homeless living on our city's streets. One winter night, at the invitation of friends who run a homeless ministry, I dressed up as a homeless person and spent the night sleeping on the streets of Newark, New Jersey. The experience was eye-opening. I met a woman who was a victim of domestic violence, an army veteran with an opioid addiction, and multiple people struggling with mental illness, and I spent the night sharing a cardboard bed with homeless friends on the sidewalk outside of Penn Station. The bone-chilling cold and sense of isolation shifted the concept of homelessness from my head to my heart.

That Sunday, I sat outside the entrance to our church in the same homeless outfit, with a hoodie over my head, as people walked into church. Most ignored me, but a few stopped and were surprised to see the face of their pastor peeking out from underneath the hood. In the worship service, I got up to speak wearing the same street clothes and taught from Matthew 25. After I shared my firsthand experience, hundreds of volunteers signed up on the spot to pray, give, and go to serve our city's homeless.

Other Churches Making Waves

As you think about a compassionate cause for your church, realize there are many leading-edge pioneers and partners who can help inspire you.

Pastors Chris Seay (**Ecclesia**, Houston, Texas), Greg Holder (**The Crossing**, St. Louis, Missouri), and Rick McKinley (**Imago Dei**, Portland, Oregon) were lamenting how Christmas had become a season of shopping, stress, and debt. They wanted to refocus their congregations on the humble miracle of Jesus' birth and direct Christ's compassion to people in need. So together they started **Advent Conspiracy** (*adventconspiracy*

.org), a movement based on four tenets: worship fully, spend less, give more, and love all. Their congregations put Christ back at the center of Christmas by spending less on gifts and used their savings to give Jesus the birthday gifts he asked for, like water for the thirsty. In partnership with **Living Water International** (water.cc), their congregations have drilled dozens of wells across Africa and ignited a global movement to serve the thirsty and hungry in Jesus' name at Christmas.

Willowdale Chapel (willowdalechapel.org) is a Pennsylvania church with one compassionate cause to end human trafficking. Each year, it sponsors a Freedom Sunday to spotlight this issue, and its missions budget designates significant money to efforts in India. Children bring in loose change week after week, which tallies to thousands of dollars every year. A lemonade stand started by one family has raised fifty thousand dollars over the years. Their partners of choice are **Bombay Teen Challenge** and **International Justice Mission** (ijm.org), the world's largest international antislavery organization. To date, IJM has helped rescue more than forty-five thousand people from slavery, working with local authorities to arrest more than thirty-five hundred suspected slave owners and other criminals. It's run by Christians but seeks justice on behalf of all people regardless of race, religion, creed, or any other status.

Hope Fellowship (hopefellowship.net) is located in Texas but regularly sends teams to serve the homeless on the streets of New York City. Through their partnership with **New York City Relief** (newyork cityrelief.org), the church helps fund and operate relief buses—mobile care centers where volunteers serve homemade soup and bread, distribute hygiene kits, and pray for the needs of homeless people living on the city streets. By setting up tables and chairs on the sidewalk, they create a space that welcomes guests and invites friendship over a shared meal. "Our members' eyes are opened to the hurting world by putting down cell phones and sharing kind words with people they would otherwise avoid. It's beautiful to see their faith grow by serving others, reading God's Word each day with others, and living out the gospel," says Launa Vaughn, missions pastor at the church. New York City Relief has mobilized thousands of volunteers to compassionately serve those struggling with homelessness, by providing hope, prayer, and resources that lead toward life transformation.

Church of the King (*churchoftheking.com*) in greater New Orleans has a vision of "Reaching People, Building Lives." When Hurricane Katrina struck its devastating blow, the church focused its efforts to respond to the dire needs of the underresourced population of the Gulf Coast. It was from that effort that the New Orleans Dream Center (*NewOrleansDreamCenter.org*) was birthed with all its healthcare initiatives. Each year, they provide free medical services to more than one thousand adults and children throughout their city. Inspired by Luke Barnett of the original Dream Center in downtown Los Angeles, this Dream Center is a nonprofit, volunteer-driven organization dedicated to helping care for the whole person—spirit, soul, and body.

ChangePoint Alaska (*changepointalaska.com*) has "demonstrating the heart of Jesus together" as one of its core values. Alaskans have the highest rates of alcoholism, sexual abuse, and suicide in the nation, and "as a church, we want to demonstrate Jesus Christ's heart to the people around us," says Pastor Joel Engle. "We're not going to sit there while our friends and neighbors suffer and die under the effects of sin and evil." They went to the mayor of Anchorage and asked what the town's top need was that the church could serve. "Homeless people," he replied. So the church zeroed in on one of the biggest creators of Alaskan homelessness: kids in foster care whom no one ever adopted and who are consequently dumped into society as they age out of the system. The church started Chosen ministry (*chosenalaska.org*) as an initiative designed to pair these young adults with trained mentors. "We want these kids to know they matter, have value, and are wanted!" Joel says.

CHAPTER SEVEN

UNITE THE GENERATIONS: MINISTRY MERGERS

One generation commends [the Lord's] works to
another; they tell of [his] mighty acts.
—PSALM 145:4

On a family trip to Italy, I had two life-changing experiences. One was tasting homemade gelato for the first time. Simply unforgettable! The other was the opportunity I had to visit several historic churches. Italy is home to some of the world's most captivating houses of worship, from soaring cathedrals to beautiful basilicas.

The largest church we visited was in Florence, home to the Duomo, described as one of the most impressive architectural projects of the entire Renaissance era. Known as the Florence Cathedral, the Gothic-style church is massive. It's the equivalent of four football fields long in either direction, earning it the title of the world's fourth largest church facility. When it was completed in the 1400s, it was the hub of spiritual life for Christians around the globe. People were baptized by the thousands in Jesus' name.

As we walked around the huge nave, I asked our tour guide, "How many people fit inside the church?"

"Over twenty thousand would pack the place," she replied.

"Wow!" I responded. "Twenty thousand people worshiping Jesus Christ in this church? That's incredible! How many does it draw on a typical Sunday nowadays?"

"About twelve," our tour guide replied.

My ears perked up. "Twelve thousand? That's got to be one of the biggest congregations in Europe."

"No, I'm sorry," the guide said. "I mean twelve people total. Mostly older women in their seventies."

I looked at the crowds of people walking around, snapping photos on their cell phones. "These are all tourists," she explained. "They help pay to keep the church open." Apparently, the twelve seniors who worship on weekends do so in an auxiliary chapel, and they volunteer to help maintain the building. They sell admission tickets and help run a gift shop that sells postcards and mementos from the church's glory days.

MUSEUM CHURCH

That shift was painful to imagine. A church that was once the nerve center of a vibrant gospel movement had turned into a museum. Sadly, the Duomo isn't alone. Europe is full of empty church buildings. Many were once the flourishing center of Christian ministry to thousands, but now their pews are barely used. These historic houses of worship now stand as silent monuments to a world that no longer exists.

> These historic houses of worship now stand as silent monuments to a world that no longer exists.

And it's not just Europe. This pattern of ministry decline can happen anywhere. Everyone reading this probably knows of a once vibrant church that's morphed over time from a thriving ministry to museum mode. It's the unfortunate life cycle of many churches.

Most churches begin as a movement born out of a fresh burst of gospel energy. There's excitement everywhere from new converts, baptisms, and life change. Churches like this can experience explosive growth, akin to how the early church began. At Pentecost, Peter preached a simple message, in effect: "Jesus died on a cross for your sins. You killed him. Now apologize to God from the heart, and get baptized!" God showed up, and "those who accepted [Peter's] message were baptized, and about three thousand were added to their number that day" (Acts 2:41). How's that for Fall Rally Day? Boom—instant megachurch!

That's the thing about evangelistic waves: they're exciting to be a part of! A church has a sense of destiny and purpose, and its eye is laser focused on winning the lost. But over time, given human weakness and the aging process, every movement eventually levels off. Vitality, passion, and focus begin to wane. Unhealthy traditions can set in. And the focus subtly shifts from pioneering the future to preserving the past. As with the Duomo in Italy, the ministry begins functioning as a museum. Churches with massive sanctuaries that were once filled find themselves selling off assets to stay alive. Many museum churches have an "edifice complex"—an unhealthy focus on preserving the physical building and protecting the church's glory days.

In a museum ministry, people object to new ideas that might upset the status quo. If a young leader wants to try something new to engage outsiders with the gospel, insiders cry, "But we've always done it this way!" Jesus warned the church leaders of his day against a subtle shift. "You have let go of the commands of God and are holding on to human traditions" (Mark 7:8). This is a sobering picture of where many churches and denominations in America are headed if new leadership isn't empowered to create change. A ministry can stay stuck in museum mode for decades, running on the glory of past successes. We all know churches in which a few core families or volunteers run themselves ragged trying to keep things afloat. But deep within, the focus has shifted. They're no longer reaching the lost; they're preaching to the choir. They're not necessarily dead, but they're stuck in museum mode. The longer they soldier on, the harder it is to introduce the changes necessary to regenerate gospel vibrancy.

ZOMBIE CHURCH

My Italian adventure didn't end at the Duomo. In Rome, we stumbled into one of the creepiest churches I've ever visited.[1] Like the Duomo, it thrived and ministered to thousands of worshipers when it first opened, but today the church functions primarily as a museum.

By this point, we'd seen enough church museums. But our tour guide had a surprise in store for us. She looked down at my nine-year-old son as he finished his gelato. He was rapidly losing interest in our "boring" tour of old churches.

"Would you like to see something spooky?" she asked him.

My son nodded eagerly. So did I.

She led us downstairs to the lower level. "Be careful and be quiet," she whispered. We held our breath, anticipating what we might see. Was it an ancient fellowship hall or choir rehearsal room?

Entering the room, my son gasped. So did his mother. And his sister.

To our utter shock, the basement was filled with the decomposing bones of more than four thousand priests! Everywhere we looked, we saw corpses—skeletons still clothed in brown friar robes, their hands stiffly folded in the position of prayer.

Our guide explained how the friars began burying their dead underneath the chapel in the sixteenth century as a memorial to those who had led the church in the past. Once a monk died, the still-living leaders moved his decaying bones to the basement as a memorial.

As I looked around at the bones fastened to the walls—and hanging from the ceiling—I thought of the TV show *The Walking Dead* and the 8:00 a.m. service at some churches. This was a zombie church for the twenty-first century. The doors were still open, but the Spirit had clearly left the building! And that's when the symbolism hit me. This church's current life stage wasn't even a museum anymore. It had become a morgue, a place of death. Jesus had warned the church leaders of his own day against this very thing. "You are like whitewashed tombs—beautiful on the outside but filled on the inside with dead people's bones" (Matt. 23:27 NLT).

A zombie church is what I call a church where old Christians go to die. Most of the time, they simply decide to hunker down and enjoy their peculiar traditions until the end comes. Churches like this have become irrelevant to the surrounding community, which is often desperately in need of Christ's living water, not lifeless traditions. These are churches with a rich history but no future. In a morgue ministry, there's no momentum left to resurrect the church. There are no new families or young adults attending. There are no dreams for the future, just a macabre memorial to a storied past. A ministry that once brought life to the local community is now just a mausoleum.

In the Ezekiel 47 vision we unpacked earlier, there's an image that haunts me. While the divine river that flows out of the temple brings new life and vitality to everything it touches, there is one exception—a place that is immune to the water of life. "The swamps and marshes will not become fresh; they will be left for salt" (Ezek. 47:11). What is a swamp? It's a place where a river once flowed but has since slowed and now has stopped! It's a place where the waters quit moving—a stalled church. Once upon a time, it may have flowed with the Spirit and saturated its community for Christ, but over time it slowed, and now it's stuck. Sadly, in North America this condition is becoming more and more common. It may even describe a majority of churches. Some 80 percent of churches are categorized as plateaued or declining—no longer keeping pace with the growth or demographic changes in their surrounding community.[2]

> Some 80 percent of churches are categorized as plateaued or declining—no longer keeping pace with the growth or demographic changes in their surrounding community.

Jarringly, Ezekiel prophecies that the swamps will be left for salt, a sad future that none of us want. This life cycle can hit any church as it transitions through stages from movement to museum to morgue. Even Liquid, which began with a fresh burst of gospel energy, will eventually decline under my care if I don't take steps to empower new leadership.

RISK TAKER? CARETAKER? OR UNDERTAKER?

As go the leaders, so goes a church. As I began thinking and praying about what I had witnessed in Europe and started looking at the hundreds of churches in our area that are in a similar state of decline, I realized that the response of a pastor and the leadership of a church is pivotal in changing this pattern. In the early days of a new church, or during a time of renewal, the role of the leader is to be a risk taker. In the early days of Liquid, we took lots of risks. Our church met in a tavern (no beer, just Bible study), moved to a hotel, and even cancelled Sunday services to go out and serve our neighbors!

We were willing to do anything short of sin to reach a new generation for Christ. We had a burning passion to reach people of any age or life stage who had given up on church but not on God. Risk takers regularly ask the question, "What if we tried such-and-such?" We weren't afraid to try half-baked ideas and boldly fail forward.

But as leaders age along with the ministry, if they aren't careful, this role can slowly begin to shift. In a museum church, the pastor is no longer a risk taker but becomes a caretaker. That's who ran the Duomo in Florence, by the way. It wasn't the pastor but the museum caretakers caring for the facility and its dwindling congregation.

> In the early days of Liquid, we were willing to do anything short of sin to reach a new generation for Christ.

Eventually, the leader moves into the final stage—undertaker. This is the hardest stage for any pastor to experience. They see families move away, watch young adults leave, and begin burying older members. Their job is primarily to preside over funerals, caring for the skeleton congregation as the church ossifies and dries up financially. It's a sobering cycle of leadership, from risk taker to caretaker to undertaker. Which kind of leader are you right now?

3 STAGES OF CHURCH'S LIFE CYCLE

MOVEMENT	MUSEUM	MORGUE

TYPE OF LEADER

RISK TAKER	CARE TAKER	UNDERTAKER

ROLE OF LEADER

PIONEER THE FUTURE	PRESERVE THE PAST	PRESIDE OVER FUNERAL

Sadly, this sequence is not unusual. On its own, any ministry experiences the pull of entropy as it peaks, plateaus, and then declines over time. And I'm not writing this to lay blame on struggling pastors or suggest that every situation or context can be revived. My heart goes out to many personal friends in ministry situations like this. I think of a recent conversation—a pastoral couple with only a handful of kids in Sunday school, running out of money and dealing with a facility that's run down because they don't have the funds to maintain it. The cost of maintenance is now exceeding the ministry taking place in the church. They desperately want to reach new people but don't know how to overcome the inertia.

THE CHALLENGE OF CHANGE

Let's be frank. Change is hard in any church, not just those in the stage of being a museum or morgue. In most churches, any attempt at change is instantly challenged. You can't even change a lightbulb without calling a vote on it. My Baptist friends are nodding at that. (I was a Baptist pastor once, so I can poke fun at my own tradition. *Q: How many Baptists does it take to change a lightbulb? A: Change? Who said anything about change?* Don't laugh too hard, charismatics. Here's a follow-up. *Q: How many Pentecostals does it take to change a lightbulb? A: Ten. One to change the bulb and nine to pray against a spirit of darkness.* Smile! It's amazing Jesus uses any of us, isn't it?)

Change is hard. But it is vital for a ministry's long-term health and growth. The older a church gets, the more its focus shifts from who they're trying to reach to who they're trying to keep. Over time, decisions are no longer viewed through the lens of growth and outreach but instead are viewed through the lens of protecting the church's legacy. Proposed changes may suffer death by committee. I've been in congregational meetings in which members debated whether to allow music posters in the youth room, while thousands walked by outside, lost and perishing without Jesus.

Catch this: the church lost its sense of mission in order to preserve tradition!

You know you're leading a museum church when you start doing ministry by memory. Leaders run the same plays as the year before—the same curriculum in Bible classes, VBS in the summer, choral concerts at Christmas. There is little innovation or fresh thinking. New ideas and technology are viewed with suspicion. (A preacher on a video screen? That will never work.)

If you're a leader, this shift may happen gradually. It can be easy to miss. Most evangelical pastors still see themselves as part of a vital movement. Once upon a time, they were part of a vibrant Jesus movement, but then, over time, the focus of the church shifted from forging the future to preserving the past. You can almost hear the lay leaders at the Duomo saying, "Remember when this place was packed in the 1400s?" It's the same song but a different verse today when people today say, "Remember back in the 1980s when Sunday school was humming? We had tons of young families and singles. But wait. That was almost two generations ago. What happened?"

> The older a church gets, the more its focus shifts from who they're trying to reach to who they're trying to keep.

DOES YOUR CHURCH HAVE AN R&D DEPARTMENT?

Thankfully, some leaders are spiritually perceptive and can take steps to intercept this entropy. In chapter 2, I introduced Pastor Peter Pendell as the godfather of Liquid Church. Liquid Church would never have existed without his risk taking. And the river of momentum we're experiencing today at Liquid is directly related to the risks he took to empower me, twenty-seven years his junior, as a younger leader. When Colleen and I first visited Millington Baptist Church, he had been pastor there for more than twenty years. Yet he quickly made us feel like honored insiders and gave us a seat at the leadership table.

Under Peter's leadership, Millington funded Liquid like an R&D (research and development) department. Not only did they never charge us a penny of rent, but they soaked up all our costs as we researched and developed new approaches to engaging the next generation, from paying for damage to the sanctuary carpet from our candle wax to buying ash cans for parking lot cigarette smokers. (We formally thanked the church later by remodeling their sanctuary.) Peter and his elder team led with an open hand in every way, even blessing Liquid as we launched out to become an independent church. I marvel at that generous, risk-oriented kingdom mindset. God used Peter's big pastoral heart and ability to build consensus to bless both congregations. Incredibly, neither Liquid's presence nor its departure resulted in a church split.

By letting Liquid leave, Millington took a risk of dying. When we were there, the church could feel good: "We're reaching twentysomethings." But after we left, people began looking around and realized that nothing had changed in their overall operating system. They had to start all over to reach a new generation. After Liquid left, it felt like the waters of Ezekiel 47 had receded, and for Peter, our departure represented the death of a dream. "I thought Tim or one of his young leaders might become my successor," he said later.

Millington, already more than 150 years old when I arrived, could have followed the downward spiral of those churches I visited in Italy, moving from gospel movement to museum to morgue. Likewise, Peter's role could have easily morphed all the way to undertaker as the church aged under his leadership. Instead after thirty years of loving leadership, he resigned and did what he refers to as "retreading." Today Peter serves as an interim pastor for churches in transition. He also continues to provide me with spiritual accountability, not just as a mentor and friend but more formally as a member of Liquid Church's board of trustees.

Today Peter's successors at Millington Baptist are more than thirty years his junior. What Peter did for me, he likewise does for the pastors who followed him. Their young team has developed all kinds of ministries for a new generation while still honoring the seniors who came before.

A MERGER CAN JUMP-START THE FLOW

My point in this story is that it's entirely possible for churches to begin a new life cycle at any age or stage. The road to the morgue is not irreversible or inevitable. Even if the generational flow of a ministry has diminished from a river to a trickle, the current can strengthen and grow.

EVERY RIVER
Starts with a Trickle

Through a series of events that could only be explained as a God-incidence, Liquid was approached by the leaders of a historic, 191-year-old church about merging our ministries. It all began ten days after a churchwide Easter fast, when we had been seeking God for revival. A leadership expert named Dr. Warren Bird came to visit our staff—yes, the same Warren Bird who is the coauthor of this book. We hosted Warren for a lunchtime training in the hope that he could equip our staff to serve our congregation and community more effectively.

We had a wonderful visit. As Warren was about to leave, he asked a question in front of our entire staff. "By the way, have any churches approached you about a merger?" I quickly said no, caught off guard by his question. "Someone will," he predicted with a confident smile, "because God is up to something here, and a merger could multiply your kingdom impact. And when they do, you'll need this." He handed me a copy of a just-off-the-press book he had coauthored titled *Better Together: Making Church Mergers Work*.[3]

I had never heard of a church merger before. And frankly, the idea of Liquid merging with another church had never even crossed my mind. I thanked him politely and put the book on the stack of fifteen other books piled high on my desk, waiting to be read.

None of us anticipated that we'd desperately need his book less than twenty-four hours later.

At six-thirty the next morning, Pastor Mike Leahy (who oversees our campuses) received a call from an elder at a local church called Mountainside Gospel Chapel. The two of them had known each other from prior ministry together at a Christian school. "Mike, I know this might seem like a call out of the blue—a crazy idea, a shot in the dark—but would you guys be open to exploring the possibility of our church becoming a campus of Liquid Church?"

Mike almost dropped the phone. He immediately called me, and I scrambled to locate Warren's book. We scratched our heads, wondering,

"What in the world is God up to?" and agreed to meet with the pastor and board of this church.

MIRACLE AT MOUNTAINSIDE

Mountainside Gospel Chapel had been birthed in 1821 out of a passion to communicate the Bible to children. Beginning as a Sunday school, the Chapel morphed into a full-blown church, and this community hub in north central New Jersey had grown over the years into a healthy congregation of three hundred to four hundred people. Through several missionaries it generously supported and prayed for, it impacted distant corners of the earth for Jesus.

This pioneering church was the first religious institution to be founded in its town. It had begun as a simple stone chapel, and over the years the church had acquired acreage and built a new sanctuary, fellowship hall, classrooms, and gym, all with ample parking. Yet sadly, the Chapel had been forced to make some difficult decisions in recent years. Though they had been instrumental in championing the Sunday school movement of the 1950s, the congregation had peaked in the 1970s and 1980s and then had begun a gradual decline in the 1990s. By the time they called us, this once thriving church had dwindled to twenty to thirty weekly attendees. They were thinking about closing their doors.

What is most heartbreaking for me in situations like this is the sincere dedication of the people who remain. The folks still at the Chapel were on their knees and in the trenches. One of those amazing people is June Burggaller, a pillar of the church and longtime Sunday school teacher. "Teaching those kids has been my life for more than forty years, and I have loved every minute of it," she says. If only we could transplant that kind of beautiful love for children into a new generation of church leaders! It took courage and honesty for the church to recognize that change was needed. The congregation of a few dozen people was no longer viable as a self-sustaining church, and in our meetings, the Chapel leaders acknowledged that though they were once a powerhouse congregation, they now needed outside help to survive.

What happened next was nothing short of a miracle. We call it our Miracle at Mountainside. (To watch a sixteen-minute video documentary

of the revitalization story, visit *LiquidChurch.com/HelpForChurches*).
Dr. Gregg Hagg, a gifted Bible teacher who had served as senior pastor
at Mountainside for the previous two decades, described the decline
this way: "The 1970s and 1980s were our best in terms of numbers and
effectiveness. Then the culture changed, but we didn't. We were more
concerned with preserving the past than forging the future. While we
tried to maintain our traditional approach, the world around us shifted,
and ministry ossified beneath our feet." It pained my heart to hear
their story. After our meeting, the leaders at Mountainside followed
this confession with something miraculous. They voted unanimously
to pursue a merger with Liquid. It was, they hoped, the rebirth of a
dying congregation.

The good news of Jesus promises that there is always hope for
resurrection! At its core, the gospel is about life, death, and then resurrection to new life. For Ezekiel, the trickle from the Lord's temple
transformed into a current and grew into a raging river that brought
new life to everything it touched.

If a leader is willing to sacrifice what's familiar to reach a new generation, God can jump-start a new season of Spirit-empowered ministry.
Those caretakers and undertakers who are willing to once again become
risk takers can experience a miracle known as a rebirth. That's when
God's Spirit does something miraculous and reignites their church into
a fresh season of gospel ministry. That's exactly what we experienced at
one of Liquid's fastest growing campuses.

REBIRTH STRATEGY

A rebirth is what happens when a struggling or dying church gets a
second life. This can occur when it is restarted under the guidance
and support of a stronger, vibrant, and typically larger church. In
Warren's coauthored book *Better Together*, the authors popularize
several terms, including "lead church" and "joining church," as they
describe a model frequently used today in church mergers that have
the highest success rates. They also highlight some of the research
conducted by Leadership Network indicating that more than one in

three new campuses in multisite churches across North America are birthed through a merger.

The Bible tells us that a church is a living organism, not a sterile organization. The "body of Christ," as Paul frequently refers to the church (1 Cor. 12:27), is in many ways similar to the human body, which naturally experiences growth spurts and seasons of decline.

The idea of rebirthing Mountainside as a new campus of Liquid Church was possible because of synergy between both of our leadership teams. Our younger team of leaders saw the rebirth as an opportunity to combine the rich history of the Chapel with the fresh ministry momentum of Liquid. We weren't interested in erasing the identity or the heritage of Mountainside. Rather we hoped to resurrect the dream of the founders and inject the community with fresh hope and vision for the future.

> More than one in three new campuses in multisite churches across North America are birthed through a merger.

But there was a steep sacrifice involved in all of this. The rebirth model follows the pattern of Christ's death, burial, and resurrection to new life. If Mountainside was to be born again, it would first have to die to itself, dissolving its ministry and donating its assets to join the lead church. This is a scary proposition for many aging congregations, not least because it requires a radical shift away from an internal focus on congregational survival and building maintenance to an external outreach to the surrounding community. When I asked Mountainside's leaders, who favored organ music and hymns, if they would be comfortable with Liquid's more contemporary worship style, they spoke honestly.

"We're not big fans of your music," one elder said. "It's too loud. I wear earplugs whenever I visit."

"Respectfully, may I ask, then why do you want to merge?" I asked him.

"Because," he said with teary eyes, "you're baptizing our grand-children."

The other leaders nodded in agreement. They had a huge heart for passing on their faith to the next generation and the one after that. That's often the show-then-tell factor that convinces a declining church to make the sacrifices necessary to merge: they've seen the lives of their loved ones impacted by the gospel (the show), and that makes them want to hear more about the idea of merging with a growing church (the tell).

So with grace and courage, the leaders of Mountainside gently shepherded their congregation to trust God and heroically pass the baton to their kids and grandkids. Although their ministry had dwindled to a trickle, we saw unmistakable evidence of a new current forming as we began laying plans to rebirth Mountainside as the fourth campus of Liquid. Although we had markedly different worship styles, we were compatible in several key areas, including our historic, orthodox theological beliefs and evangelical doctrinal statements. We both were Bible-based, Christ-centered churches committed to the gospel and lordship of Jesus Christ. And we loved people.

MESSAGE VERSUS METHODS

We discovered that several Mountainside members had children who attended Liquid as young adults with their own families. Although Liquid was certainly louder, the Mountainside leaders understood that music and media were a big part of the way God had called our church to communicate the gospel to the next generation. At Liquid, we are closehanded about our message (never changing) and openhanded about our methods (always changing). While the gospel is timeless and unchanging through all generations, our methods for communicating its truth must adapt to the current culture. As I shared in chapter 5, we routinely employ video clips, social media, onstage props, and creative illustrations to bring the Bible to life for a visual generation.

When I met with Pastor Gregg, I discovered we had something else in common—his son Andy. Andy had been a part of the original team of volunteers that had launched Liquid in a tavern more than a decade ago, when there were forty people in their twenties. Andy had married and moved to Texas, and I hadn't seen him in more than ten years. But when Gregg and I met, Andy happened to be in town on business. We greeted each other with big hugs, like old friends, and everyone had a sense that this was right. We had come full circle.

> At Liquid, we are closehanded about our message (never changing) and openhanded about our methods (always changing).

You might call these events coincidences, but I believe they are God-incidences. I think God arranges all these details out of sight, behind the scenes, and waits to reveal them at the proper time so we don't miss his hand steering the story.

THIRTY-THREE DAYS

Thirty-three days after Warren Bird's visit, the Mountainside elders called a congregational meeting of their remaining members, and twenty-seven people showed up, the majority of them seniors in their sixties. After opening in prayer, the church members voted unanimously to donate their entire church to Liquid. The building, property, parsonage, assets—all of it—were given away to us, a gift worth roughly four million dollars.

I sat next to Gregg and looked at him in stunned disbelief. I'm still shaking my head, as I write this years later, at how quickly all of this came together. I can't even get my kitchen painted in thirty-three days! In my entire life, I've never seen the Holy Spirit move so dramatically. It was breathtaking, shocking, and—most of all—deeply humbling. It's impossible to overstate the courage, generosity, and sacrifice shown by the Mountainside seniors in voting to give their church away, all so that it could be born again.

On the Sunday of the vote, Pastor Gregg invited me to preach. I shared a message from Nehemiah about rebuilding the city walls for a new generation. In Nehemiah's day, the holy city of the Jews had fallen into disrepair. "The wall of Jerusalem is broken down, and its gates have been burned with fire" (Neh. 1:3). When Nehemiah heard about the glorious city's decline, he sat down and wept. Broken gates were a symbol of spiritual atrophy; something that was once strong and thriving was now weak and in decline. The broken walls were a sore spot to the Jews, a daily reminder of their lowly condition. If you had asked God's people at the time, "Are the best days ahead of us or behind us?" they might've

> It's impossible to overstate the courage, generosity, and sacrifice shown by the Mountainside seniors in voting to give their church away, all so that it could be born again.

pointed to the hollowed-out shell that was Jerusalem and said, "You tell me."

Enter Nehemiah. He didn't just stay depressed about the situation; he decided to do something about it. "For some days I mourned and fasted and prayed before the God of heaven" (Neh. 1:4). I don't think it's a coincidence that the Miracle at Mountainside began ten days after our church completed our Easter season of prayer and fasting for revival. I believe that God loves to fill empty vessels. Most of the time, we're so consumed by the challenges in our situation, we miss the power God's waiting to unleash.

God gave Nehemiah a fresh vision, and Nehemiah shared it with his people. "Then I said to them, 'You see the trouble we are in: Jerusalem lies in ruins, and its gates have been burned with fire. Come, let us rebuild the wall of Jerusalem, and we will no longer be in disgrace'" (Neh. 2:17). Spiritual renewal begins when one person is courageous enough to believe God has a fresh vision for the future. When a man or woman is brave enough to honestly survey the landscape and say, "Let's forget the former things and begin a new work in this place. Our best days are not behind us; with God's help, we can rebuild and restore this ministry!"

Nehemiah had guts, and he was willing to move out of his comfort zone. At the time, Nehemiah held a privileged position in the royal court of the Persian king. He had power, influence, and likely great wealth. And yet God put it in his heart to forsake all that to rebirth Jerusalem. It meant leaving behind the things he'd grown to love—the food, the fellowship, the traditions that had been with him since childhood.

> Spiritual renewal begins when one person is courageous enough to believe God has a fresh vision for the future.

But Nehemiah stepped out in faith and conviction, and the rest is history. When he summoned the people to start rebuilding, they responded in unity. "So they began this good work" (Neh. 2:18). The result? The rebirth of Jerusalem was completed in record time. It took fifty-two days from start to finish for the people to rebuild the walls and repair the gates of the holy city. This was surely a miracle for a powerless people who'd been demoralized for decades. But Nehemiah shows us what God can do when his people fast and pray and come together for a common vision, making sacrifices and linking arms to build the kingdom for a new generation.

One reason we call the merger our Miracle at Mountainside is that it didn't even take fifty-two days; it took thirty-three! Both our teams marveled at the Spirit's leading as we pledged our commitment to Christ and each other. We realized we'd been blessed to witness a modern-day miracle of biblical proportions.

WASHING THE FEET OF HEROES

I get choked up every time I see the picture of the congregational vote at Mountainside. Twenty-seven seniors heroically raising their hands to give away their church. Most viewers of that cherished photo notice a lot of white hair. But I see so much more than an aging congregation in decline. These aren't simply gray-haired saints; these are our spiritual fathers and mothers who have faithfully served God for decades.

The seniors at Mountainside Gospel Chapel are my heroes. Can you imagine being in your sixties or seventies and voting to hand your ministry over to the next generation? That's humbling. That's inspiring. That's who I want to be like when I grow up. We aren't worthy to untie their sandals! But we wanted to wash their feet. In a final service, inspired by Jesus' example to his disciples in John 13:1–17, I got down on my hands and knees with the rest of Liquid's senior leadership team, and together we washed the feet of the Mountainside saints. I washed Pastor Gregg's feet while Mike Leahy, our pastor of campuses, washed June's, and we worshiped the Lord for his great mercy to our new family. Gregg's wife, Linda, said, "This day could've been one of sadness and dread for us. But our mourning has turned into joy for what God has done and is preparing to do in our future. I can't believe we get to witness a miracle in our time!"

CELEBRATING A LEGACY

When news of the merger got out into the community, word spread like wildfire. For five years, our church had been 100 percent porta-ble, meeting in hotels, schools, and anywhere we could fit. Now, in thirty-three days, God had blessed us with our first-ever permanent facility. Providentially, Mountainside was located smack-dab in the center of all three other campuses. It was equal driving distance from each and instantly solved several logistical problems. We now had a central meeting location for our youth and a rehearsal space for our bands, and our engaged couples were thrilled with an actual chapel for weddings!

But amid the excitement about the future, I cautioned our people not to forget the past. We taught our young adults to approach the rebirth with humility and the understanding that God had been at work at Mountainside long before they were born. It was critical for our people to understand that we weren't just inheriting some brick-and-mortar building. We were inheriting all the spiritual history, all the testimony of changed lives, and the rich legacy of men and women who invested their lives over the years at Mountainside.

We arranged a special barbecue to celebrate 191 years of ministry at Mountainside. After their final service, we treated the seniors to a pig roast with all the trimmings, and an army of Liquid volunteers were thrilled to serve their spiritual fore-bears. Over pulled pork, we listened to story after story from saints in their sixties and seventies: "I was born in this church." "I met my spouse here." "I was married in the Chapel." "My children were baptized here."

> We taught our young adults to approach the rebirth with humility and the understanding that God had been at work long before they were born.

It was deeply humbling to realize God had been at work for almost two hundred years before Liquid ever arrived on the scene and that we were simply joining the good work that had been going on there for many decades. Gregg showed me a time capsule outside the church, stamped with the dates 1821–2021.

"This will be yours to open," he said.

I wondered what might be inside. The bones of Moses? A flannel-graph? It was inspiring to think that the founders of the church had the foresight to envision a day—two centuries in the future—when a new generation of leaders would take up the mantle of ministry.

Gregg and I committed to wait and open the capsule together, Lord willing, when the time comes.

BORN AGAIN . . . AGAIN

That summer, we closed Mountainside Gospel Chapel to lovingly renovate, repair, and upgrade the facility in anticipation of launching what we initially called Liquid Mountainside for a new generation. We hosted several work days that helped bond our congregations as young people and seniors linked arms to "rebuild the walls" together. It was moving to see Bob, a retired eighty-seven-year-old laborer, working side by side with a group of our college students—a powerful visual of the unique generational partnership we had forged. We replaced the stained glass with flat-screen TVs and carefully archived many of the Chapel's historic ministry mementos in a special hall of history. While forging the future, we believe, it's also important to celebrate the past.

The week before the grand opening, we fasted and prayed for God to move powerfully once again. And boy, did he ever! As I pulled my car into the parking lot on opening Sunday, the energy was electric and there was a buzz in the air. A local paper had run a feature story on the merger, and it seemed like the entire community had come out to see for themselves what God was up to. Walking up the front steps, I was greeted by none other than Gregg and his wife, Linda. But instead of wearing a suit and tie, Gregg was proudly wearing a Liquid volunteer T-shirt and passing out programs to new guests. We hugged and he said, "Tim, we are here to serve in any way you need. Whether it's handing out programs or helping teach the kids, we'll do whatever it takes to see this place thrive again!" (And on the side, he's now helping a new generation of church leaders by working as an adjunct seminary professor.)

Our goal that Sunday was simple. We hoped to launch Liquid Mountainside with a birth weight of four hundred men, women, and children. But God had other plans. When we opened the doors, more than one thousand people poured through them for four worship services! In its first year, Mountainside became our fastest growing campus, all because a group of twenty-seven seniors was willing to sacrifice their comfort and take risks for the gospel again.

Those senior saints are kingdom heroes. Decades before, their ministry began as part of a vibrant gospel movement. But over the years, it cycled through the museum and morgue stages. Instead of simply selling off assets to survive, they took the heroic step of "dying" so they could be born again (again!) to reach the next generation for Christ.

Their sacrifice reminds me of what Jesus said in John 12: "I tell you the truth, unless a kernel of wheat is planted in the soil and dies, it remains alone. But its death will produce many new kernels—a plentiful harvest of new lives" (John 12:24 NLT). That fall, we baptized dozens of new believers at Mountainside, including a family of four (a father and three sons), surpassing one thousand baptisms in Liquid's history. The campus is now brimming with new Christians and young families. As the congregation grew, many of the senior saints stayed as well. As June, the longtime Sunday school teacher, commented, "Many times with a contemporary church, we think the message is watered down. Not so here! Pastor Tim's messages are right out of the Bible, and the Word of God is foremost. That's how I knew I was in the right place. From day one, everyone was so supportive, encouraging, and respectful. I think it's important to have a multigenerational congregation, because each generation has something to give. It is such a joy to see this place as we always dreamed it would be: filled with people coming to hear about Jesus Christ."

We thanked the Lord for the miraculous rebirth, and I thought of Psalm 145:4: "One generation commends your works to another; they tell of your mighty acts." Isn't that how it's supposed to be in Jesus' church? Every generation—builders, boomers, gen X, millennials, gen Z—young and old, coming together and merging streams to create a powerful river that flows with new life and gospel vitality. Because of those seniors' kingdom sacrifice, a ministry that had once dried up is now again saturating its city for Christ.

THE RIPPLE EFFECT

If God had chosen to limit the miracle to the Mountainside rebirth, we would have been thrilled. But it turned out that the Spirit was just getting started. Only a few miles away, the merger had a ripple effect.

Unbeknownst to us, another dying church about fifteen minutes away was watching our ministry merger with great interest. As they witnessed the generations locking arms to revitalize the church, they too approached us about becoming a campus of Liquid.

The success of our Miracle at Mountainside inspired the Gift of Garwood—our second merger, with a 120-year-old, dying United Church of Christ congregation. The Garwood congregation had dwindled down to a handful of people attending on Sundays. But they too shared a heart to reach the next generation. After our teams met, they followed Mountainside Gospel Chapel's example and voted to dissolve and to donate their building. A second miracle! Just as we had done at the Chapel, we lovingly renovated and upgraded the Garwood facility for the next generation, and it became Liquid's fifth campus, launching with more than four hundred people in attendance.

We didn't realize it at the time, but God was laying the groundwork for a third miracle. As a young church, we had no money in the bank and zero assets. But after receiving the gift of our first two permanent buildings (Mountainside and Garwood), we suddenly had five million dollars in assets on our books. Three years later, these properties provided the collateral by which we were able to secure a bank loan and sell bonds to purchase our 165,000-square-foot broadcast campus in Parsippany, New Jersey. Only God could've architected such a plan; we're simply not that smart!

Since these two ministry mergers, we've been approached by dozens of ministries in the museum or morgue stage that are interested in joining Liquid's movement to saturate our state for Christ. One fascinating observation in the book *Better Together* is that many mergers happen while the joining church is still strong, but they merge with a lead church as a strategic decision to become even more viable as they prepare to pass the baton to the next generation. Such mergers often occur at the retirement of a long-term pastor.

Revitalizing dying churches is one of the most rewarding things a Christ follower can do. You get to have a front-row seat to witness the gospel cycle of voluntary death, burial, and resurrection to new life. The result? Older churches are replanted and become fruitful again as a river of younger leaders revitalize their ministry.

Are you ready to imagine a new future for your church? Draw inspiration from the words of God in the book of Isaiah: "Forget the former things; do not dwell on the past. See, I am doing a new thing! Now it springs up; do you not perceive it?" (Isa. 43:18–19). I believe we are living in one of the most exciting times to be in ministry. Like Europe, North America is rapidly becoming a post-Christian culture, and a strategic baton pass between generations is desperately needed. Thankfully, I see God pouring out his Spirit, giving younger people fresh visions and older people new dreams and performing merger miracles for which only Christ can get the credit. I mean, who wants to be part of a church where everything is explainable?

> Like Europe, North America is rapidly becoming a post-Christian culture, and a strategic baton pass between generations is desperately needed.

THE BROADER CURRENT

Every year in America, more than 3,500 churches close their doors.[4] I'm sure you can think of some in your area that already have. Many declining congregations are left with no choice but to sell their facility, often to a developer who repurposes the church property, building condos, offices, or a strip mall. What a huge loss for the kingdom! The spiritual legacy of that sacred space—all the priceless years of faithful witness, outreach to the community, and transformed lives—is forever gone.

However, the rising tide of ministry mergers offers a hopeful alternative. I believe we are living in a time of unprecedented generational transfer, with enormous kingdom potential. Older congregations that have assets (but lack people and momentum) have the opportunity to team up with younger congregations that have people and momentum (but lack assets). When they link arms and merge ministries, it's a win-win for Christ's kingdom!

The current wave of healthy, successful mergers sweeping across our country presents a unique opportunity for declining churches to start a new life cycle. The result? The spiritual legacy is not only preserved but revitalized to reach a brand-new generation for Christ. Please understand, though: for a ministry merger to succeed, timing is critical. So is the attitude of the key leaders from both sides.

Looking back, I consider it a blessing that God made Liquid patiently wait for seven years as a tear-down-and-set-up church before bringing free buildings into our life. Those seven years were the anvil on which God forged our patience, humility, and character. I see this waiting time as a gift—loving evidence of God's father heart in developing our maturity.

Sadly, we've all heard horror stories of young pastors at fast-growing churches whose charisma outpaced their character. The church may have grown quickly and multiplied campuses, but it eventually imploded because their leadership lacked maturity, wisdom, and a humble spirit. So be patient. Don't rush things or try to make a merger happen. God is writing the unique story of your church, and believe me, his timing is always better than your plans!

> We are living in a time of unprecedented generational transfer, with enormous kingdom potential.

My friend Brad Leach, lead pastor of City Life Church in Philadelphia, can testify to God's perfect timing in the merger process. In 2018, Brad was approached by a historic congregation in the heart of south Philadelphia about potentially merging. Calvary Temple, in Packer Park, was founded in 1925 and served six hundred families at its height. However, the aging urban church had plateaued in the '90s and contracted to a congregation of 150, including children. Together, Pastor Brad (City Life) and Pastor George (Calvary Temple) built a friendship and began dreaming about revitalizing the aging church to reach a new generation of city dwellers. Nine months later, the two congregations formally joined forces and merged ministries. City Life, the lead church, received its first building—an eight-million-dollar facility—in exchange for a symbolic one-dollar bill. Calvary Temple, the joining church, received an influx of young families and singles with a fresh passion to reach their urban neighbors. Another amazing win-win for God's kingdom!

The life stage and calling of your church may be different. Maybe you're in the position to come alongside another church in your area or denomination, playing the role of a stronger older brother or sister. Perhaps the two of you can work together in ways that bring living water to your greater community. Often, one church has the energy and personnel, and the other church has a great location and better inroads into the community.

Maybe your situation is different, such as the congregation becoming more receptive to younger generations, as explained in *Growing Young: Six Essential Strategies to Help Young People Discover and Love Your Church* by Kara Powell and her team.[5] See the story of Lee Kricher and his turnaround of an older, dying church in the "Other Churches Making Waves" section that follows.

Perhaps you have individual ministries that are graying and need revitalizing. Do various staff and volunteer leaders at your church need to be more intentional about finding and mentoring a new generation as apprentices, interns, and ministry residents? For help getting started, check out the books *Reverse Mentoring* by Earl Creps and *Hero Maker* by Dave Ferguson and Warren Bird. Whatever you do, don't limit your millennials and gen Z members to college ministry or student ministry. Trust God and give them a seat at the table earlier than you feel comfortable with. Be intentional about creating a secondary stage for the development of new musicians, teachers, evangelists, administrators, and those with gifts of compassion. As a fortysomething pastor, I'm working with our team at Liquid to raise up the next generation of leaders. I don't want to wait until Liquid levels off to museum mode or I'm in my sixties and suddenly have to scramble to find a successor.

The opening line of the book *Next: Pastoral Succession That Works* reads, "Every pastor is an interim pastor."[6] As staff and volunteer leaders realize their position is temporary in God's eyes, the priority of strengthening the leadership bench at all levels of ministry takes on fresh urgency. Don't miss the wave that the Holy Spirit is whipping up as generations unite around Jesus to saturate their city together!

Dive Deeper

In our first ministry merger, I drew inspiration from Mark Jobe, an urban pastor in Chicago, whom I view as a pioneer of church rebirths. Mark helped us see how God was already at work in declining congregations and embrace the opportunity to build on their spiritual legacy.[7] He did this nine times during his pastorate at New Life Community Church (in 2018, he became president of Moody Bible Institute), with seven of New Life's first ten campuses being restarts. His humble approach of celebrating the past but not being bound by it helped enlarge my vision and provided language to deepen discussions with our rebirth partners.

How about you? What are your next steps regarding potential partnerships? Consider these possibilities.

ANKLE DEEP Read Nehemiah chapters 1–2. Nehemiah looked at the data (1:2–3), prayed (1:4–10), built goodwill and gathered assets (2:4–9), and then cast a vision for what God would do (2:17). In these chapters, what do you see that your church could do to intercept entropy in your ministry? How could your church tap into the stream of revitalizing God's work for the next generation?

Do your own data gathering by taking a survey. What's the average age of people in your church? Now look at census data to find out the average age of people in your community. Is the gap between the two something you need help to close?

KNEE DEEP Identify what stage your church is at in the life cycle of movement, museum, and morgue. Have an open, honest discussion with two or three other leaders at your church, especially someone who sees your church at a different stage in this cycle. Or invite someone objective from outside your church. Begin a discussion about mergers with a time of prayer and spiritual discernment. Have a few facts on hand, such as how many local visitors your church had over the last six months. Then ask, "Are we headed in a direction where merging is an option we should consider?"

If your answer is yes, continue exploring by reading the book *Better Together*, coauthored by Warren Bird.

If your answer is no, what needs to happen so that your church will be a greater blessing, bringing more of the living water to your community?

WAIST DEEP Visit a church that has merged and ask them some questions. What worked well? What didn't? What would they do differently? More important, what has been the resulting impact on their community? Have they seen an increase in evangelism, new believers, baptisms, and outreach? How has combining streams with another ministry created a ripple of momentum?

Talk with denominational leaders about options they see for your church in a possible merger. If you're not part of a denomination, find someone who can wisely advise you. Either way, have someone at your church become knowledgeable about your church constitution and bylaws, to understand what they say, if anything, about such a process.

If a merger is not in your short-term future, what options from the "Broader Current" section in this chapter apply best to your church?

Pastors, whatever your role in your church, what is your succession plan? What do you need to do over the next six months to take the next steps in training potential successors?

Other Churches Making Waves

Amplify Church *(amplifychurch.com)*. In 2003, Pastor Lee Kricher invited his aging congregation in Pittsburgh to take on a huge goal: do whatever it takes to become a multigenerational church in which the average age is at least as young as the average age of people in the surrounding community. It worked. He then wrote *For a New Generation: A Practical Guide for Revitalizing Your Church*[8] to tell the inspiring story. In the book, he outlines the five aspects of their strategy. See also *future forwardchurches.com*.

Ginghamsburg *(ginghamsburg.org)* is a United Methodist church. It has sponsored four restarts (and it also does church planting). Each time, the bishop has come to Ginghamsburg's leadership to ask if Ginghamsburg would take a dying congregation under its wing. Each then became a campus of Ginghamsburg during a revitalization process. Two have grown to become self-standing United Methodist churches again, one of which has grown from twenty-five to thirteen hundred on a weekend. The other two experienced revitalization and have remained as Ginghamsburg campuses.

CenterPoint Church *(cpchurch.com)* is a fast growing multisite congregation on Long Island, New York. It currently has four campuses, all of which came through some form of merger. Two were churches that were headed toward closure. Two others are repurposed Jewish synagogues, both of whose owners merged with other synagogues. In the first case, CenterPoint bought the vacated facility, and in the second, the church rents the empty space throughout the week.

The Chapel *(chapel.org)* was a pioneer in pursuing church adoptions as a component of their multisite strategy. Four of their seven campuses across metro Chicago came about through conversations initiated by the Chapel. In essence, they had a staff member who made dozens of contacts with area churches to find those who might be willing to consider being adopted by The Chapel.

Woodside Bible *(woodsidebible.org)*, based in greater Detroit, Michigan, and founded in 1955, first went multisite in 2005. Today nine of its fourteen campuses are the result of mergers. Longtime senior pastor Doug Schmidt has never initiated a merger; instead as he has encouraged, supported, and resourced local pastors, a few have proposed merger as the best path forward for the congregations they've served. For more on the Woodside story and the pastoral heart it tries to communicate, see the lengthy write-up in the book *Better Together*.

CHAPTER EIGHT

INSPIRE GENEROSITY: GUILT-FREE GIVING

The generous will prosper; those who refresh others
will themselves be refreshed.
—PROVERBS 11:25 NLT

A s CNN's hot studio lights glared down on my head, I started
sweating. I thought, *What am I doing here?*

It was Sunday morning, and I was in a Manhattan television studio
an hour before Liquid Church's worship service was scheduled to start
just across the Hudson River. As I sat on a stool in front of a digital
backdrop of the New York City skyline, a makeup artist powdered my
shiny forehead to reduce the glare. A few feet away, a TV producer
with a headset waved to get my attention. She held up three fingers and
began mouthing a silent countdown: *three . . . two . . . one.* She pointed
to the studio camera, and the light on top turned red.

"Pastor Tim Lucas is about to change things up this morning at
his church," CNN anchor T. J. Holmes announced. "At the Liquid
Church congregation, he sees the congregation putting money in the
collection plate every single week, even though he knows some of them
are struggling financially." The Sunday morning anchor grinned
broadly. "But this week, instead of collecting money in that plate, the
church is giving it away. We're talking about thirty thousand dollars
here."[1] Talk about a show-then-tell approach that really piqued people's
curiosity!

My Sunday sermon on generosity was about to go viral. That week, I had planned to teach on Jesus' parable of the talents from the gospel of Matthew. In Jesus' story, a man going on a trip "called together his servants and entrusted his money to them while he was gone. He gave five bags of silver to one, two bags of silver to another, and one bag of silver to the last—dividing it in proportion to their abilities" (Matt. 25:14–15 NLT).

This is a familiar Bible story for a lot of congregations, so our teaching team was looking for a fresh way to capture the imagination of our modern audience. That week, a member of our creative team had pitched a novel idea during a brainstorm session. "What if we actually gave away God's money?" he said. We all laughed, but he pushed in. "I'm serious," he said. "What if we put our money where our mouth is and give back God's money to God's people and ask them to invest it?"

Around the room, a few eyes rolled. At first glance, the idea seemed outlandish. Our church was only four years old, and we needed every dime just to make payroll. On top of that, our region had been hit hard by the Great Recession of 2008. Many people had lost their jobs, home values had plunged, and so had our weekend offerings.

"I love it," I said. Everyone turned and looked at me like I was crazy. "Don't get me wrong. It's a big risk. But it'll bring God's Word alive for folks. Plus I think Jesus is honored when we take him at his word." We called in our executive pastor and pitched the idea. "We want to hold a special offering this Sunday, only in reverse," I explained. "Instead of people putting an offering envelope into the bucket, they'll reach in and take one out. We can fill them with different amounts—tens, twenties, and fifty-dollar bills—just like Jesus' parable, and then I'll challenge our people to creatively invest the money in God's kingdom."

Our team studied the Scripture a bit more and began to see Jesus' dramatic story about stewardship with fresh eyes. When the master returned home, Jesus explained, he asked his three servants for an account of the money he had entrusted to them. The first two servants explained that they each put his wealth to work and doubled its value. "The master was full of praise. 'Well done, my good and faithful [servants]. You have been faithful in handling this small amount, so now I will give you many more responsibilities. Let's celebrate together!'" (Matt. 25:21 NLT).

But the third servant, afraid that his master was a harsh man (v. 24), dug a hole and buried his money in the ground. Jesus was unflinching in his judgment. "You wicked and lazy servant! . . . Why didn't you deposit my money in the bank? At least I could have gotten some interest on it" (vv. 26–27). The master took the money from the man and gave it to one of the servants who had creatively invested his wealth and made a good return.

The lightbulb went on for our team: God (the master) had entrusted us (his servants) with some of his money as we waited for Christ to return. We decided to challenge our congregation to creatively invest God's money and turn a spiritual profit for Christ and his kingdom.

So we took the biggest risk of our young church's life. That week, we went to the bank and withdrew thirty thousand dollars—the previous week's offering. Under the watchful eye of our executive pastor, our finance team stuffed two thousand unmarked offering envelopes, putting in each one a ten-, twenty-, or fifty-dollar bill.

> We decided to challenge our congregation to creatively invest God's money and turn a spiritual profit for Christ and his kingdom.

Somehow the media caught wind of our plan, and CNN brought me in for a prime-time interview on their Sunday morning program. The TV host was gracious but curious about what motivated our reverse offering.

"A lot of people are cynical about religion," I explained to him on camera. "They come to church expecting to be shaken down, but we're saying, 'You know what? It's all God's money and he trusts you.'" I noted that every bill in the American economy says, "In God We Trust" and we were about to put that conviction to the test.

As soon as the interview ended, I jumped in a car and hightailed it from Manhattan back to Morristown, New Jersey, just in time for our first service. As I entered our rented ballroom, people were buzzing, as some had seen the CNN broadcast before coming to church. When I got up to share Jesus' teaching, I noted that today we were taking a risk to put our faith into action. Before distributing the cash, I challenged the congregation to creatively invest the money in one of three ways.

For those in need, I said, "Maybe you're a single mom, and you're going to use a fifty-dollar bill to fill your tank with gas this week or pay for a babysitter. That's awesome. Today's gift is from God directly to you. We want you to know how much God loves you and that he can provide for your needs."

I challenged others to look outside our church walls and think about helping a neighbor in need. Our area was still recovering from the devastating impact of Hurricane Irene, a major catastrophe on the East Coast that had caused $13.5 billion in property damage.[2] "Maybe you can use the money to buy groceries or cook a meal and bring it over to a hurting neighbor," I said, trying to spark out-of-the-box thinking. "Be creative. It's God's money, but he trusts you to put it to work."

And finally, I issued a challenge to the businesspeople and marketplace leaders in our congregation. "Invest God's money for three weeks and multiply it like the faithful servants in Jesus' story," I said. "In three weeks, bring back the money you multiplied, and we'll donate it to help rebuild a homeless shelter."

The air was electric with anticipation. I called our ushers forward and instructed each worshiper to reach into the offering bucket, take out a single envelope, and ask God what he wanted them to do with it. You should've seen the looks on people's faces as the bucket was passed down each row. I watched an older woman's eyes grow wide as she reached in, looked both ways, and pulled out an envelope. I think she expected lightning to strike her! A row of high school students were not so bashful. Each one ripped open their envelope, and they immediately compared the collection. "I got a twenty!" one exclaimed. "I got fifty!" cheered another, and then he taunted his friend. "I guess God trusts me more than you." I realized I had some more teaching to do in the days ahead.

In the weeks that followed, we were blown away by the creativity of our congregants. The owner of a hair salon decided to use his fifty-dollar bill to offer free haircuts for the homeless that Saturday. The stylists at his salon were so moved by the idea of compassionate care for the homeless, they each donated their own services that weekend. They cut hair, trimmed beards, and gave free salon services to more than three dozen homeless people in their city.

A pair of young moms at one of our campuses combined their

cash—one received a ten-dollar bill, and the other a twenty-dollar bill—in a delicious way. The two friends shared a passion for baking and were locally famous for creating designer cakes (for weddings, birthdays, and other special occasions) that often sold for more than a hundred dollars apiece. They combined their thirty dollars and purchased all the ingredients necessary for a *Cake Boss*–style masterpiece. They posted photos of their delectable creation on Facebook and offered it for sale to the highest bidder. They declared that all proceeds would be donated to a shelter for battered women in their town. Someone immediately offered one hundred dollars, another offered two hundred and fifty dollars, and by the following weekend, an anonymous donor had bought their cake for four hundred dollars. The thrilled moms joyfully donated the proceeds to a safe home for victims of domestic violence.

Stories began pouring in. In the wake of the greatest financial recession of our generation, God's people stepped up and captured Christ's heart of generosity and compassion for their neighbors in need. A river of generosity rippled out of our church that fall, and our congregation grasped a fundamental truth that has guided our church ever since: you can never outgive God!

MY OWN 180-DEGREE TURN

Our reverse offering was not a stunt; rather it was an innovative way to teach our people to take God at his word and put their faith into action. We did it to demonstrate how God's perspective on money is dramatically different from how most people—including Christians—think about money. It also represented a shift in my own thinking, and I wanted others to experience the same "aha!"

> Our reverse offering was an innovative way to teach our people to take God at his word and put their faith into action.

I grew up in an environment where discussions about money always involved guilt, duty, and obligation. At one church we attended, a big thermometer was brought onstage to raise funds for a new building campaign. Each week, the "mercury" in the thermometer inched upward to match the congregation's giving toward the project. One week, there was no progress, and an elder chastised the congregation. "This thermometer doesn't just measure dollars; it measures your passion for God!" A wave of shame washed over the room. Ouch.

When I became a pastor, I vowed to never use guilt or shame to motivate people. But as I was unaware of any life-giving alternatives, my solution was simply to say nothing about money. In my preaching, I avoided the topic of money like the plague. But silence is never a good corrective to abuse, and I quickly realized that my avoidance kept me from challenging the unhealthy consumer mindset so many people brought to church. We wanted people to be free in Christ, but this was an area of discipleship where I wasn't allowing God's truth to set people free from materialism (John 8:31–32).

In my personal study, I was struck by how frequently Jesus talked openly about money and possessions. It was the main subject of almost half of his parables. As Greg Laurie observes, the Bible offers five hundred verses on prayer, fewer than five hundred verses on faith, and more than two thousand verses on money. A whopping 15 percent of everything Jesus ever taught was on the topic of money and our stuff—more than his teachings on heaven and hell combined![3] Why the emphasis? Because, Jesus noted, there's a direct spiritual link between money and our hearts (Matt. 6:21). Tradition tells us that Martin Luther once said, "There are three conversions a person needs to experience: the conversion of the head, the conversion of the heart, and the conversion of the pocketbook."

As I studied Scripture, I began to notice a pattern. Over and over, when God asks his people to give to his house (whether the temple in the Old Testament or the church in the New Testament), we see how he wants to use those funds. The first time it dawned on me was when I learned the background of God's call for tithes to be returned to the storehouse (Mal. 3:8–12). The purpose was to feed the poor who otherwise couldn't eat. God commanded people to bring the whole tithe into the storehouse "that there may be food in my house" (v. 10). In that era, there were no public safety nets like Social Security checks and disability insurance. The only social assistance came from the place where people were fed spiritually. The temple (and later the early church, as we see in Acts 6:1) used the gifts from God's people to, among other things, take care of widows, orphans, and others in need. I saw the importance of always connecting people's giving with the compassionate need that will be met because of their generosity.

Similar verses in the New Testament began to pop off the page as I read them. I noticed the apostle Paul's instructions to former thieves to get a job and earn money legitimately, and then saw the reason he gave them—so they could bless others. "Use your hands for good hard work," he commanded, "and then give generously to others in need" (Eph. 4:28 NLT). And as the Spirit opened my eyes, I made a 180-degree turn in my teaching. Now I use an inspirational show-then-tell approach to replace my childhood memories of guilt-laden giving appeals to pay church bills. Instead I say, "See this dilapidated women's shelter in our town? Here's a before-and-after photo. Your generosity transformed it. You gave your treasure, and look how God used it to help vulnerable families." At Liquid, our offering time has become much more focused on what God wants for you—learning to bless others—than what he wants from you.

The biblical connection between generosity and compassion has empowered me to boldly ask people to give sacrificially. When you connect generosity to the discernable difference it makes, people naturally open their hearts as well as their hands.

My friend Juan Galloway leads a life-changing ministry to the homeless that Liquid Church supports with volunteers, materials, and finances. New York City Relief's mission is compelling: it's a mobile outreach that compassionately serves homeless people living on the streets, by offering hope and resources that lead toward life transformation.[4] As president, Juan spends a lot of his time building relationships with business leaders and high-capacity donors. He once remarked to me, "How many leaders of Christ-centered nonprofits would give their right arm to be able to stand up before their constituency each week to show givers the lives changed by their generosity? A church is one of the few nonprofits where we can do just that."

> When you connect generosity to the discernable difference it makes, people naturally open their hearts as well as their hands.

GOD'S M&M'S

One weekend I was teaching our congregation how to handle God's money God's way. To drive the point home in a memorable way, we gave everyone an envelope containing ten M&M's candies. I held up ten M&M's and said, "If this represents your household budget, let's imagine where the money goes." I had people pop three M&M's into their mouths to represent the average costs gobbled up by housing. Two more were eaten to symbolize food expenses. Transportation consumed another M&M, and so forth. Although everyone loved eating M&M's in the service, they ran through their supply pretty quickly!

Next, I held up a glass cup labeled "Me" and poured ten M&M's into it. Then I pulled out a giant bucket labeled "God." It was brimming with thousands of colorful M&M's (our volunteers had a wonderful time getting this prop ready for me!). I read Malachi 3:10, where God challenges his people to test him by bringing a tithe to the storehouse: "See if I will not throw open the floodgates of heaven and pour out so much blessing that there will not be room enough to store it."

The point was simple: when we carve out one M&M from our budget for the Lord's use—representing 10 percent (the tithe)—God promises to bless the rest. To simulate the opening of heavenly floodgates, I began slowly pouring M&M's from the "God" bucket. The rainbow-colored M&M's quickly filled the "Me" cup. But I had only begun! I kept pouring and pouring and pouring. Hundreds of M&M's overflowed the "Me" cup, spilling onto the table and across the stage, and kept scattering onto the floor—a trickle that became a current that became a rainbow river of God's blessing.

I still had more of God's M&M's in my big bucket that I kept floodgating into that little cup. "This is a picture of surplus! Of blessing! Of abundance! Of more than enough!" I preached, as the congregation visually processed the glorious mess I was making. "Our world tells you to spend every last cent on yourself. But when you put God first in your finances and give generously from the heart, you demonstrate that your greater trust is in God. And guess how he responds? Your heavenly Father blesses you with more because he knows you won't spend it all on yourself!" Our dollar bills may say,

"In God We Trust," but did you ever consider that with every paycheck, God trusts you?

I landed the message by announcing a Ninety-Day Tithe Challenge, inviting people to take God up on his challenge to "Try it! Put me to the test!" (Mal. 3:10 NLT). For those who returned a tithe (10 percent) for three months, we offered a money-back guarantee. "If God doesn't bless you as he promised, we'll refund 100 percent of your money, no questions asked," I said (with the prior arrangement of our financial team, who later reported that no one asked for a refund). We made this crazy offer because we want people to experience financial freedom by learning to honor God first in their finances.

> Our dollar bills may say, "In God We Trust," but did you ever consider that with every paycheck, God trusts you?

And they did. Beth, a mom in our church with a son who has special needs, took the tithing challenge. Then after the ninety days, she continued to tithe, even when her marriage broke up. "My first thought was to feel like I might need to keep more of my income," she says. "I was scared. But then I said to myself, 'God wants me to give obediently and joyfully.'" She stayed with her commitment. "Looking back, it drew me closer to the Lord, helping me to realize what was important, and to trust him with my finances. I've learned that it's not even about the money but how God wants my heart. I'll tell anyone today, 'You can't outgive God!'"

TRAINING WHEELS FOR YOUR HEART

The ancient practice of tithing is like training wheels for our heart. It's a spiritual discipline that trains us to trust God with all we have and place our dependence on him. Tithing 10 percent is the ground floor of generosity for Christians; offerings are given above and beyond the tithe. (And we never collect tithes and offering in our church; we receive them.)

We've offered a Ninety-Day Tithe Challenge several times over the years. It's always thrilling to see a new wave of people trusting God financially for the first time. The testimonials are energizing to everyone! The blessings we see God pour out aren't always financial; sometimes they are relational harmony in a home, a spiritual break-through in a family or marriage, or just a sense of God's peace as people give him first place in their lives.

Another spiritual discipline we encourage is fasting. Abstaining from certain food for a season is a powerful way to whet the spiri-tual appetite of a congregation. We've done several churchwide fasts, some for ten or twenty-one days. In spring 2018, we did a forty-day fast that had a huge impact on the generosity of our church. We had just moved into a new building, and our weekly giving had grown by 12 percent—a blessing for sure. But there was one problem: we had projected a 24 percent increase that was necessary to sustain all six of our campuses at the time. That shortfall of 12 percent worried our senior leadership team. As we crunched the numbers, we realized we might have to lay off staff members if giving didn't increase.

So we hit our knees in prayer and leaned into a season of fasting. Our senior team felt the Spirit leading us to hit the pause button on lay-offs for forty days and see what God might do as we sought his provi-sion to fill the financial gap. We prayed the words of Jehoshaphat, who called God's people to fast in a time of need: "Our God, . . . we do not know what to do, but our eyes are on you" (2 Chron. 20:12). Incredibly, halfway through the fast, general giving increased to 20 percent, then 25 percent, then 35 percent. By the time fall arrived, an outbreak of generosity had infected our church, resulting in a 45 percent increase year on year! Prayer, fasting, and tithing are a powerful combo and set the stage for God to move in miraculous ways.

An additional discipline we encourage is online giving. Currently, 70 percent of our weekly income comes online through our website or mobile app. Our prayers during the traditional offering time at church acknowledge those who have already given even before they came to church. Every company that offers software to support online tithing soon begins to claim that overall giving is up, often substantially. The reason is simple: online giving helps people be more consistent. If they're traveling or on vacation, they're still able to prioritize generosity. Plus many young adults don't even own a checkbook. How else can they give?

EVERY RIVER
Starts with a Trickle

From the beginning, Liquid has been committed to being a tithing church. That means we give away the first 10 percent of our income to people who couldn't possibly pay us back. The Bible describes people like that as the "least" (those society views as adding the least value; Matt. 25:40), the "last" (those who are typically last in line or last to benefit from upturns in the economy; Matt. 19:30; 20:16), and the "lost" (those who need an eternity-changing faith relationship with Jesus Christ; Luke 19:10).

We've always wanted to invest that first 10 percent outside our church walls—even when we were renting and borrowing the walls where we met!—in order to demonstrate God's heart for outsiders. We serve a God of radical grace and generosity. If we represent God, we might be the only Bible some people will read. So no matter how little we began with, I wanted us to model generosity from the start.

We began living out that value even before we became a church. In the weeks leading up to our launch, we were handing out free granola bars and water at the train station a few blocks from where we'd be meeting. When morning commuters asked what was behind our no-strings-attached gift, our volunteers told them, "Because our God is a giver. He gave his son Jesus to show us his love. So we're here to share his love with you!" Some were thankful, others were skeptical, and some came to check out this new church.

Here are some of the no-strings-attached outreaches we launched in our early days to open the floodgates of radical generosity at Liquid Church.

GAS BUYDOWN

In keeping with our commitment to invest 10 percent of all church income outside our walls to bless our neighbors, we used some of those funds to buy out a local Exxon gas station one Saturday morning. We called the outreach Pray at the Pump. We explained to the station owner, "We'd like to buy so many dollars' worth of gas and then give it away for free to the community." Volunteers stood on the street corner with signs: "Free Gas! No strings attached." And it quickly took off. Word of mouth and a local radio station spread the word. "A local church is giving away free gas!" Soon a line of cars and SUVs wrapped around the gas station and two city blocks.

Our gas buydown took place right after the 2008 Great Recession hit. It was a time when some people didn't know how they would fill up their tank, and we wanted to show them God's love in a practical way.

When people pulled up to the gas pump, they wanted to know why we were being so generous. Our volunteers replied, "We're giving away gas for free because God's love is free. While we're filling up your tank, how can we pray for you?" We prayed for more than four hundred motorists that weekend; not one turned us down for prayer. People were genuinely touched that a church would love without strings and not solicit a donation. Even when people tried to give us money, we turned it down, again saying, "We just want to meet needs in a practical way to show you that Christ's love is free, no strings attached." (Show-then-tell.)

By noontime a crisis had developed, with people waiting in line forty-five minutes for the gas. What started as a wonderful gesture to warm hearts was now angering impatient people. So our volunteers improvised on the spot, running to a nearby store for glass cleaner and paper towels. We went up and down the line of cars, asking, "While you're waiting, can we clean your windshield? We've also got some Armor All wipes. Can we shine your tires and dashboard?" Volunteers in Liquid T-shirts also served donuts and hot coffee to those waiting in line. It was easy for them to "prime the pump" so that when drivers got to the point of receiving gas, they were open to being prayed for as well.

FREE MARKET

One of our first outreaches cost us practically nothing, except time and repurposed treasures. In chapter 3, I described how we reversed the idea of a flea market and instead hosted a free market. Instead of bringing their junk, our people brought their best, and we gave it away for free to the urban poor. Soon we had collected clothes, baby cribs, strollers, bikes, and more—each item cleaned and packaged attractively. We held the giveaway outdoors in the public park at the center of our city.

What was so powerful is that our people caught the heart of it. I had taught, "This is not a dump for cleaning out the junk in your attic. God gave us his firstborn Son; let's give people our very best." I asked them to imagine blessing an immigrant family of eight people living in a one-bedroom apartment.

We partnered with local social service agencies to identify specific families in need. We also asked one of the social services staff, "What do people need the most?" She said quality winter coats.

In response, one family dry-cleaned and donated all their ski coats, first mending any minor wear in them. Another family, in which the wife was part of the church but the husband was not yet a believer, was so touched by our effort that the husband went out to a local clothing store, bought three hundred coats, and donated them to our free market! He was so moved that this wasn't a fundraiser but a way to treat our city's poor with compassion and dignity. He's not yet a follower of Jesus, but to this day he continues to give generous gifts as long as they're part of our no-strings-attached outreach ministries.

CHRISTMAS SHOPPING

The outdoor free market was such a huge win and blessing for our church that we morphed it into a Christmas event for single parents and low-income families. This time, we hosted it inside a hotel ballroom and catered a delicious meal to accompany the giveaway. Volunteers dressed up in ties and white gloves and acted as personal waiters to serve the families orange juice, bacon, and delicious omelets. Other volunteers served as personal shoppers, taking each family first to the toy room and then to the clothing room to select custom gifts for their children. Again, we partnered with local social service agencies to identify families living below the poverty line and personally invited them to come.

> We don't believe in random acts of kindness; we believe in strategic acts of kindness that let us serve our way into the hearts of our neighbors.

It's amazing how many creative ways exist to serve your city with little or no money. But as fun as it might be to dream up ideas, we avoid operating in a vacuum. Partnering with municipal agencies is the key to strategically saturating your city. Typically, we begin by contacting the mayor's office or meeting city officials. We introduce our church and ask, "How can we meet the needs of underserved people that no one else is meeting? What's on your wish list?" In most cases, city officials are elated that our church is stepping up to help families that they lack the budget to resource in generous ways.

Too many churches have their hearts in the right place but lack strategic thinking. They reason, "We'll put up some posters in local shops and then pray that people will show up to our outreach." This is good-hearted but almost always ineffective. By not having strategic partnerships, they miss out not only on serving a critical mass of residents but also on the goodwill they could have gained regarding their relationship with their city.

At Liquid, we don't believe in random acts of kindness; we believe in strategic acts of kindness that let us serve our way into the hearts of our neighbors.

PARTNERING WITH OTHERS

As Liquid Church grew, we gained more volunteers, connections, and financial resources to work with. (We continue to tithe as a church, and as our budget has grown larger, some years we have given away 12 percent or more.) The more established we become as a church, the more we seek out community partners who are killing it in their area of expertise, and come alongside them with money and manpower. Our DNA of radical generosity allows us to offer funds to do special projects for our partners, and the volunteer muscle to pull it off. Here are a couple of my favorite initiatives.

Women's Safe House Makeover

During a sermon series on biblical manhood, we decided to redeem and correct one of the tragedies created when men abuse their God-given strength. We focused on helping a home for battered women, something that wouldn't even exist if all men lived in Christ-honoring ways. So we partnered with Women Aware, a safe home for victims of domestic violence. It housed fifteen women and children, but the home itself was run-down. The deck was decaying, with nails popping up all over the place. Several steps to the house were missing, so women had difficulty lifting their children and groceries inside, and the neglected yard desperately needed attention. That Sunday we announced, "Men, let's mobilize our strength for God's glory and the good of these women and give their safe home an extreme makeover." We set a weekend and called it our Man-Made Outreach.

Earlier, we had met with the director, who was not a follower of Christ, and explained our idea. "What's the catch?" she asked. We affirmed that there was no catch. "We have an army of men who want to serve in a way that uses their God-given strength for good." She initially pushed back, explaining the problem: her residents might be afraid and feel overwhelmed by the sight of so many men descending on their safe house. Through many conversations, plus her attendance at some of our worship services, she saw our heart and gave us her trust.

It became one of our most transformational outreaches ever. On the designated Saturday, from 6:00 a.m. to 10:00 p.m., men swarmed over the property like ants on a popsicle stick. They rebuilt and upgraded the deck, powerwashed the house, and lovingly sanded and painted the home. They cleaned out a moldy, damp basement and installed flooring and new shelves and bins for residents' clothes and belongings. A crew of men transformed the back yard, pulling weeds, planting trees, installing a privacy fence and landscaping, and building a brand-new jungle gym for the kids to enjoy.

At first, the curtains inside were drawn as the men worked. But as the day went on, women began peeking through the windows to watch the men sacrificially serving them in Jesus' name. It ministered deeply to the wounds that they'd received from the hands of their abusers. Phyllis Adams, the director, was so moved that she said, "I have to come to your church and personally thank these men." Not only did she come and speak to the congregation, but she heard the gospel, gave her heart to Christ, and was baptized.

Phyllis represents exactly who we want to reach—people who have given up on church but not on God. She's why we started Liquid

Church: we want the water of life to saturate our entire community, including women's shelters, so that everyone will see the power of Christ to restore broken lives.

Jesus Loves Jersey

Another extreme makeover took place in New Brunswick, where we had opened a second campus. We learned of Elijah's Promise, a soup kitchen for people living homeless on the city streets. When we asked how we could help, they said they didn't need volunteers to serve food nearly as much as help with the facility that housed the soup kitchen. It was a dingy, poorly lit basement, where the mismatched chairs were the nicest part of the furnishings.

"What's your dream?" we asked the community leaders. The director replied, "I wish we could give them an environment like Starbucks, where it's a warm place to meet friends and enjoy a hot meal and drink, and give them a sense of dignity and community." Our teams prayed, talked about it, and then offered to supply both the money and the volunteer energy, with the goal to install brand-new café seats, booths, lighting, and more.

These types of radically generous outreaches help exercise the discipleship muscle of our congregation. We tell our community partners, "As much as it may be a blessing to you, this helps build our people's generosity muscles. We don't want them to simply give their money; we want them to invest their heart and time." When people share their time, talent, and treasure, that's the trifecta for us! We are intentional to involve men and women from all walks of life, from teens and young adults to seniors. When we do an extreme makeover, our first step often involves an interior designer who is willing to use his or her talents to create a beautiful environment. This is a very valuable resource, not typically available when serving a nonprofit.

AS FUNDS FLOW OUT, PEOPLE FLOW IN

At the risk of oversimplification, I believe that when our funds flow out, people flow in. There is an attractional power to no-strings-attached generosity. When a city sees a church freely giving of its time, talent, and treasure, people are magnetically drawn toward it, either to attend, to applaud, or to partner with us. Show-then-tell.

In the various communities where we have campuses, the mayors' offices now routinely reach out to us (initially, we were the ones reaching out to them). That's a direct result of how generously we've given to and served their city. One year, we remodeled the seniors' center in one of the cities where we have a campus. Another year, at the mayor's request, we did an extreme makeover of the town's animal shelter. Another time, we sponsored a fall festival for families with special needs and donated aqua wheelchairs to a water park for kids with disabilities. For our largest campus, we've let the city freely use our state-of-the-art auditorium to host their summer concerts. That kind of no-strings-attached generosity is deeply attractional. We've found it softens the hearts and draws the favor of even the most hardened skeptics.

> When our funds flow out, people flow in. There is an attractional power to no-strings-attached generosity. When a city sees a church freely giving of its time, talent, and treasure, people are magnetically drawn toward it.

HELP PEOPLE FIND FINANCIAL FREEDOM

The reality is that most churches are full of people who want to be generous, but they're strapped. They're drowning in consumer debt, they're swamped by poor financial decisions, and they lack healthy financial role models. So before people can become radically generous, they must take their first steps to financial freedom.

At Liquid, our main tool for teaching the basics of biblical money management is Dave Ramsey's Financial Peace University (FPU). Each year, our church offers the nine-week course, which teaches people how to plan a budget, eliminate personal debt, and save for their future. We've had hundreds of people from all walks of life receive this stewardship training, from millennials paying off college loans to families of four trying to eliminate credit cards and save for college. The results have been astounding: since we began offering FPU in 2009, more than five hundred households have retired more than two million dollars of debt. Praise God!

Rick and Cecilia are one of many couples who have made this transition. They had racked up $185,000 in debt—student loans, car loans, and credit card bills—when they took the Financial Peace University class. "Ever since I was eighteen, when I took out my first credit card, I've been in debt," says Cecilia. "No one had taught me about budgeting or personal finances." Over time, she tried to fill the emptiness she felt in her heart with shopping. "I was addicted," she says. "I was the wife who would leave shopping bags in the car because I didn't want my husband to see that I had gone shopping again." The weight of debt put a huge strain on their marriage.

At the urging of a friend, they went to FPU, hosted at a Liquid campus. When the class presented the idea of tithing 10 percent of their income—the first thing you do when you get a paycheck—Rick was stumped. He was certain they couldn't afford it. But he did it in faith. "I realized it's about our hearts, not our money," he says. "We could give our hearts and trust God to take care of the rest." So they did, and they've already paid off more than half their debt. More important, Rick and Cecilia both trusted Jesus to pay their spiritual debt to God and became Christ followers! Their marriage is stronger, and their family is as well. "If we could do it, anyone can," says Cecilia.

SACRIFICE IS MORE IMPORTANT THAN SIZE

Imagine that Jesus walks into your worship service this weekend. He quietly observes the worship and sits back to listen to the sermon. But when it comes time to pass the offering plate, Jesus gets up and notes exactly what each person puts in or gives on their mobile app. Awkward, right? Yet that's exactly what Jesus does in Mark 12:41–44. In this revealing story, Jesus "watched the crowd putting their money into the temple treasury. Many rich people threw in large amounts. But a poor widow came and put in two very small copper coins, worth only a few cents" (vv. 41–42).

Jesus is so impressed that he calls to his disciples. I can just imagine him saying, "Come here. I want you guys to see this!" What's the big deal? A widow drops a couple of pennies into the offering. Poor lady didn't even have two nickels to rub together. Then Jesus delivers an unexpected punch line. "Truly I tell you, this poor widow has put more into the treasury than all the others. They all gave out of their wealth; but she, out of her poverty, put in everything—all she had to live on" (vv. 43–44).

The application? When it comes to a generous spirit, God counts not the amount but the willing, heartfelt sacrifice to his house. Do you have a heart for his house? Bigger offerings don't necessarily mean a bigger heart toward God. Jesus doesn't count the amount; his concern is whether we sacrifice our comfort to put God first. How much do we hold back as a safety cushion? That's where true faith is revealed.

God is after our hearts, not our wallets. Radical generosity is an ongoing exercise in stretching our faith, deepening our trust, and believing that God will show up in what remains after we've given. When the numbers don't add up, we're fully dependent on God to show up. That's where Jesus wants us. That's how we become more like him. And that's where our communities "see your good deeds and glorify your Father in heaven" (Matt. 5:16).

> Jesus doesn't count the amount; his concern is whether we sacrifice our comfort to put God first.

THE BROADER CURRENT

In many fast-growing churches, radical generosity is a core value that grows like a trickle into a current and then a raging river that saturates their city for Christ. In Maple Grove, Minnesota, Passion Church decided to powerfully demonstrate God's generous heart to families in need. According to their state's department of education, more than two hundred thousand students depend on free school lunches, and another sixty thousand depend on reduced-price lunches. Passion Church learned that many students who don't qualify for a meal subsidy are unable to pay for their lunch.

So they contacted their local school district to ask about helping families who couldn't afford lunch for their kids. At first, school officials were wary of the church's motives. But lead pastor Jonathan Brozozog met with the board of education to share his church's heart to help. Passion Church offered to monthly pay off the debt of every family who couldn't afford school lunch, no strings attached.

The board was floored and embraced the idea. Jonathan explains, "Each month, the school district sends a letter to families that says, 'Passion Church has paid your debt in full.' We think this is a great representation of the gospel. As believers, we had a debt we couldn't pay, and Jesus wiped it clean."

What a powerful witness! For those who worship a Savior who paid our debt to God, what a practical way to demonstrate God's grace to families in need. Passion's free lunch deal has become so popular, they've established a program *(SchoolLunchMatters.com)* to encourage other churches who have a similar heart.

At churches like Passion, meeting a practical need through radical generosity is often the first step in ministering to spiritually hungry people. Pastor Jonathan observes that Jesus fed the multitudes before he ministered to them. "Churches that focus only on spiritual needs tend to reach hundreds of people," he notes. "But churches that meet physical needs first reach thousands."

The current wave of radical generosity in growing churches is opening fresh, new inroads into a post-Christian culture skeptical of institutional religion. It shatters the popular stereotypes of oily evangelists who fleece the flock, as well as megachurches that appear to use their flock's funds simply to build larger buildings. When God's people are seen sacrificing deeply, from the heart, to give to those who can't possibly pay them back, even skeptics sit up and take notice. As it turns out, generosity isn't just good for the recipient and giver; it is a powerful witness to the unbelieving world.

Dive Deeper

When it comes to generosity, I've discovered it's impossible for pastors to lead their congregation any farther than they've personally been willing to go. That's why generosity has always been part of my walk with Christ. In college, Colleen and I both committed to be tithers, and—once we eliminated our stupid consumer debt—by God's grace, we've increased the amount we've returned to God's house through our offerings each year. One book that has inspired me is The Treasure Principle by Randy Alcorn. In Matthew 6, Jesus offers life-changing investment advice. He says to store up treasures for ourselves, just not here on earth. Instead he tells us to store our treasure in heaven, where it will await us and last forever. According to Jesus, we can't take it with us, but we can send it on ahead!

Here are ideas that can help you and your church practice giving that grows from a tiny trickle into a current and, finally, a rising river of generosity that impacts your community with the gospel.

 ANKLE DEEP Read 2 Corinthians 9:6–15. Name all the positive outcomes of giving generously and cheerfully. In light of all those good results, do you or your church put enough priority on sacrificial generosity? If not, what keeps you or your church from giving it more attention?

Select a onetime idea from this chapter (or come up with one of your own) that would be new for your church and would be realistic for you to implement in the next six months. Most important, pick one that would train your congregation in the practice of no-strings-attached generosity in a way that would spill outside your church walls and bless people in your community.

KNEE DEEP Create a track specifically for discipling donors. At Liquid Church, we launched what we called the Legacy Team. It's a Dream Team made up of people who have the spiritual gift of giving and believe wholeheartedly in Liquid's God-given vision to saturate the state with the gospel of Jesus Christ. Legacy Team members lead the way in financial generosity and build a spiritual portfolio of their eternal investment in the kingdom of God. In 2018, we held our first breakfast meeting, at which I forecast some ideas for upcoming initiatives and asked for their input and insights (not their money). As a pastor, it's so valuable to get candid feedback from dedicated leaders as well as affirm their calling in the marketplace. Because we involve insiders in the early stages of our planning, their hearts help shape our ministry as we brainstorm projects that are still in the whiteboard phase of discussion. Want an idea for a book to give donors and core supporters? *The Treasure Principle* by Randy Alcorn. Want a book for your church's executive team? Try *Contagious Generosity* by Chris Willard and Jim Sheppard.

Be generous in a way that blesses other churches. In 2019, we started a Pastors Coaching Network at Liquid Church. Because of our people's generosity, we're able to give away free resources such as sermon series, systems content, graphics, curriculums, and more. We also donate a certain portion of staff time to help other churches and coach their ministry leaders.

WAIST DEEP Earlier in this chapter, I said that "when a city sees a church freely giving of its time, talent, and treasure, people are magnetically drawn toward it." When funds flow out, people flow in. Can you imagine a churchwide effort in a big-scale venture to bless a specific "last" or "least" group in your town, with no strings attached? This would involve vision casting from the pulpit, mobilization of many teams from inside the church, and sacrificial, heart-motivated generosity of time, talent, and treasure. Ideas might include an extreme makeover of a soup kitchen or domestic violence shelter, a free market for city residents living at or below the poverty line, or a special trip or meal for residents of an adult daycare center. As a first step, remember to reach out to your mayor or city officials or partner with a social services group that could use help serving an underresourced demographic. Set realistic expectations for something you can do well.

Other Churches Making Waves

In 2008, **Life.Church** (*life.church*), based in Edmond, Oklahoma, created the YouVersion Bible App, a free mobile app which has been downloaded more than 365 million times since it launched as one of the first apps on the Apple App Store. YouVersion started with one teenage developer's part-time focus and has grown into a dedicated team of full-time developers and designers and hundreds of volunteers. All this is possible because one permission-giving senior pastor, Craig Groeschel, had a heart to bless other churches. Likewise, as the church grew (it's one of the most widely attended churches in America), leaders at other churches wanted to use their resources, from children's and youth ministry curriculum to web graphics and worship. But instead of selling their ministry materials, Life.Church decided to make them available for free. Groeschel says the decision to give away their church's content ushered in a season when God began to do more through them than they ever could have imagined, and they saw explosive growth throughout their efforts.

Salem Baptist Church *(sbcoc.org)* in Chicago looks forward to any "National ___ Day" if it enables the church to serve its community with generosity. For the most recent National Law Enforcement Appreciation Day, the church honored the police officers at the local precinct by sending flowers, lunch, and a note delivered by one of the officers who is a member at the church. Sadly, street violence that morning resulted in a fatality, and it was the job of the police to inform the parents of their son's death. Returning to the police station, the two officers saw the flowers, food, and note and were all but moved to tears. One of the officers posted on social media how the church had made his day. Once again, the church's no-strings-attached generosity had made a difference.

Vineyard Columbus *(vineyardcolumbus.org)* in Ohio runs a giant community center that offers everything from immigration counseling, free medical and dental clinics, a free legal clinic, after-school programming, a huge ESL program, citizenship classes, and job training, to basketball leagues. It is subsidized by the church so that it can do many things for free or at a subsidized rate for people participating in the programming. The church did a capital campaign for global and local missions to send out forty missionaries and to construct the community center.

Christ Community Chapel *(ccchapel.com)* has learned that regularly giving away the church's Sunday offering increases the congregation's generosity rather than decreases it. Three or four Sundays a year, the Hudson, Ohio, congregation donates 100 percent of the day's giving to local and global causes such as orphanages, hospitals, and ministries that free children from sex trafficking. "For whatever reason, this has inspired our people to give more all around," says lead pastor Joe Coffey. "We've tapped into a different kind of generosity, and it inherently increases the trust people have in our leadership. People get pumped when they hear we're going to give away all our money from the week's offering with no strings attached." The church calls the campaigns Micah 6:8 Sundays, and amazingly, the church's giving on those weeks averages 50 to 70 percent more than a normal Sunday. "We think it's having a profound impact on becoming a generous church, and our people are giving more than they ever have," Joe says. "Giving to justice and mercy ministries in the name of Jesus is one of our favorite things as a church. We feel that generosity makes us kinder, more loving, and better for the world."

The Life Church *(theLifeChurch.com)*, in Memphis, Tennessee, discovered that it was a short drive from the hungriest zip code in the United States. "We talked to schoolteachers in our church, and they told us some of the children show up Monday in the same clothes they wore Friday, and they hadn't eaten all weekend. Their stomachs were growling, it was impossible to teach, and the kids were not learning," says Pastor John Siebeling. "On Friday afternoons, volunteers line up outside the school with food bags," he explains. "When the kids come out, they give them hugs and pray for them." The volunteers tell the children, "You're a champion" and share free lunch bags and God's love.

CHAPTER NINE

DEVELOP UNTAPPED TALENT: LEADERSHIP CULTURE

> Their responsibility is to equip God's people to do
> his work and build up the church, the body of Christ.
> —EPHESIANS 4:12 NLT

I don't see how we can do this without more volunteers," said the leader of our kids' ministry in the middle of our strategy session.

"How many do we need?" I asked, taking a sip of coffee and leaning in.

"Double what we've got," she said with concern in her voice.

The room went silent. Team members shifted uncomfortably in their chairs. This was not happy news.

Clearly, we had a major problem. Our church was six months away from the grand opening of our new broadcast campus, but there was a serious volunteer gap, and we were coming up way short.

Time to pray. Honestly, our first instinct was to panic!

There's not a church leader I know who wouldn't love to magically double their volunteer base overnight. But of course, it doesn't work that way. Like me, many pastors are unaware of the acute need for leaders, until there's a crisis.

Our kids' ministry at Liquid had been growing steadily for five years, but then it took off like a rocket ship in the last two, growing more than 30 percent annually. Our nursery was brimming with babies. Infants and toddlers outnumbered frazzled volunteers. And our high school program was desperate for new mentors to lead small groups.

SIZE DOESN'T MATTER (SORT OF)

In our case, doubling meant going from three hundred to six hundred volunteers. You may be thinking, *Well, at least you had three hundred volunteers; that's an army!* Not really. Size is just a matter of scale. Don't be thrown by the extra zeroes. Maybe you have three volunteers today and need six tomorrow. Or thirty and you need sixty to take your ministry to the next level. Doubling the volunteer base would be a massive challenge for a church of any size.

Our circumstance was unique (and so is yours). It was the spring of 2017, and we were on the cusp of a growth curve jump in the life of Liquid. We were about to finish renovating a giant warehouse that would serve as our main broadcast campus and permanent staff offices. After a roller-coaster three-year search, the Lord had miraculously led us to a beautiful building in north Jersey, near the intersection of four major highways.

Our staff was excited, but intimidated by the size. The facility was 165,000 square feet—bigger than a typical Walmart (105,000 square feet). It would provide plenty of room for new classrooms and kids' spaces to alleviate the crowding. But as we tripled our seating capacity, we realized we had to double our volunteer ranks.

Kids' and students' ministries were both growing explosively, and we knew the grand opening would attract many new guests and families. Sure, these are normal growing pains for an expanding church—"Good problems to have," as my pastor friends would say. But a platinum problem is still a problem.

And we had a big one. Plus our main campus had been portable for all ten of its years. Portable church requires an extraordinary amount of volunteer muscle. Roadies are needed to set up an empty ballroom at 5:00 a.m. with staging and audiovisual lighting equipment (AVL). Banners and signage, kids' books, toys, snacks, and teaching tools must all be schlepped in every Sunday to start from scratch.

I was so proud of our volunteers. They were 100 percent committed, and dedicated, resilient. They'd do whatever it takes to make church happen. But each time we onboarded five new leaders, two would exit out the back door. Yes, our church was growing, but our leadership ranks were churning. And the churn rate was uncomfortably high.

And now we were about to move into a brand-new building that we had to learn to operate ourselves. Previously, we'd enjoyed a few perks of doing church in a rented hotel ballroom: we never had to worry about parking (there was a covered garage) or security (the hotel supplied its own) or building maintenance (major mess in the bathroom? Just dial "H" for housekeeping and it was magically cleaned up. Thank you, Jesus!).

> Our church was growing, but our leadership ranks were churning.

TEAMWORK MAKES GOD'S DREAM WORK

So that spring, we made a gutsy decision. Instead of making a few temporary tweaks, our team decided to reboot our volunteer system. We planned a special sermon series called *Dream Team* and set an ambitious goal: to turn our depleted ranks of volunteers into a steady stream of leaders to achieve our vision to saturate our state with the gospel. We chose the symbolic name Dream Team (an idea we gleaned from Church of the Highlands, noted in the "Other Churches Making Waves" section at the end of this chapter) to rebrand the dozen or so ministry teams led and run by volunteers, from children's ministry to guest connections to media.

We realized there were scores of people sitting in the seats on Sundays who had one-of-a-kind talents and gifts that were going unused. It was our job to challenge the spectators to come down from the bleachers onto the field and get in the game! Before casting the vision, we asked God for special grace in mobilizing his people on mission, following Jesus' instruction in Luke 10:2: "The harvest is plentiful, but the workers are few. Ask the Lord of the harvest, therefore, to send out workers into his harvest field." We knew it would take everything we had to mobilize the masses and that we were playing catch-up, since we were starting from a volunteer system that was solid but not reproducing at the rate needed to realize our vision.

This was another "all hands on deck" moment in the life of our church. That Sunday, I rang the bell to get everyone's attention. As I preached, I carefully avoided using guilt or duty to motivate people but instead called them to God's grander vision of reaching our unsaved neighbors and raising up the next generation of leaders. In the series, we shared a brief overview of the many needs we had. We needed people to park cars, greet guests, serve coffee, register new families, take care of toddlers, mentor middle schoolers, operate lights, cameras, and video, do midweek data entry, translate the message for Spanish-speaking guests, and pray with people after the service.

"We can't make this happen without every person playing a part," I said. I shared how most churches operate on a 20:80 rule—20 percent of the people do 80 percent of the work. "We want to flip that ratio around," I said. "We want eighty percent of our congregation doing the work of ministry together. Our vision is too big and too important to leave in the hands of a select few. Teamwork makes God's dream work! And we need every able-bodied man, woman, and student to step up, join a Dream Team, and sign up to serve."

To show how serious we were, I cut the message short and we ended the service early (but told parents not to pick up their kids). Instead people left the service and went out into the lobbies at our campuses, where we staged a Dream Team expo, showcasing all the volunteer teams and roles available to fill. Team leaders came up with creative ways to communicate the heart of their ministry. Male leaders carried dolls in BabyBjörn carriers to show how men could make a difference working with infants. The Spanish translation team offered lime chips, salsa, and homemade guacamole to share their passion for serving Latino guests.

We branded the Dream Team experience with a college football look. Varsity banners proudly waved over each team. Electric-blue T-shirts emblazoned with the Dream Team athletic logo were offered to those who signed up to "shadow serve" (learn the role as an apprentice). Although the need was most acute at our main location, we cast vision at all of our campuses and asked God to stir people's hearts to action.

AN AVALANCHE OF NEW VOLUNTEERS

The result? Over the two-weekend series, a whopping 815 new volunteers signed up to serve in our church that spring. Hallelujah! We were blown away. Our entire staff thanked the Lord of the harvest for answering our prayers with an avalanche of potential new volunteers. We praised Jesus for doing "more than all we ask or imagine" in an Ephesians 3:20 breakthrough moment. But in the elation, we also made a sober resolution: never again would we allow so much untapped talent to remain warehoused, sitting stagnant and underutilized in our congregation.

The short-term crisis led to a long-term overhaul in our leadership development culture. Out of the 815 people who came down from the bleachers and got in the game, several emerged whom God had planted in advance to lead our church to the next level. One of them was Robert Barba, a corporate executive who had started attending Liquid a little more than a year before but had never volunteered to serve.

> We made a sober resolution: never again would we allow so much untapped talent to remain warehoused, sitting stagnant and underutilized in our congregation.

"It wasn't for lack of interest," Robert explained. "I'd just never been asked."

Who would imagine that a CFO by day would have a passion for protecting God's flock by leading a volunteer security team? But that's how God had wired Robert. "My day job is to keep things in order by policies and procedures, so why not use the same approach with protecting the house of God?" he asks. He had become a follower of Jesus on the other side of the country and had volunteered to be on a church security team there. He absolutely loved it. After he and his family moved to New Jersey and decided on Liquid as their church home, he had offered to help with our security team. "We don't have one," Pastor Mike Leahy told him. Security simply wasn't on our radar, because the hotels provided it at our rented venues.

Yet many months later, as we renovated the giant warehouse and prepared to move into our new broadcast campus, we were keenly aware that churches are a soft target, as mass shootings in Charleston, South Carolina, and Sutherland Springs, Texas, had reminded us. Pastor Mike remembered his conversation with Robert and approached him about creating and building a brand-new security team. "I was thrilled to be asked," Robert recalls.

So we let Robert loose. We empowered this talented entrepreneur to use his organizational know-how to develop security plans, procedures, and a trained team. This amazing and knowledgeable volunteer did in six months what it would have taken paid staff two to three years to figure out! Today we have security teams at all campuses that are screened, trained, and equipped with the right technology. These women and men keep an eye on all classrooms, hallways, entrances, backstage rooms, offices, bathrooms, and even the grounds. Robert set up a security camera system that can even be monitored remotely via phone. His team has also partnered with local police to have them walk our building, identify vulnerabilities, make recommendations, and coordinate emergency response should it be needed. Talk about a guardian angel. Robert even coordinated active shooter training by local law enforcement for our campus staff.

More important, Robert integrated faith at every step. He tells his people that they don't do anyone any good on the team if they're not growing in the Word. "We hold each other accountable," he says. "We poke at each other to make sure we each get to the services, not just walk around them. It's become a brotherhood and sisterhood, growing in our passion for the things of God." Robert did all of this as an ordinary (okay, extra-ordinary), unpaid volunteer. This is the power of tapping into hidden talent in your congregation!

Most churches lack a steady flow of volunteers. But your next wave of volunteers (and many of your future staff) are already sitting in your seats this Sunday. What practical steps can you take to unleash top-talent leaders like Robert and create a steady stream of volunteers in your church? Mobilizing high-capacity leaders to saturate your city with the gospel has five elements.

1. The role of the lead pastor
2. Developing paid staff (if your size warrants)

3. Cultivating volunteer staff
4. Recruiting and retaining Dream Team volunteers
5. Attracting and training interns

UNCORKING THE BOTTLENECK: ME

It's been said that you can structure for control or structure for growth, but you can't do both. Sadly, many senior pastors favor a "high control, high command" leadership style that creates a bottleneck that makes it hard for new leaders to emerge. A few years ago, I discovered I was doing just that as a lead pastor, often without realizing it. Every new project and program had to come across my desk for review, suggestions, and approval.

And here's the thing: I loved it. I wasn't on a power trip, but as founder of the church, I was used to having my fingerprints on every new initiative. I recalled the early days when I created the worship programs on my laptop and chose the color of outreach T-shirts. But now my founder's passion to sweat the details was being perceived as micromanagement by staff and volunteers. Ouch.

As our church grew larger, I had to admit that my span of care needed to grow smaller, since I could no longer control (or even know about) everything happening in each ministry. At first, I felt guilty, as if this were a leadership shortcoming. But from coaching by other senior pastors, I realized how critical it was for me, as the senior leader, to acknowledge my limitations and voluntarily "give up to go up" and uncork the bottleneck.

Yes, I can still be hands-on and available. On weekends, I love to wander the hallways, greeting families and praying with people. It's my favorite kind of hands-on ministry. But I've learned that any follow-up from those conversations is best handled by specialized staff; otherwise I become a bottleneck. Instead of offering to counsel an engaged couple, I connect them to volunteer marriage mentors who can offer longer-term friendship and support. In my message illustrations, I work hard to shine a spotlight on the staff or volunteer leaders who are the real frontline heroes. Instead of being a bottleneck for leaders, I've become their biggest cheerleader!

EMPOWERING ENTREPRENEURS

So I started letting go of the day-to-day details of ministry and empowering key staff and volunteers to do the work. And I made a shocking discovery: in so many ways, they did a far better job than me! Thank you, Lord, for a lesson in humility. At Liquid, we love to empower volunteers.

When my coauthor, Warren, and his wife, Michelle, made a first-time visit to one of our newest campuses, they tested our system by parking in the area designated for newcomers. A greeter named Pat Collins walked over, welcomed them, and struck up a conversation. When Warren asked how Pat became part of Liquid Church, Pat gave a quick witness of how Christ had changed his life and that of his family. Obviously a people person, Pat seemed like the perfect first-impression volunteer: outgoing, authentic, a good listener, and someone who immediately made Warren and Michelle feel at home. When Warren thanked him for his warm welcome, Pat said, "I can't think of anything at church I'd rather do than what I'm doing right now."

Pat did not go through a checklist or script in welcoming Warren and Michelle. Instead he had been fully empowered by the campus pastor, who recognized Pat as a mature believer and high-capacity leader. As with Robert Barba, Pat was cut loose to do ministry. And what a difference people like Pat make!

LET THE NEED BE KNOWN

One of the biggest bottlenecks to engaging new volunteers is that people don't realize there's a need that they have the ability to meet (or could be trained to meet). We love to do things with excellence at Liquid, because we believe excellence honors God and inspires people. We love to have guests experience our personal care and attention to detail—from outside landscaping to artful interior design to bright, clean, well-staffed kids' rooms—from the moment they arrive.

The problem is many then assume, *Wow, these guys have it all together! Guess they don't need any help.*

Nothing could be farther from the truth. However, we need to break that misconception by regularly communicating both our need for new volunteers and the opportunities to make a difference. One of the ways we do this is by rotating ministry leaders as onstage host of our weekend services. In addition to normal hosting duties (welcome, prayer), they share a quick story of life change from their ministry (special needs, kids', small group) and invite people to get involved after the service. In addition, our social media channels regularly spotlight open roles we're hoping to fill, and include links to apply.

MASTER THE ART OF SHOULDER TAPPING

However, the most powerful way to recruit new volunteers and leaders is to learn the art of shoulder tapping. We train each of our leaders to look for emerging talent among their friends, especially those spectators sitting in the stands, and to tap them on the shoulder and have an ICNU conversation. ICNU stands for "I see in you . . ." and we encourage a leader to use the idea to call out the gifts and potential they see in a friend or unengaged member.[1] Once they do that, we follow it with a practical next step in which the person can hone their gifts and not keep them hidden.

Kayra Montañez, whom you met in chapter 4, started as an attendee, then became a volunteer with Spanish translation, and is now one of our campus pastors. I love the way she and her team help potential volunteers find a place for their gifts. One of her favorite examples is the data team now headed by Tiffany Zappulla. Like most churches, we put huge value on following up with new guests, and we've had to adjust our system many times as we've grown or added campuses. Transferring information from our "new here" card to computer had previously been done by various volunteers. But as the weekly total of first-time guests continued to grow, we began praying and looking for a volunteer with data expertise and team leadership skills to take us to a new level.

Enter Tiffany. Her volunteer profile suggested a great fit: someone who loved data, who preferred behind-the-scenes work, and who knew how to scale and improve a system. From her volunteer work, she seemed wired with the gift of data management. The person who would be her supervisor approached her with the challenge, affirming, "We see this in you." Tiffany said yes and has done a fantastic job creating a robust team of fellow volunteers. Let's be honest, data entry isn't glamorous. Inputting information from a "new here" card into a computer could feel lonely and strictly transactional, but not with Tiffany. Yes, her people largely do their work individually, but she casts vision to them, communicates in creative and humorous ways, and gathers her team for in-person celebrations, recently taking them out for a celebration dinner and night of games. "She has been the perfect person for this crucial task," Kayra says.

DON'T MAKE NEW RECRUITS JUMP THROUGH TOO MANY HOOPS

One sure way to discourage new volunteers is to make the onboarding process unreasonably long: "Wanna serve? Great, just sign up for this eight-week class, complete a gifts inventory, take a personality test, and read two assigned books on the theological significance of spiritual gifts."

"Sounds fun!" said no one ever.

Don't make new recruits jump through a long series of hoops. At Liquid, we have a quick onboarding process for people to join a Dream Team. Yes, they need to fill out a very short application and do a one-on-one interview with the team leader, but this is primarily for building relationship, not training. Training is best done on the job, because that's how people learn best. If you ask a busy adult to learn a new skill, most won't study it until they have to perform it.

At Liquid, we err on the side of saying yes to leaders too early. We'd prefer to have an eager young leader get involved right away and, as we take time to discover their strengths and areas for development live, on the job, adjust their role and responsibility as we lead together. Although the fit may not be perfect at first, we train our leaders to play to strengths and adjust roles accordingly.

> At Liquid, we err on the side of saying yes to leaders too early.

Newcomers especially need to have R&R—a role and a relationship—within their first few visits if they're expected to stick. People may come to your church for practical teaching or killer worship, but they stay when they have relationships (friendship) and a responsibility (others counting on them to fulfill a key role). To mature as followers of Jesus, people need to see how their practical gifts contribute to something much bigger than themselves, such as building up Christ's body or touching our city with the gospel. That's why serving on a Dream Team is a key part of our discipleship process at Liquid and why we onboard people quickly.

> To mature as followers of Jesus, people need to see how their practical gifts contribute to something much bigger than themselves.

It's different for some ministries, of course. Working with children and students in Liquid Family involves a more detailed onboarding process. We require thorough background checks for each volunteer and provide watertight training (security protocols for working with children). Teams that involve specialized talents such as singing or playing an instrument (worship team) may require people to go through auditions and apprenticing for a season before becoming active members.

THE SMELL OF STINKY FEET

Most important, we ask our team leaders to model servant leadership—to use their power humbly serving those who are under their care. In some churches, younger staff and volunteers are left to do the "dirty work" of ministry, while the veteran leaders in charge tend to the more "important matters" of speaking, planning, and governing.

But in John 13:1–11, Jesus demonstrated to his disciples what true servant leadership looks like, by washing their smelly feet. What's even more shocking is that he did this aware "that the Father had given him authority over everything" (v. 3 NLT), which is to say, he was at the height of his power! So what did Jesus do with his authority and influence? He tied a towel around his waist, knelt down, and began to wash stinky, filthy feet. In first-century culture, this was scandalous behavior. In dusty Palestine, feet came covered in grime and dirt from the road, and I can just imagine Jesus taking off the sandals of his disciples. Undoubtedly, there were cracks and calluses, blisters, and dirt between their toes.

Washing feet was the stuff of low-level house servants, not respected rabbis and certainly not self-proclaimed kings! But after toweling off their tootsies, Jesus puts a point on his object lesson. "Now that I, your Lord and Teacher, have washed your feet, you also should wash one another's feet. I have set you an example that you should do as I have done for you" (vv. 14–15). Jesus essentially says, "Here's an example, a model, a template for leaders to follow. If you want to lead, spend your power humbly serving those who follow you. If you wanna be great in God's house, roll up your sleeves and do the dirty work."

NEVER TOO BIG TO DO THE SMALL STUFF

I'm never more proud of our leaders than when I see them doing "dirty work" that falls outside their job description. I think of Mike Leahy (pastor of campuses), who helped start our church and launch our first multisite campus. Volunteer roadies would come at 5:00 a.m. to unpack trailers full of equipment—wheeling road cases, running wires, setting up the stage, truss, sound system, projectors—to get our portable campus ready for the 9:00 a.m. service. It's heavy work and receives little public applause, since it occurs mostly behind the scenes.

When the bleary-eyed roadies arrived one Sunday morning, guess who was already there, waiting for them? Pastor Mike had arrived at 4:30 a.m. to prepare hot coffee and egg sandwiches to fuel our troops. As campus pastor, he was the first to arrive and the last to leave on that day. Often, it's not the grand gestures that inspire volunteers; it's the little things that communicate care, that say, "I see you. I notice. And I appreciate you."

> Often, it's not the grand gestures that inspire volunteers; it's the little things that communicate care, that say, "I see you. I notice. And I appreciate you."

Our roadies Dream Team has become the backbone of our portable campuses and has forged unusually strong community. These humble servants do life together, sharing prayer, food, fellowship, and the care of great leaders who take time to wash their feet.

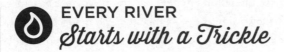

EVERY RIVER
Starts with a Trickle

Have you ever seen a whirlpool at the bottom of a bathtub or sink that's draining, or on a grander scale, in a river or ocean? Whirlpools are typically formed when conflicting currents meet and create a rapidly rotating mass of water into which objects get sucked down and eventually churned out.

A whirlpool is a good image to represent churn in your organization. Imagine your staff, leaders, and volunteers moving through your church or ministry over a five-year period. Some stick and stay long-term. Others churn out rapidly, resulting in high turnover. In business, churn rate (sometimes called attrition rate) measures the number of people moving out of a group over a specific period of time. Churn is a normal part of any organization, but a high churn rate is unhealthy and often symptomatic of a larger problem in the culture.

At Liquid, we had our highest staff turnover in the first four years of our church's life (2007–2011). We were a fledgling organization, and it was the first time in ministry for many of us. Most of our staff wore multiple hats, led teams of overworked volunteers, and juggled half a dozen responsibilities just to make weekend services happen. Our leaders were stretched too thin, and we hadn't yet developed any systems to make things sustainable for volunteers. As a result, our church sucked down developing leaders and churned them out. Sadly, for too long we didn't notice or understand what was happening.

Our young staff felt like they were caught in a whirlpool, with new hires arriving just in time to replace the previous group who churned out. Our worst year was in 2010, when 38 percent of the staff churned out in twelve months. This was deeply disturbing to our senior team, and we vowed to find a solution. But first we had to discover the causes. Through exit interviews and super honest conversations with key leaders, we discovered several negative factors.

We weren't hiring well. As a scrappy start-up, we lacked a robust interview process and often hired anybody we could find. "Love Jesus? No criminal record? Welcome to the team." It wasn't that bad, but we did hire staff whose gifts didn't match their roles. Worse, because our church had a shallow talent pool at the start, we made the mistake of hiring people from outside our church, even outside our state. We learned the hard way that folks who aren't from the Northeast typically do not flourish in our spiritually dry region. Our churn rate with the first ten outsiders we brought onto our staff was 90 percent; nine out of ten left within three years. Today we avoid recruiting from other parts of the country and have an extreme bias for hiring homegrown talent raised from within.

It was a crappy work environment. We joke that our first church office looked like a crack den, but that may be too generous. We rented a storefront across from the hotel where our church met on Sundays. While happy to finally have our very own home, the building was barebones and falling apart. The floorboards were warped. Heat was spotty. Mice scampered across the meeting room. And it was in a rough part of town. One night, after Thursday Night Gospel (chap. 5), someone threw a brick through our storefront window. Thieves didn't even bother to steal anything; the only thing of value was our used copy machine.

I realize it's romantic to think about the good ol' days when leaders were so focused on the mission that they didn't care about the crappy conditions of their workplace. But the truth is we didn't prioritize a professional environment for our staff. We felt we couldn't afford it, and that affected morale. When we ran out of space, we moved some offices to the windowless basement, which had no heat and contained traces of black mold. We liked to rationalize, "We don't invest in buildings; we invest in people!" But part of investing in people means creating an environment where they feel comfortable, safe, proud to come to work each day, and well-resourced to do their job. Our offices today not only check off the basics (like sunlight and heat), but we try to include some fun creature comforts that encourage community, creativity, and collaboration among our leaders. These include a free coffee bar, whiteboard walls, whimsical meeting rooms, and yes, a few scooters to ride around our hallways like they do at Google.

We had immature systems and structure. As a start-up, we asked people to do more with less resources. Looking back, we probably stretched them farther than we should have, without offering support.

We felt like novice pilots who were building the plane as we flew it. "Whatever it takes to get the job done," we reasoned. But a lack of systems (structures, strategies, policies, and procedures) hurt us. Well-defined job roles and systems are critical to ensure leaders don't burn out and to make ministry sustainable.

We had inexperienced management. Our turnover rate was also impacted by inexperienced management. Many of our younger leaders (myself included) didn't have experience leading or managing people. Our pastors, in particular, had a difficult time navigating the management of volunteers. Most wanted to be friends with congregants and consequently avoided conflict or hard conversations. There was a lack of accountability, and some took a hands-off approach, rarely communicating expectations up front but instead waiting until there was a crisis. Hurt feelings and tangled lines of communication were common. No wonder both volunteers and staff churned out at an alarming rate.

ALLEVIATING THE CHURN

So in year five, we took several bold steps to correct these missteps and alleviate the churn. First, we moved offices to a more professional (and cleaner) environment. That was the easy, cosmetic part. The hard part was changing the leadership culture—or lack thereof. We started to see that we were so focused on "getting 'er done," we were failing to develop the leaders who were doing the heavy lifting. We committed the cardinal sin of volunteer care: putting task ahead of relationship. This is a very real temptation for church planters, and we were guilty.

> We committed the cardinal sin of volunteer care: putting task ahead of relationship.

As the founding pastor, I take responsibility for this early mistake. I naively assumed that if you hire healthy, spiritually mature people, a healthy, spiritually mature culture would automatically develop. Not so much. At first, I attributed our high churn rate to the growing pains of a young church, and to be sure, some of it was because of that. But the blame lay squarely with me: for our first four years, I was guilty of neglecting to build a robust culture that nurtured young leaders and cared for the whole person—physically, emotionally, and spiritually.

Our entire senior team humbled ourselves before the staff, apologized, and pledged to do better. Of course, true repentance involves much more than words; it requires action. So we spent months developing training for our staff and managers to equip them with the tools and skills to develop our people. We learned that the typical turnover rate for staff at nonprofits and churches is around 15 percent annually.[2] People will always leave organizations because of change, but we wanted them to transition for positive reasons such as moving, family expansion, or a Spirit-inspired career change (not because they were burned out by our church!).

HIRE AROUND YOUR VALUES

So we revamped and professionalized our hiring process. We added multiple layers of interviews, focusing on culture fit and chemistry as much as the applicant's capabilities. We trimmed our church's core values from a list of nine (which no one could remember) down to three essentials (grace wins, truth is relevant, church is fun) and hired around those values.

When onboarding new hires, we began offering a First Ninety Days training so leaders knew what to expect, and we even offered them a buddy on staff who would take them out to lunch and check in monthly to see how they were doing relationally and spiritually (apart from their work). We introduced a tool called RACI to our staff members so they could understand the areas for which they were *responsible* and *accountable* as well as which things they needed to *consult* or *inform* others about.

CREATE A CULTURE OF FEEDBACK

We also created a culture of feedback, which was sorely missing in the early days. Previously, we played church on Sundays like smashmouth football; there were plenty of head-on collisions each weekend, but if services came off okay, we felt like we won. But come Monday, our staff felt banged up and bruised, and we rarely took the time to appreciate people's contributions and brainstorm how we could do things better.

So we instituted SMART (specific, measurable, achievable, relevant, and time-based) goals and performance reviews, which offer a chance for every leader to both receive and give feedback. By formalizing this process, we ensured that managers took the time to let leaders know they were appreciated, supported, and valued and had the opportunity to develop new skills. The feedback flowed both ways; workers were invited to candidly tell their manager about what tools and support they needed to do their job better. Together, our teams learned to speak openly about alignment, confront conflict, and collaborate on ways to improve the leadership experience at Liquid.

EMPOWER YOUNGER STAFF TO CREATE CULTURE

Perhaps the biggest innovation was the creation of our Staff Culture Team, which was tasked with the job of helping make Liquid "the best place to work and lead in the Northeast." We selected key staff for this special team—a majority of them young adults—and empowered them to make significant changes to our staff culture.

Their first target was our staff meetings. Previously, our monthly meetings were information dumps. For two hours or more, we'd bore our staff with endless updates, missing the opportunity to cast vision and build camaraderie. The Culture Team pulled me aside for a candid conversation. They wanted me to pour as much effort into motivating our staff as I did into feeding our congregation during weekend services. That had never occurred to me. I assumed that if people worked here, they would be naturally motivated and stay that way (duh!). So at their request, we added live worship to start each meeting, followed by a time of "God sightings," when we shared about moments when we saw the Holy Spirit at work, changing the lives of our people. We began emphasizing prayer, and we gave a Culture Award to those who embodied our staff values. The winner was brought onstage for special recognition and a surprise reward, like a day off or free lunch with a friend.

The Culture Team also added a splash of fun to encourage our leaders to let their hair down and laugh. We encourage our leaders to take God seriously—ourselves, not so much. Over the years, staff meetings have featured cornhole contests, a make-your-own-sundae bar, wiffleball games, karaoke sing-alongs, and even a giant sumo suit wrestling contest among pastors! I love it when I walk through our offices nowadays and hear the sounds of belly laughter spilling out of team meetings.

Notice something important: Our senior team didn't crack the culture code. It took a team stocked with empowered younger leaders to do it. Their passion to create a winsome, authentic staff culture was a game changer for our entire organization. It transformed our church into a healthy, highly attractional place to work and lead. "The creation of the Culture Team has changed the landscape for our staff experience," says Hyo Sil Siegel, pastor of Liquid Family, who serves on our senior leadership team. "Simply put, what they do is contagious and flows down to our volunteers." To keep our staff values of trust, excellence, and humility top of mind, the Culture Team even attached those words in giant tin letters on the walls of our office. But they also ensure that our organizational language isn't empty rhetoric. The job of the Culture Team is to make sure what's written on the wall is happening down the hall!

By 2012, we had reduced our churn rate to 13 percent, which is in the normal, healthy range for a nonprofit. Morale was up, and our staff felt supported and appreciated and that leadership lids had been removed so they could grow. But the real breakthrough came with our volunteers.

Another Sunday, I was wowed when a member of our senior leadership team stepped in to serve in the nursery at our most crowded service. He received a double blessing—the chance to mop up vomit and lovingly change a poopy diaper. Our volunteers could talk about nothing else that Sunday; it meant the world to see a pastor get down and dirty with them.

I'll never forget the sight of Dave Brooks, our executive pastor, carrying stacks of extra chairs on his back one Easter Sunday to provide overflow seating for our capacity crowds. A former corporate CFO of Dave's stature and position easily could have said, "Seating is outside my scope of responsibility; I deal with numbers and budgets and strategic planning." But Dave is one of my personal role models for humble servant leadership, and his willingness to do the heavy lifting (literally!) communicates something powerful to leaders.

We tell our senior leaders, "Never get too big to do the small stuff."

At Liquid, we try to champion humble leaders. It's not the flashy ones onstage who are truly great in Jesus' kingdom; it's the guy who empties a Diaper Genie, or the first-to-arrive volunteer who stands in the parking lot during a January snowstorm, waiting for cars to greet and guide into a parking spot. Humility is one of our staff values (along with trust and excellence) and something we want leaders to model through their actions. Here's a question we often ask staff: Are those you lead routinely wowed by your humility? If not, you're missing out on a powerful motivator for staff and volunteers.

> Are those you lead routinely wowed by your humility? If not, you're missing out on a powerful motivator for staff and volunteers.

TAPPING INTO HIDDEN TALENT IN YOUR PEWS—VOLUNTEER STAFF

We realized there was an untapped reserve of leadership horsepower inside Liquid Church with many of our lay leaders. Up to that point, we had used volunteers only in functional roles such as greeting, parking, running media, teaching kids, or leading a small group. But we were increasingly attracting professional people who had leadership skills and abilities they wanted to share with the church while keeping their full-time jobs in the marketplace.

So our executive pastor, Dave Brooks, created a new category called volunteer staff, setting it up in a way that gave more flexibility to the roles we could include at a leadership level. Suddenly we had at our disposal high-capacity executives, business owners, and marketplace professionals who had both great experience in leading effective teams as well as a passion for serving the Lord. We piloted the volunteer staff program and asked its members to donate ten to fifteen hours a week of their unpaid time so they could use their gifts to lead our volunteer teams. In return, we treated them exactly as we did salaried, full-time staff, including them in staff meetings, internal communications, and leadership development classes. We also provided job descriptions and performance reviews and empowered their leadership, freeing them up to make decisions and "to equip

[God's] people for works of service, so that the body of Christ may be built up" (Eph. 4:12).

Elizabeth Chang is one of those people. She's a high-powered attorney in one of the world's top-tier law firms from Monday to Friday and an associate pastor at one of our campuses on weekends. Not only had she been active in various churches while growing up, in a campus ministry at college (where she met her future husband), and in a thriving church plant while building her legal career, but Elizabeth was "poured into," as she describes the mentoring she received at various points in church. "One pastor saw God's gift of teaching in me, and I fought it a lot," she says, but she stepped forward into ministry leadership when invited, and she blossomed.

After she and her husband moved to New Jersey, they asked friends and relatives to pray with them that God would lead them to a church close to their new home. They landed at Liquid Church's Essex County campus and soon became involved in leading the marriage mentoring ministry there as volunteers. "This began a path of leadership at Liquid Church for us both," says Elizabeth. The next steps in her path included leading a small group and serving on the prayer team. Along the way, Elizabeth was affirmed by Liquid's staff: "You're gifted and equipped." Together they explored more ministry opportunities at her campus.

Today Elizabeth serves as an associate pastor at that campus, a volunteer staff position. She's responsible for the spiritual care of the people, including prayer team and lay care ministry, life events like weddings and baby dedications, and teaching Liquid's leadership development class on campus. "My job is to apply my gifts wherever I am: as a mom, as a lawyer, or as a pastor," she says. "People like me get to be the hands, feet, and voice of God as we allow him to work through us wherever we are."

One time, a couple approached her after a service. "We want to renew our wedding vows," the husband told her. Elizabeth knew from her role on the prayer team, to which he had come for prayer several times, that this was a big step of faith for this couple. There had been infidelity, repentance, and counseling to help restore the broken trust. Now this couple wanted a rededication ceremony, one involving their two teenage children, who were shattered by the infidelity. Elizabeth agreed to perform the rededication ceremony, in which she shared God's message of healing with the family. "What a holy moment when they re-exchanged rings and felt God's love, approval, and forgiveness," Elizabeth says. "As an associate pastor, I love getting to spend time learning people's stories and showing them who they are in God."

The addition of highly talented, spiritually mature volunteer staff like Elizabeth revolutionized our leadership culture. They added depth and bench strength at every level, stepping into key roles by caring for volunteers, providing lay counseling, and leading prayer, outreach, and technical teams. Some volunteer staff eventually transition out of their careers to become professional ministers. Our innovation was to create the associate pastor role for spiritually gifted people who previously were not serving as pastors and give them pastoral training.

> Currently, we have about fifty unpaid volunteer staff at Liquid, which makes up almost a third of our overall staff team!

As of this writing, more than half of our campus pastors came from a career in secular business but first began developing their pastoral gifts by volunteering as associate pastors at their home campus. After two years of spiritual development and pastoral training, each left their secular job to join our salaried staff as full-time campus pastors. Currently, we have about fifty unpaid volunteer staff at Liquid, which makes up almost a third of our overall staff team!

INTERNSHIPS AND RESIDENCIES

In addition, over the last five years, we've developed a robust internship program, bringing scores of talented college students onto our staff for the summer. In summer 2018, we had five interns in our video department who produced killer content. The interns sat at the main table in all our creative meetings, pitched ideas, led brainstorms, sketched storyboards, shot testimony videos, and edited series trailers. The influx of millennial and gen Z interns is our emerging pipeline for homegrown talent and gives our staff the chance to invest in future colleagues.

We're also laying the groundwork for a residency program at Liquid. The goal is for our church to one day function like a teaching hospital, providing practical, on-the-job ministry training for aspiring leaders apprenticed to experienced veteran leaders. We're learning from thought leaders like Community Christian Church (Illinois) and 12Stone Church (Georgia), who have cutting-edge residency programs and a track record of reproducing leaders at all levels. We realize that if we're going to saturate our state one day—by having at least one campus in each of New Jersey's twenty-one counties—our pipeline needs to be multiplying new leaders. Our aspirational goal is to one day reproduce more leaders than we need at Liquid campuses and send them out to transform other regions of the country.

> The influx of millennial and gen Z interns is our emerging pipeline for homegrown talent and gives our staff the chance to invest in future colleagues.

Back in 2010, when our churn rate was 38 percent, I had doubts we'd ever see the day when both marketplace professionals and college kids would be clamoring to join our church staff. But by God's grace, we've reversed the whirlpool of leadership churn. Now we're drawing in top talent, developing our people at a much deeper level, and unleashing a growing river of humble, qualified leaders to saturate our cities for Christ.

CLOSE THE BACK DOOR WITH VOLUNTEER CARE

It's one thing to recruit and develop new leaders; it's another to keep them healthy and engaged over the long haul of ministry. Long-term relationships require personal care, especially in larger churches, where people perceive it's easy to fall through the cracks.

Fortunately, our Mountainside campus was the first to seize the opportunity to close the back door by creating an amazing culture of volunteer care. They created a new Dream Team called Volunteer Care that has a singular focus: to treat our volunteers like gold, because they are! Early in the morning each Sunday, Volunteer Care begins frying up eggs, potatoes, and bacon before anyone else arrives. As volunteers arrive, they stop by and grab a plate of warm food and hot coffee.

A volunteer named Al actually wears a backpack of coffee and visits each table to top off volunteer coffee mugs as our troops fuel up to serve. Food is a love language, and we love on our volunteers with chocolate chip pancakes and sausage-egg-cheese wraps.

SURPRISE AND DELIGHT YOUR LEADERS

When we moved into our broadcast campus, our Care Team started something called Surprise and Delight to shower appreciation on our volunteers in creative ways.

- We sent notes of heartfelt gratitude to the spouse and kids of a rock star leader, thanking them for sharing their wife and mom with us. Team members included a gift card to a local Funplex, something the whole family can enjoy together because their mom has given up nights at home to serve others.
- To celebrate a volunteer who went above and beyond in organizing a churchwide event, we sent an Edible Arrangement to her workplace. As her coworkers munched on yummy chocolate-dipped strawberries, they asked who the gift was from, and she got to share about her faith in Christ and serving at our church.
- Before team huddles, we'll sometimes ask Dream Teamers to write one thing they appreciate about a specific volunteer. To the person's surprise, we read them aloud at the huddle. Volunteers cherish those words of affirmation from peers.
- We'll send central staff to visit campuses with a surprise volunteer breakfast—hot waffles off the grill, bacon, omelets, all the fixings. Senior staff wear aprons and wait hand and foot on our Dream Teamers.
- We blow up a red balloon, and on it staff write a personal note of thanks to a volunteer. We then deflate the balloon and mail it to their home, along with a handwritten thank-you note and Starbucks gift card.
- Sometimes the leader we pick to surprise and delight is a ministry leader or staff member. One of our staff recently did an

outstanding job leading her campus during a time of transition. Her team knew she loved to drink Coke, so they purchased a twelve-pack and attached personalized tags that said, "Best Pastor Ever" and "Prayer Warrior Zzzz" (her passionate prayers are sometimes extra long!).

- During the year, we host a special VIP event for Dream Team members only and mail personal invitations to honor our volunteers. In fall 2018, we brought in New York Yankees pitching legend Mariano Rivera to speak to our Dream Teamers about serving the Lord with all their heart. We chose a baseball theme for the event, and our staff served our volunteers hotdogs and Cracker Jacks, and our pastors even serenaded our volunteers onstage in song!

TAKE TIME TO SAY THANK YOU

Writing to the Philippians, the apostle Paul began his letter with the words, "I thank my God every time I remember you" (Phil. 1:3). At Liquid, we have a culture of handwriting personal thank-you notes to our leaders who go above and beyond in their roles. Every. Single. Week. It may be to celebrate a volunteer who coordinated a stressful event, like campus baptisms or extra guests at Easter. Or it may be to simply acknowledge the faithfulness of office volunteers who stuff programs or roll T-shirts behind the scenes.

In our weekly staff surveys, we ask, "Who can our pastors personally thank on your team? Please list specifics." Campus pastors and senior staff then take the time to handwrite five thank-you letters each week. Including the senior pastor.

This has become one of my favorite things to do each week—to tell our Dream Teamers, "I heard what you did to serve Jesus on Sunday, and—wow!—what a difference it made!" In a world awash in emails, emojis, and short texts, a handwritten note is experienced as deeply caring and personal. I've even been in the homes of some volunteers and seen my thank-you note taped to their refrigerator door like a badge of honor. This is a bonus benefit to mailing handwritten thank-you notes to leaders' homes—their spouse and family get to experience your gratitude too.

"HERO" YOUR VOLUNTEERS BECAUSE THEY'RE THE STAR OF YOUR STORY

My friend Wayne Francis, lead pastor of Authentic Church in New York, is a social media ninja with thousands of Instagram followers. But Wayne doesn't just post pics of himself preaching or use his feed to promote church events. Rather he leverages his platform to "hero" leaders on the church's volunteer teams. Each week, he posts a photo of an Authentic volunteer and tells a story. Perhaps it's about a man who used to do drugs but found Christ and sobriety and now serves on the church parking team. Wayne sent public birthday wishes to a kids' volunteer described as a "crazy-creative, kids-serving, soccer-ball-kickin' culinary queen" and then invited others to comment and send some birthday love her way as well.

In a digital world, there are so many ways to shine a spotlight on your volunteers. So shine it on them, because they truly are the stars of your church. Celebrate, applaud, cheerlead! Feature them in highlight videos, weekly emails, and on your website, especially those who serve anonymously behind the scenes. Publicly thank them for the eternal difference they're making. Remember, what gets rewarded gets repeated.

PROACTIVELY PROTECT AGAINST BURNOUT

Finally, if you really love your leaders, take proactive steps to safeguard their long-term health. I thank God we're light-years away from our early season of staff and volunteer burnout. Over time, we've trained our staff to look for telltale signs that leaders are running out of gas and need a break: physical and emotional exhaustion, spiritual apathy, a cynical spirit, missed commitments, irritability, and increasing isolation.

Church leadership ain't for the faint of heart. While deeply rewarding, it also is deeply demanding, and it can be downright dangerous when a leader is running on fumes. So we routinely offer on-ramps and off-ramps for long-term volunteers, encouraging them to take time off from their ministry role, guilt free. We model Sabbath keeping to our staff and teach volunteers that it honors God to simply be still and cease from serving during various seasons in life. This surprises many people, and some pastors might be scared of sending the wrong message to volunteers. But this comes from a spirit of fear, not genuine love.

Encouraging leaders to take a break helps volunteers who encounter a season of crisis, such as illness, divorce, family trouble, or stress at work. In those times, we have the opportunity to come alongside and minister to our ministers in a special way, lavishing the love of Jesus on them. At the same time, we also encourage high-achieving leaders to take periodic breaks after busy seasons like Easter and Christmas to spend extra time with their families and friends. They are not only super grateful for this proactive care but often eager to return once they're replenished, because they've been loved well on the back end of serving (not just during onboarding).

THE BROADER CURRENT

How would you describe your current leadership culture? Do you have a healthy staff with a normal churn rate? Do you have a steady stream of volunteers, or is it just a trickle?

Wherever you're at, don't forget: People are the lifeblood of your church and ministry. And Jesus gave his life for each and every one. For some reason, in God's great plan of love and salvation, he chose ordinary men and women with dirty feet to share the message of Jesus and saturate our thirsty world with the Savior's love. When we unleash new leaders to advance Christ's kingdom, everyone wins: your people win, your church wins, and the world is increasingly won for Christ. Love your people well, then step back and trust the Holy Spirit to do his most dazzling work through them. That's how you create a rising river of healthy, high-capacity leaders to realize your church's vision and saturate your city for Christ!

Dive Deeper

Church of the Highlands, led by Chris Hodges, has mentored and inspired me in the culture they've created, in which newcomers feel inspired to volunteer.[3] Their strategy involves a Growth Track (a four-session class) to introduce people to the church and to match them by gifts rather than by needs. They call their volunteers a Dream Team (one of the inspirations for our use of the term), and they truly do ministry in teams. They also have a pathway that can lead from volunteer to lay leader to staff member. Here are some ideas that might inspire your own thinking.

 ANKLE DEEP As a first step to get your feet wet, evaluate what percentage of your people are engaged in serving or leading. Is it closer to the classic 20:80 ratio, or have you moved toward 80 percent participation? Don't answer alone: to avoid perception gaps, compare notes with key leaders who represent major ministries (such as kids' or outreach) to see what ratio they would propose. Pray and talk about Matthew 9:35–38, identifying both opportunities and leadership gaps where you long to see God at work.

 KNEE DEEP There is untapped talent warehoused in your church right now. Review the relevant material in this chapter, and then develop a track for volunteer staff, including job descriptions and a way to meaningfully support talented volunteers. If you need more ideas, challenge some volunteers to read and report on the book *Hero Maker* by Dave Ferguson and Warren Bird, or *Empowering Leadership* by Michael Fletcher.

WAIST DEEP Liquid's dream is to build a training pathway that includes a residency model. Could you start with the idea of reproducing one ministry resident per year? Research says the key to success is not a written curriculum so much as simply giving someone the opportunity to do hands-on frontline ministry as part of a team. For ideas, see "Leaders in Training: Internships and Residencies Help Churches Shape Future Leaders" by Warren Bird (free download at *leadnet.org/intern*).

Other Churches Making Waves

Community Christian Church *(communitychristian.org)* is a multi-site church saturating the Chicagoland area with eleven local campuses and counting. They are taking seriously the idea of redefining their ministry scorecard. Yes, each guest, baptism, and dollar donated still matters, but even more important are the sons and daughters of the church who are released elsewhere into ministry (whether as volunteers or staff), and through their NewThing church multiplication network, they're expending major resources to support church-planting teams, many of which aren't even part of their denomination and are located around the world.

12Stone *(12Stone.com)* developed a program called the Residency—a two-year, full-time leadership training program designed to provide hands-on experience working with one of the staff teams of the church, personal mentoring, and leadership training to equip emerging leaders for a lifetime of ministry impact. Residents work approximately thirty hours a week and gain experience by serving as part of a staff team in one of the ministry departments of the church. Six months before the end of their residency, they begin looking for full-time employment in a local church. For a small cost, 12Stone shares their training resources with other churches hoping to start a successful residency program *(church residency.com/partnership)*.

Church of the Highlands *(churchofthehighlands.com)* started a ministry school in its first year as a church. Pastor Chris Hodges, mentioned previously, had a vision from day one to raise up the next generation of leaders. The result today is a training school that has become a full-fledged college *(highlandscollege.com)*. It is producing more leaders than their campuses need, thus becoming a major feeder system into the ARC network of church planting (arcchurches.com). The college also sets up interviews with graduates to help place them in other local churches.

Manna Church *(manna.church)* is located near a major military base in North Carolina, which means the church constantly faces a high turnover. The average stay of just two to three years could have been a liability and discouragement, but Michael Fletcher, whose book was mentioned previously, decided to capitalize on the possibilities. He's made it his major focus to train military members to know Jesus and become church leaders wherever they are deployed. Their big vision is to plant a Manna Church near every US military base in the world, along what they call "the Military Highway."

The Journey *(yourjourney.tv)* does ministry through their J-Team, or "army of volunteers"—people who use their gifts, passions, and skills to make a difference in the lives of others. Each J-Team area has multiple volunteer leaders, and staff then lead those leaders. Abby Ecker, a full-time staff member who oversees serving and leadership development, has served in multiple levels of leadership. She came to the church as a college student, put her faith in Jesus, began to volunteer, began leading a team, and went on staff to lead several teams. Lead pastor Mark Johnston summarizes how his view of ministry has changed: "I used to lead the church," he says, "but now I lead my team, and they lead the church. What a world of difference, and I love it!"[4] The Journey also offers a nine-month, hands-on leadership intensive called Potential, in partnership with Highlands College, designed to equip young leaders with hands-on ministry training, character formation, and spiritual development.

Part Three

FLOWING WITH THE SPIRIT

CHAPTER TEN

A RIVER RUNS THROUGH IT

> Then the angel showed me the river of the water of life, as clear as crystal, flowing from the throne of God and of the Lamb down the middle of the great street of the city.
> —REVELATION 22:1-2

Have you ever noticed how many great cities of the world have a river running through them? I think of the Thames running through the heart of London under the watchful eye of Big Ben. The ancient Tiber in Rome. The Nile snaking its way through Cairo. The Danube, Europe's second longest river, flows through four capital cities, including Vienna and Budapest. There's also the Yangtze River in Nanjing, China, the Hooghly (Ganges) in Calcutta, the Saint Lawrence River in Quebec City, and the Yarra flowing through Melbourne.

Then there's the famous river Seine—widely considered the most romantic river in the world—that runs through the heart of Paris. My family and I recently visited France's capital city to celebrate a milestone wedding anniversary, a birthday for our daughter, and a graduation for our son. Like many tourists, we included a visit to Notre-Dame Cathedral, located right on the riverbank of the Seine.

On the inside, the famous cathedral was dark and dimly lit. As we followed our guide around the ancient altar, we could sense gargoyles glowering in the gloom. But soon the midday sun sent shadows scurrying and lit up the magnificent rose windows. As the sunlight filtered through the stained glass, the air was suddenly filled with a kaleidoscope of colors—dazzling purples, pinks, reds, and blues.

"Construction of Notre-Dame, which began in 1163, would have been impossible without the Seine," our guide informed us. He noted that the ancient river was used to transport construction materials for the cathedral, as well as food, water, and supplies for the workers. He told us that historians have traced the use of the river back to the Iron Age, when Celts transported tin across present-day Europe. The Romans fortified settlements and increased trade along the river. Villages and towns along its banks blossomed like flowers. Eventually, shops, schools, restaurants, inns, and a thriving farmers' market helped establish the city of Paris. There's a reason why rivers often run through major cities: they function like a carotid artery. Only instead of delivering a vital flow of blood to the brain, the river provides a steady flow of goods, transportation, food, and water straight to the heart of the people and their culture.

After touring Notre-Dame, we walked down a set of cobblestone steps to sit by the Seine and share lunch. We took off our shoes, dangled our bare feet in the ancient waters, and gazed up at the cathedral. The pairing of Paris's life-giving river and grand house of worship brought Ezekiel 47 freshly to mind. Here we were, next to a world-famous church, in the middle of a world-class city with a river running straight through its heart. I pulled out my Bible and reread the striking Old Testament vision.

As commercial riverboats glided by, I closed my eyes and imagined a river the size of the Seine gushing out of a modern church building—flowing from the sanctuary, down the steps, and flooding the city streets. In Ezekiel's vision, the river is a symbol of the life-giving presence of God that is available through faith in Jesus Christ.

THE RIVER OF LIFE IN REVELATION

But Ezekiel's city-saturating river isn't just an ancient prophecy. It's also a foretaste of our future heavenly home. According to the book of Revelation, Christians will one day live together in a beautiful, expansive city known as "the new Jerusalem" (Rev. 21:2), where God will be seated forever on his throne.

And guess what? A river runs through it.

According to the apostle John, a raging river of life flows down the center of heaven's main street. Like Ezekiel, John received a powerful revelation from God, and an angelic tour guide gave him a future vision of our heavenly home. The last chapter of the Bible presents John's powerful picture: "Then the angel showed me the river of the water of life, as clear as crystal, flowing from the throne of God and of the Lamb down the middle of the great street of the city. On each side of the river stood the tree of life, bearing twelve crops of fruit, yielding its fruit every month. And the leaves of the tree are for the healing of the nations" (Rev. 22:1–2).

Sound familiar? It should: it's the fulfillment of Ezekiel's prophecy. The river of life in Revelation 22 is the same river featured in Ezekiel 47. Only instead of flowing from God's temporary temple on earth, the river in heaven flows from God's eternal throne. Think of it: God's heavenly city is saturated with a river of living water, and he wants your city to be too!

> God's heavenly city is saturated with a river of living water, and he wants your city to be too!

Until Christ returns, it's up to you and me to bring up there to down here. Just as God saturates his city in heaven with the water of life, we are called to saturate our city on earth with the life-giving presence of Jesus.

Both Ezekiel and John point to three blessings that flow from the divine waterway.

- *Flourishing trees.* Both prophets see trees that are growing and flourishing on both banks of the river (Ezek. 47:12; Rev. 22:2). When churches are connected to the Holy Spirit's flow, they naturally grow and are fruitful.
- *Spiritual fruit.* The trees produce a monthly harvest of fruit. In Ezekiel's vision, the angel tells him, "Every month they will bear fruit, because the water from the sanctuary flows to them" (Ezek. 47:12). John says the tree of life bears twelve crops of fruit,

"yielding its fruit every month" (Rev. 22:2). Spirit-saturated churches never fail to produce spiritual fruit—a steady stream of salvations, broken addictions, resurrected marriages, healed lives, and serving saints. Even in dry times, when spiritual fruit is less evident, God is working to produce the fruit of the Spirit in his people (Gal. 5:22–23).

* *Healing leaves.* John writes, "The leaves of the tree are for the healing of the nations" (Rev. 22:2), echoing Ezekiel 47:12, where water flowing from the temple produces trees with healing leaves. What a beautiful picture of Christ's curative power to heal the sick, mend the broken, and even raise the dead to life.

Friends, this is God's dream for our broken world: the healing of our nations! But it starts with your city.

Wherever God's river flows, strength and healing follow. If it brings spiritual blessings like these, who doesn't want a river of living water running through their town? To prepare the way for our Savior's return, God has called your church to saturate your city on earth with Jesus' love and power, just as God's city is saturated in heaven. Your mission is to bear spiritual fruit that will last and bring God's healing to the broken people living around you. Whether you're aware of it yet or not, you are surrounded by spiritually thirsty people who desperately need Jesus' healing touch.

> This is God's dream for our broken world: the healing of our nations! But it starts with your city.

WHICH OF THE SIX STREAMS IS CALLING OUT TO YOU?

In this book, I've introduced you to six ministry currents that God is blessing and using to reach new generations, transform communities, and saturate our region for Christ. Which of these six streams are you drawn toward? Is God's Spirit whispering to you about serving people with special needs? Perhaps he's laying the groundwork for a ministry merger in your future. Or maybe you felt your heart stir as you thought about bringing clean water to the global poor.

Follow that whisper. If Jesus is calling you to step into the water, don't delay. Get your feet wet and obey.

Recently, I spent a week fly-fishing with a group of pastor buddies on the Little Bighorn River in Montana. It was a spiritual retreat with no agenda other than to be alone with God, connect with each other, and simply enjoy God's glorious creation. The movie *A River Runs Through It* was filmed in Big Sky Country, and many of the city slicker pastors in our group had dreams of landing a giant rainbow trout like Brad Pitt did. Each morning, we'd put on our hip waders, tie some flies, drink black coffee, and meander down the chilly river, trying our best to land a monster trout.

At night, we'd come back to our rustic retreat lodge to watch the sun set and swap stories around a firepit. After we laughed about the bigguns that got away (there were a lot of them!), our conversation frequently turned to the joys and pains of ministry. One millennial pastor from North Carolina described how he took over his father's position as lead pastor in his early twenties. His dad had founded the church two decades ago but died tragically of a sudden heart attack. His youngest son (my fishing partner) eventually stepped in, but the transition was traumatic, and more than two thousand of the older members left.

"Those were tough times with a lot of churn," he said quietly as we gazed into the fire. "But now I see God's hand in it." Although the ministry struggled and downsized for three years, a brand-new generation of millennials was attracted to my friend's collaborative leadership style and started streaming in.

"The average age of our congregation probably went down by twenty years," he said with a chuckle. "Our team is now full of young adults and college kids that reflect our downtown demographic." A painful season of pruning had done its work, and the church was now positioned for a new season of growth and outreach to its community.

The conversation turned to how the Spirit was speaking to each of us. A pastor from Canada looked at me and said, "Tim, I feel so excited that my heart might burst! I know our church is being called to special needs ministry. I grew up with ADHD and really struggled to fit in church. I was always the one getting in trouble."

During the week, we had become friends while playing cornhole at the lodge. As we casually tossed bags on the lawn, I had shared about Liquid's growing ministry to families with special needs. Hearing about our Night to Shine outreach to the community, he seemed to come alive. Later, while fly-fishing, he asked me all sorts of questions about our buddy system on Sundays and how we train our volunteers.

"You have ADHD?" I said. "Sounds like your interest in special needs is personal."

"No, it's more than that," he explained. "As we've talked this week, I felt my heart burning. Our church plant meets in a city school. For the last two years, I've been wracking my brain trying to figure out how to reach out and meet the needs of our neighbors in practical ways."

As he spoke, someone tossed a fresh log on the fire, and sparks flew up.

"While we were fishing on the river, it dawned on me." He paused and leaned forward in his chair. "Our church just happens to meet in the best special needs school in Calgary!"

I love it when the Holy Spirit connects the dots in a leader's soul. He excitedly began talking about how his church could naturally minister to the needs of families who attend the school Monday through Friday, by offering special programming on the weekends.

"I love the idea that our church could build a natural bridge to that community," he said. "I know it will require a ton of work, but I'm going to share my heart with our team, and I know they'll catch the vision." We prayed together, hugged, and I promised to share whatever resources his team needed as they got their feet wet in special needs ministry in the months to come.

AN OPEN INVITATION

God spoke to my Canadian friend about serving families with special needs in his city. What is the Spirit saying to you? Take a look around. In chapter 11, we'll ask three revealing questions: What is the Holy Spirit already blessing? What needs are being overlooked? Where is God directing your path?

Your answers to those questions may provide a clue to where the

Spirit is leading next or simply confirm a burning conviction God's been stoking in your soul. Maybe the Spirit has been nudging you to go all in and pour more energy and resources into a ministry that is unexpectedly thriving. Maybe it's time to take a risk and dive in over your head. However God is speaking to you, move forward with confidence, knowing that he is already at work in your city and that this is your chance to join Jesus on his mission to bring up there down here, touching earth with heaven and saturating your city for Christ.

We live in a world desperate for living water, and people in your neighborhood are dying of spiritual thirst. But it's not too late to respond to Jesus' generous invitation: "Let the one who is thirsty come; and let the one who wishes take the free gift of the water of life" (Rev. 22:17).

If the Spirit is speaking to you and you're ready to take your next step, keep reading. In the next chapter, we'll answer the practical question, how do you saturate your city?

Dive Deeper

Ezekiel and Revelation both share a vivid vision of a rising river gushing out of God's presence down the street of a great city. It is a word picture of Jesus' love dominating a city so completely that all the people and all aspects of the culture draw their life directly from God. These passages have stretched my vision. How will they enlarge yours?

 ANKLE DEEP Read Revelation 22:1–5 and compare it with Ezekiel 47:1–12. In your own words, what do you think the river symbolizes? At which depth in God's river—ankle deep, knee deep, waist deep, or deeper—are you today? How deep is God calling you to go this next season?

KNEE DEEP God's river of life produces fruit-bearing trees, and "the leaves of the tree are for the healing of the nations" (Rev. 22:2). Get a few leaders together to make an honest assessment: How fruitful is your church in its current state? Is your ministry a source of healing in your city, town, or neighborhood? What are the broken places in your community that need fixing or healing? Pray together and ask God how he has positioned your church to help bring healing to people in your community.

Is your church doing something that is unexpectedly effective? Do you have a grassroots ministry that is growing or meeting a vital need? Sometimes the next growth curve jump in ministry isn't part of a strategic plan but something simply blessed by God's hand. Identify what the Holy Spirit is already doing in your midst. As a leadership team, ask God if he wants you to dive in deeper through a greater commitment of time, talent, and/or money.

WAIST DEEP You can't lead others where you haven't gone yourself. Before a church can expand its vision, the leaders must be willing to go there, and even to start the journey. As you dream about what God wants to do through the church you serve, what needs to grow first in you? On a scale of one (not even ankle deep) to ten (over your head), where are you? How strong is your conviction that God can use you and your church to flood your city with the gospel? What is your next step?

CHAPTER ELEVEN

HOW DO YOU SATURATE *YOUR* CITY?

> So the word of God spread. The number of disciples in
> Jerusalem increased rapidly, and a large number . . .
> became obedient to the faith.
> —ACTS 6:7

When I talk about a strategy for saturating your city with the living water of Christ, what does that mean? For starters, you don't have to live in a major metropolis to do it. When most people hear the term city, they immediately envision an urban jungle of skyscrapers and streets clogged with traffic and pedestrians. But I'm not talking solely about modern population centers like New York or Chicago. Rather let's go back to biblical times and broaden our concept of city living.

New York pastor and author Tim Keller reminds us that in the Old Testament, "the main Hebrew word translated 'city' refers to any human settlement surrounded by a fortification or wall. Most ancient cities numbered only about 1,000–3,000 in population. 'City,' therefore, meant not so much population size as density."[1]

So when I refer to saturating your city or mine, I'm pointing to wherever people are clustered. You may live in a small town or village, a quiet suburb or sprawling metropolis. Even if you live in the Big Apple or the Windy City, you likely identify with a smaller, specific neighborhood or community that you call home. That's your city.

Your city—your sphere of influence—is the place where your people live, work, play, go to school, make art, eat in restaurants, and raise their families.

Your city is very likely packed with spiritually thirsty people. They are all around you—in your office, your classroom, your coffee shop, your workout studio. Some live right next door to you. Just as Colleen and I sat despondent and dehydrated on the side of that Grand Canyon trail (opening story of chapter 3), they are thirsty for the water of life that quenches their soul's thirst at the deepest level. As Jesus modeled with the Samaritan woman (John 4), our job is to build a spiritual bridge to thirsty people in our community—those who may have given up on church but haven't given up on God.

> Our job is to build a spiritual bridge to thirsty people in our community—those who may have given up on church but haven't given up on God.

In Ezekiel's vision, the river flowed eastward out of the temple. That direction is significant. In Hebrew thought, the east was considered evil; that's where one's enemies lived. The east was home to godless sinners and pagans—the spiritually lost. Yet this is the direction that God's Spirit flows, out of the church and toward a city filled with lost and thirsty people.

FROM RELIGION TO RELATIONSHIP

We're talking about thirsty people like Tawana. When Tawana first visited Liquid, she wasn't completely clueless about Jesus. "Growing up in church, I was under the impression that I knew everything there was to know about God," she says. "Because my mom was a die-hard Christian, I, at a young age, thought it automatically made me one." Tawana represents a large swath of people best described as cultural Christians. Although she lacked a personal, saving relationship with Jesus Christ, Tawana assumed that her family's religious background automatically made her a Christian. Call it the friends and family plan.

However, Tawana instinctively realized something was missing. "I was attending church, but that's all it was—attendance. I was reading my Bible but never really allowing it to read me. It was all just . . .

religion. Then one day, I realized that I knew a lot about how to be a good churchgoer but not much about Jesus! I was dry and felt a thirst to know him!"

In our region, many people grew up like Tawana did, with a Christian background, but it makes no discernable difference in their daily lives. Many of my friends were raised as a nominal Catholic or occasionally attended a Methodist or Episcopalian church or one belonging to some other mainstream denomination. They've heard about Jesus and know the basic gospel story, but they've never encountered the Lord intimately on a personal level. We often joke that Liquid is filled with CEOs—folks who used to attend church twice a year: Christmas and Easter Only.

When Tawana came to Liquid, she immediately sensed a difference. "It was a new beginning. I saw all nationalities worshiping and praising Jesus," she says. His love penetrated her heart. Tawana asked Christ to be her personal Lord and Savior and offered her life to his service, moving from dead religion to a life-giving relationship. She was transformed as God's love flooded her thirsty soul. "I joined a small group, and the encouragement that I receive from those amazing people is second to none. Today my life as a Christ follower is filled with purpose, joy, and a peace that surpasses all understanding. I am certain of Christ's love for me and certain to go home with him when he decides to come." In fall 2018, Tawana was baptized, and now she serves Jesus as a volunteer leader on a campus Dream Team.

A CULTURE SHIFT . . . AND A HUGE OPPORTUNITY

Tawana's story represents a cultural shift and a huge opportunity for re-reaching a growing swath of people who were raised with a knowledge of Christianity but have no personal relationship with Christ. Ed Stetzer, popular author and chair of the Billy Graham Center at Wheaton College, describes this trend in his book *Christians in the Age of Outrage*.[2] He breaks our nation into four groups.

1. *Convictional Christians.* Roughly 25 percent of Americans may be described as convictional Christians who take their faith

seriously. They actively read the Scriptures, plan and shape their life around their personal faith in Christ, and try to incorporate biblical values into all they do. They would describe their relationship with Jesus as intimate, vibrant, and life-changing. Hopefully, that's you and me.

2. *Cultural Christians.* Another 25 percent of Americans check the box "Christian" on most surveys, primarily because they aren't some other religion (Jewish, Muslim). As with Tawana, Christianity is part of their family's background, and so in their mind, they must be Christian. But the reality is, they are Christian in name only; it makes no difference in their day-to-day lives.

3. *Congregational Christians.* Another 25 percent of Americans self-identify as Christian because they are connected to mainline Protestantism (United Methodist, Episcopalian, Presbyterian, etc.). Their family's heritage is tethered to some congregation, even if they aren't actively involved or only attend on holidays. Although they may not describe their relationship with God as personal or vibrant, they have loose affiliation with a Christian denomination.

4. *Non-Christian.* The final fourth of Americans are complete non-Christians. They belong to another religion (Jewish, Hindu, Muslim, Sikh, Baha'i). Or they're atheists or describe themselves as "none of the above" on surveys when provided with a list of faiths to choose from.

The big shift, according to Ed, is that the first three groups used to have a general consensus in their spiritual beliefs. The cultural Christian and congregational Christian historically sided with the convictional Christian, forming one team, which is why demographers often report that around 75 percent of Americans are Christian.

But our nation is rapidly secularizing. The result? The cultural and congregational Christians are splintering away and shifting toward a more secular perspective. That's why it feels to many like the church in America is dying. These cultural and congregational Christians are increasingly siding with secular worldviews. I often hear them make statements such as, "I'm a Christian, but I don't force my beliefs on anyone. I think there are many ways to God. I'm spiritual but not religious."

Their increasing identification with a secular perspective represents a tectonic cultural shift. Convictional Christians are now standing alone outside mainstream culture in the United States, which means that only 25 percent of Americans possess a scripturally rooted, Spirit-filled, personal faith in Jesus.

YOUR TARGET AUDIENCE JUST DOUBLED

On one hand, this shift is sad news: half of our population is now moving away from the church and traditional Christianity. But on the other hand, it's good news: your target audience just doubled! Fifty percent of Americans are signaling that they're giving up on church as they know it, but they haven't given up on God yet.

These cultural and congregational Christians are increasingly up for grabs. They may have some memory of church (to which they said no thanks), but they are ripe for personally experiencing Jesus in a fresh way. Are we ready to re-present Christ to them? To employ a show-then-tell approach to ministry that earns a fresh hearing for the gospel?

> These cultural and congregational Christians are increasingly up for grabs. They are ripe for personally experiencing Jesus in a fresh way. Are we ready to re-present Christ to them?

This massive shift opens a huge door of opportunity to engage our rapidly secularizing culture for Christ. For Liquid Church, this realignment is key to defining our target: the spiritually thirsty who have given up on church but not on God. Both cultural and congregational Christians who are drifting away represent our target market. When we encounter those who are cynical about religion, are apathetic, or have only a nominal faith allegiance, they are much easier to identify, and often they are more receptive to a Christian faith expression that emphasizes refreshing relationship over dry religion, often by showing the gospel in a compelling way before telling it.

Our challenge—and perhaps yours as well—is how to re-present Jesus to them and win a fresh hearing for the true gospel. Your city can be saturated in a revitalizing way if you're able to harness this important current presently churning through our culture.

THE TIPPING POINT

So what will it take to saturate your town, your city, your state? In chapter 3, we spoke of Malcolm Gladwell's tipping point idea. In the context of evangelizing your city, a tipping point is reached when the message of Jesus spreads like a virus does, infecting a community so widely that its impact is undeniable.

Tim Keller notes, "When a gospel movement is underway, it may be that the Body of Christ develops to the point that a whole city tipping point is reached. By that I mean the moment when the number of gospel-shaped Christians in a city reaches critical mass. The Christian influence on the civic and social life of the city—on the very culture—is recognizable and acknowledged. That means between 10 and 20 percent of the population."[3]

What would it look like if 20 percent of your town became authentic followers of Christ? It may help to narrow that down to an image you can see in your mind's eye: what if 20 percent of your neighbors or people living in your apartment complex shared a vibrant, personal faith in Jesus? How would that transform your community, its schools, its businesses, and the wider city?

THREE IMPORTANT TRENDS IN THE GREATER CULTURE

At Liquid, we try to capitalize on what's happening in the overall culture whenever it can help spark interest in the gospel. Let me highlight three trends that help explain why the six currents described in this book are having a heightened impact on re-presenting Jesus to our nominal neighbors.

1. Overcoming Skepticism with Compassionate Action

Gone is the day when churches had the home court advantage of guaranteed favor with our communities. As two authors who surveyed more than two thousand postmodern people who have come to follow Jesus, summarizes it, "In another age, God, religion and church enjoyed the respect of culture. Not today. Religion is suspect, church is weird and Christians are hypocrites. Distrust has become the norm."[4] A prominent researcher of religion concludes that over the last several decades, "public confidence in religious leaders has declined precipitously."[5]

Therefore we speak to a culture that's grown skeptical of churches, one that assumes churches to be self-focused, existing primarily to meet their own needs. When people see that a church is not about itself (it cares for people with special needs, builds clean water wells), it challenges their negative notions of church. They take note. People who have given up on church but not on God become more open to be re-churched.

Envision the cracked desert floor in Death Valley. The ground is dry and hard, perpetually parched, and it needs to rain for a long time for water to penetrate the surface. Compassionate action is what breaks up that hard-packed soil. In the old days, churches could saturate their communities just by proclamation evangelism or witnessing to neighbors, getting the word out. In a few places that might still work, but in regions like the Northeast or Pacific Northwest, if you ask a stranger as a conversation starter, "Hey, where do you go to church?" people are more likely to suspiciously put up their walls or dismiss you as an unsafe fanatic.

Instead we've learned to lead by demonstration. We've found that compassionate service is the best cure to cynicism in our post-Christian culture. When non-Christians see no-strings-attached generosity and compassion, it undermines their skepticism and opens them up to considering church as a viable source of love and acceptance. We show, then tell.

2. Families Are Looking for Support

Where do Americans today find meaning in life? What makes life most meaningful? In a major survey, 69 percent said family provides them with a sense of meaning, while only 20 percent said spirituality and faith do.[6]

We can build on that deep desire for family. God created the family, and churches can be the world's greatest parent training centers and the best support networks for developing healthy family relationships. They say it takes a village to raise a child. We want parents to view our church as a partner to help them parent, not as a place (like their parents' church) that will reject them if their marriage fails or they're struggling as parents. We want people to see that our church can actually help them raise their kids.

On a recent weekend, we hosted a meaningful child dedication with more than forty sets of parents and kids. After parents pledged to build a Christ-centered home, our entire congregation stood to vow to help them. Later in the service, we promoted an upcoming missions trip designed so that parents and teens can travel together to serve in places where poverty abounds.

That same weekend, we also highlighted an opportunity for families to pack nutritious meals for the global poor. We're always a bit surprised when all the volunteer spots for an outreach event "sell out" quickly, but one reason is that we set it up so singles and families, including children of all ages, can work together. While modern families have no shortage of entertainment, gadgets, and distractions, they are desperate for opportunities to serve together and make a difference.

> While modern families have no shortage of entertainment, gadgets, and distractions, they are desperate for opportunities to serve together and make a difference.

Our 2018 Christmas outreach drew more than five thousand volunteers who, for two days, packed and shipped more than 1.1 million nutritious meals to feed starving children around the globe. At this outreach, I met multiple families from our city who had never stepped foot in our church for Sunday worship (yet), but the parents were open to working side by side with their children to help serve the poor. I'd go so far as to say that family-supportive events are a key aspect of our appeal to non-Christians. It's been a trickle that became a stream that now contributes to a raging river of touching family and friends with the gospel.

Another variation on our show-then-tell ministry approach.

3. Belonging Before You Believe

Every church lays out a pathway for discipleship. When someone begins to follow Jesus, what are the things they do first? As they mature and become more like Christ, how do they keep growing? In many traditional churches, the discipleship pathway is straightforward and linear. The first step is becoming a Christian, followed by going through some membership process, formally joining the church, progressing to a Bible study or classes on doctrine, and then perhaps volunteering. In many churches, going on an overseas missions trip to an impoverished country is the ultimate step in maturing one's faith.

At Liquid, our approach is often the exact opposite. We've found that many lost people want to belong before they believe. One twenty-something told us, "I'm not sure if I'm interested in attending your church yet, but I'd love to go to Rwanda to dig a clean water well with your team." (We unpacked the power of a compassionate cause in chapter 6.) We have dozens of people in our church who didn't meet Jesus in a Sunday worship service; rather they first encountered Christ at our Night to Shine prom for people with special needs. (Learn more in chapter 4.) There's something about seeing the love of God in action that earns room for a fresh hearing of the gospel in a post-Christian culture. Once again, showing, then telling.

Don't miss this flip-flopped sequence: today more people want to belong before they believe. They are attracted by compassionate outreach and service and want to experience the demonstration of the gospel before the proclamation of its meaning. And that's fine with us. At Liquid, service is the tip of our evangelism spear, especially with younger generations, who highly value a cause to believe in. They don't just want to hear the gospel explained; they want to experience it firsthand, rolling up their sleeves and getting dirty to serve the homeless and hungry or to fight for the global poor. This paradigm shift has dramatic implications for churches.

In the recent era of attractional evangelism, a "come and see" approach drew many people to church and to the Savior the church

> Don't miss this flip-flopped sequence: today more people want to belong before they believe. This paradigm shift has dramatic implications for churches.

proclaimed. From there, discipleship followed a predictable, linear path—from belief to membership, classes, and eventually serving. But we've found that many young adults aren't interested in going from first base to second to third to home. As a first step, they want to slide headfirst into third base and begin with serving. Sometimes even before believing!

There are some churches today that won't let you serve anywhere unless you're a member. If you offer to help serve coffee to new guests, you'll be told, "Not until you've gone through a seven-week membership class." It sounds extreme, but that's reality in some churches, and frankly, that's how non-Christians perceive reality in many churches.

> We've found that many young adults want to slide headfirst into third base and begin with serving. Sometimes even before believing!

However, at Liquid we have the exact opposite philosophy. While guests are certainly welcome to come and see, we have strategically chosen a more experiential *"taste* and see" approach (Ps. 34:8, emphasis added). Because we've discovered that young adults want to belong before they believe, we create opportunities for people to serve or participate at whatever level they feel inspired to try, even before they receive Jesus, believe in his name, and become children of God (John 1:12). Whether they want to go on a missions trip or serve coffee in our café or paint faces at our festival for kids with autism, we welcome them to use their gifts and serve shoulder to shoulder with authentic believers who know Christ personally. It's been a highly effective way to break down stereotypes about church and Christians, as they get to see our faith in action but also contribute at the same time.

SERVING AS A POWERFUL DOOR FOR EVANGELISM

Serving others is a powerful form of evangelism and levels the playing field. It's a very natural way for the water of life to flow from one person to another. I think of Jen, who invited her friend Lisa to church. Lisa said she'd come, and in planning when and where to meet, Jen said,

"Hey, this week before church I'm scheduled to make magic in the parking lot. Wanna join me for that?"

"What's making magic in the parking lot?" Lisa asked.

"We wear these giant, puffy Mickey Mouse gloves with four fingers. Kids love them! When parents pull in, we smile and wave and go a little crazy trying to make kids feel welcome, especially kids with special needs."

Lisa perked up, so Jen kept talking. "If they roll down their window, that means their child wants a high five—or with our Mickey gloves, a high four! That's making magic!"

Lisa was intrigued and said yes. It was her first visit to church since graduating college. Lisa joined Jen for the preservice huddle, during which the team prayed over each other. They also prayed for the people who would momentarily be pulling into church, that they would feel like VIPs, because that's who they are in God's sight.

Like a trooper, Lisa put on a parking vest and the Mickey gloves and gave out lots of high fours. She even had a teary moment as she saw the impact on one child in a wheelchair, who wouldn't stop giggling and trying to hug her.

To me, this was the ultimate first impression. Lisa hadn't heard one sermon yet (or had she?), and she hadn't yet sung one song. But I believe that Jen, along with the rest of our hospitality team, had already preached to her powerfully. The case for Christ had its foundation laid through joyful, sacrificial service and side-by-side relationship. The teaching pastor had a very easy job that morning with Lisa!

Lisa had a sense of belonging before she believed. She said, "This is the most fun I've had in years. You do this every Sunday?" I hope and pray she'll be back, and I know that Jen is walking alongside her in her journey to meet Jesus. This is the best kind of showing, then telling.

A GOOD THING? OR A GOD THING?

To be clear, we don't oppose discipleship pathways that begin with becoming a member, followed by learning the Bible, then serving or going on a missions trip. We're simply finding that many people—young adults especially—are initially more open to compassionate causes.

They say, "I'm not sure yet about your church, but I heard you're having a 5K run to bring clean drinking water to Africa. I'm in, and I'll invite my whole office to join me." As Christians, we serve the global poor because Jesus promised, "If anyone gives even a cup of cold water to one of these little ones . . . truly I tell you, that person will certainly not lose their reward" (Matt. 10:42). We see our clean water projects as a God thing. But pre-Christians often see it first as a good thing. And that's okay. We are happy to meet them on that common ground, trusting that the current of compassionate service will ultimately lead them to embrace a compassionate Savior.

Serving is the new evangelism. Cause is the key to engaging the rising generation and is often the first step toward introducing them to Christ. This is a generation that naturally gravitates toward values like empathy, generosity, and service. They have grown up in an experience economy,[7] and causes often drive their consumer choices. Many in the next generation don't just buy any socks; they might favor Bombas socks, because the company that makes them follows a one-for-one business model, like TOMS Shoes. For each pair of socks purchased from Bombas, a pair is donated to the homeless. Liquid's outreach to our city's homeless population[8] features Bombas socks. Only the best as we clothe the needy in Jesus' name!

> Serving is the new evangelism. Cause is the key to engaging the rising generation and is often the first step toward introducing them to Christ.

THREE CRUCIAL QUESTIONS AS YOU SATURATE YOUR CITY BY SERVING

How do you find a current of service that will help you saturate your city? In a post-Christian culture, sacrificial service earns tremendous goodwill with skeptics and cynics. Jeremiah 29:7 instructs us, "Seek the peace and prosperity of the city to which I have carried you. . . . Pray to the LORD for it, because if it prospers, you too will prosper." Look at the city God has called you to. What are its needs? What is broken that needs fixing? Who is neglected and needs hope?

God's river of living water is waiting to be unleashed where you live, and discovering the best current of service isn't as hard as you think. Here are three questions that have helped us discern where to invest our prayer, time, money, and human resources.

1. What is the Holy Spirit already blessing? When choosing causes to champion, we don't sit around in committee meetings, debate ideas, or take a vote. Nor do we thumb through a missions catalog and randomly pick something that catches our eye. "Hey, look at these malaria nets. Let's do a fundraiser."

Instead we pray earnestly for the Spirit's discernment and look around for a groundswell. What is God already blessing in the city? Who is already there, serving effectively? What is organically happening? And how can we come alongside and help? Each of the six chapters in part 2 addressed one of those themes.

2. What needs are being overlooked? As our church enters a new city or town, we strategically serve our way into its heart. In the communities where Liquid is blessed to have campuses, we reach out to the mayor, school superintendent, or town officials and ask, "How can we serve the people of this city? We have a heart to show the love of God through service. Do you have any dirty jobs that need doing? Or a special project that your budget can't afford? What needs are being overlooked?"

Through our no-strings-attached approach to service, our church has been invited to paint schools, renovate shelters for battered women, landscape neglected playgrounds, give an extreme makeover to a seniors' center, and host citywide concerts. You'll be shocked at what doors magically open when you offer money and muscle to meet the needs of your neighbors.

3. Where is God directing your path? Chapter 6 tells the story of our clean water cause. In reading it, I hope you realized that we didn't choose this cause; clean water chose us. Our name is Liquid, after all! What started with just a trickle (a modest ambition to fund one clean water well) quickly grew, and God multiplied the impact. To date, our church has drilled more than 280 wells in Central America and Africa, bringing clean drinking water to more than one hundred thousand thirsty people. This powerful current reminds me of the verse in Proverbs: "In the LORD's hand the king's heart is a stream of water that he channels toward all who please him" (Prov. 21:1).

HOW RECEPTIVE IS YOUR CITY?

Whatever town you call home, chances are that two out of every three people didn't connect with a church last weekend.[9] The good news, according to a survey of unchurched people, is that a number of reasons they gave for not engaging can be readily addressed. Some said they "haven't found a house of worship that they like," others that they "don't feel welcome," and still others think "there's no house of worship in their area."[10]

This same survey asked those who did go to church why they did so. People could select more than one of the options, but look at the following responses (which are ranked) to see what you're already doing well.

1. To become closer to God (81 percent).
2. So their children will have a moral foundation (69 percent).
3. To become a better person (68 percent).
4. For comfort in times of trouble or sorrow (66 percent).
5. They find the sermons valuable (59 percent).
6. To be part of a faith community (57 percent).
7. To continue their family's religious traditions (37 percent).
8. They feel obligated to go (31 percent).
9. To meet new people or socialize (19 percent).
10. To please their family, spouse, or partner (16 percent).

Likewise, another survey probed young churchgoing Protestants ages twenty-three to thirty about why they stay connected with church. Those who regularly attend do so "primarily because, they said, 'church was a vital part of my relationship with God' (56%) and 'I wanted the church to help guide my decisions in everyday life' (54%)."[11] These are emphases you're probably already providing.

Bottom line: your message about Jesus, and your mission to serve others in his name, is probably already in place and is positioned for greater impact on your community than you think. In this unique moment of cultural transition, will you seize this new evangelistic opportunity?

If you're ready to set out on a new rescue mission to reach thirsty people but need some practical steps, the final chapter is for you. Together, let's explore some launch points in the river.

Dive Deeper

One of the many churches I've learned from is Crossroads Church (crossroads .net), led by Pastor Brian Tome. He and a dozen friends started Crossroads in Cincinnati with a dream to reach the city and be a church for their friends who didn't like church. Lots of their friends. Today the church meets in more than a dozen different locations, with campuses planted across two states (Ohio and Kentucky). They also lead worship services in correctional facilities to reach prisoners with the hope of Christ. They're not just trying to saturate their states; they're striving to grow into a nationwide community of Christ followers.

As I stretch my faith and think about what more God might want to do through Liquid Church, here are some ways you might dive deeper in saturating your own community with living water.

ANKLE DEEP Look back at the section in this chapter titled "Three Crucial Questions as You Saturate Your City by Serving." Reflect on Jeremiah 29:7 in terms of how well it describes your priorities or actual practice as a church. What's your next step in serving your way into the heart of your city?

KNEE DEEP Briefly review Ed Stetzer's observations about the shift that's underway, in which cultural and congregational Christians are abandoning traditional church but remain open to a life-giving relationship with Jesus. Make a list of the cultural Christians in your sphere of influence who identify nominally as Christian but don't know Jesus in a personal way. Make a similar list of congregational Christians you know who are drifting away from their denominational connections. Begin praying for each by name, and ask God to illuminate new ways (especially experiential) that you can re-present Jesus to them.

WAIST DEEP This chapter suggests that a paradigm shift in discipleship is occurring. How would you describe your church's pathway of discipleship? Does it follow a traditional, linear pattern? Have you thought about the idea that the next generation prefers to belong before they believe? What strengths are there in this approach? What dangers? If service is the new evangelism, how can your pathway incorporate easily accessible entry points so newcomers can engage in compassionate service as a first step to meeting Jesus?

CHAPTER TWELVE

LAUNCH POINTS IN THE RIVER: SUGGESTIONS FOR LEADERS

> You will be my witnesses in Jerusalem, and in all
> Judea and Samaria, and to the ends of the earth.
> —ACTS 1:8

C an you imagine having access to water that flows at the rate of fifty million gallons a day, drawing from an eight-billion-gallon lake?[1] Do you think that might be enough to fill any water needs in your life?

That's exactly what happens every day at a nine-hundred-acre reservoir less than a mile from one of Liquid Church's campuses. It's so big that airline pilots use it as a visual reference as they're flying into New York City airports. This abundant lake—releasing more than enough water daily for a half million people[2]—is a constant visual reminder to me of what God wants to do with the gospel. But God offers not just a lake but an entire ocean of compassion, grace, and forgiveness through Jesus Christ. Those who already follow Jesus get to offer God's living water (John 4:10–11; 7:38; Rev. 7:17) not just as people show up to our church gatherings but also as we go out into our city, to nearby towns, and to the ends of the earth. Acts 1:8 contains Jesus' final words to his followers before he ascended to heaven. They are his saturation strategy and represent ever-widening circles of influence:

Jerusalem is local; Judea is regional; the ends of the earth are global. This is Jesus' saturation plan for churches like yours and mine.

NARROWING YOUR OPTIONS

I hope that by this point in the book, God has stirred your spirit with the vision of trickles turning into currents and ultimately into a raging river as you take the gospel outside of your church walls to spiritually thirsty people in your city. I've wanted to equip you with both practical ideas and the courage to believe that your church can have a better future—one in which it is more outward focused and culturally engaged and meaningfully takes the gospel to dozens, hundreds, and even thousands of thirsty people who have given up on church but not on God.

You've read about six LIQUID practices that form our powerful river: Love the overlooked (chap. 4), Ignite the imagination (chap. 5), Quench their thirst (chap. 6), Unite the generations (chap. 7), Inspire generosity (chap. 8), and Develop untapped talent (chap. 9). At the end of each of the chapters about these currents, I've challenged you to venture out into three different levels like Ezekiel did, going ankle deep, knee deep, or waist deep. Three levels times six chapters is eighteen invitations to go deeper in your leadership. I've also concluded each of these chapters by pointing you to five other churches whose websites can help spark additional ministry ideas. Five churches times six chapters makes thirty more leads for you to explore.

In every chapter, I have also challenged you, asking what needs in your city can you address in Jesus' name. Maybe they are similar to the ones Liquid Church is meeting, or maybe they're unique to your town. Has the Holy Spirit used any of these gentle nudges and innovative examples to inspire you? If you have clarity in what to do and how, then close this book, pray, and dive in! This book has met its purpose for you.

However, if you're still narrowing and discerning, then read on. That's what this chapter seeks to guide you through. All you need is the conviction that God wants to use you and the church you serve to saturate your city for Christ.

ALLOW YOURSELF TO EXPERIMENT

God might help you hit a home run with the first thing you try. Or he might show you that he's placed your church on third base with no one out, with your team's best batter up next.

I hope he does. That has not been our experience at Liquid Church. We've tried a lot of things that didn't work at first or about which God seemed to answer, "Not now." I remember one campus that had to move to a new location, a hotel, but the management there kept announcing weeks when we couldn't meet. During 2015, we met in five different locations. We told people with a smile, "If you can find us, you can join us." Predictably, no one at that campus found it funny. Potential guests began to think of us as too fly-by-night, and so did some of our regulars. Today we're settled into a centrally located high school that's working really well. But things weren't so stable out of the gate.

At another point, we began a big buildup to launch a campus in Jersey City. It would be our first urban campus in one of the most racially diverse cities in the country. We prayed hard. We had secured a great rental location in the heart of the city. We did a campaign that included fundraising for the Jersey City campus. We even began to meet with a core group of Liquid attenders from that community and people with a heart to reach it. But the momentum didn't grow as quickly as we thought it would; the population in this urban center is more transient, and we lacked critical mass to launch the campus with excellence. We concluded that God's reply was, "Not yet." That was three years ago, and we're patiently laying the groundwork to launch soon. Remember, God is the author of your story, and following his timing always works out better than trying to force yours!

We learn from every experience, but we always fix our gaze outward and upward. We believe nothing produces new Christians like new campuses, so we continue to experiment with how to use that strategy to channel Christ's living water to new communities. We don't believe failure is an option when it comes to demonstrating the gospel to our neighbors, and we pair our actions with words whenever we can.

START WITH THESE SEVEN QUESTIONS

Now it's your turn to take a risk and define your next experimental step. The following material is the most prescriptive in the book. I'm being as direct as possible because the more clarity you have, the more you can confidently step into the water and go deeper with Jesus.

Would you please pause to pray that you'll walk away from this chapter having identified God's next win for your church in going from trickle to current to river? Sometimes a next step comes by first identifying a problem to solve. So as you read the following, which of these questions is easiest for you to answer? Which is hardest? Perhaps your answers will lead you to spot the trickle that will become a current that will one day become a mighty river flooding your community with the love of Jesus.

What is God already blessing?

Can you clearly discern the problems or needs in your city that God has already begun using your church to address? Suppose your church has several families, each with a child in their twenties who has the same kind of mental illness. Suppose these families know each other, informally support each other, and have already begun to reach out to other parents with a similar situation. Hmm. Is it possible that God is already connecting the dots for a potential ministry in your midst? Situations like that forecast a trickle that can naturally grow toward becoming a current.

If you simply ask, "What are the needs in our community?" you'll quickly identify far more needs than any church can meet. However, if you also ask, "Is there passion and experience in our church to meet those needs?" then you can build on something already present in your people.

How can you affirm people's desire to make a difference in the world?

One reason Rick Warren's *Purpose Driven Life* has sold more than sixty million copies is that the book points to a widespread yearning for purpose. A strong motivation for most people, especially millennials and gen Z, is to feel that they are making a meaningful difference. They want to see a trickle of hope grow into a current of healing, and they delight to know God has wired them with such a dream. Sadly, some leaders make guilt or duty the primary motivation for trying to impact their community for Christ.

I love the cartoon about two people on a beach, where the tide has washed up thousands of starfishes that are certain to die under the rising sun. One person is busy throwing the starfishes back into the water. The second person sees the challenge and asks, "How can what you're doing possibly make a difference?" The first person picks up yet another starfish and says, "It makes a difference to this one!"

If you can change the world for one person, one child, one family, one apartment complex, you've made an eternal difference in Christ's kingdom.

How can you empower people to personalize their involvement?

Today's culture has taught us to expect personalization in everything we experience. Your music playlist is customized. Your internet package offers lots of options so that, as the ads say, you can pick the one that's right for you. Even fast-food joints that used to offer a one-size-fits-all burger now allow you to customize each item on the menu.

Likewise, any churchwide ministry initiatives need variety, allowing the experience to be tailored to the time, talent, and level of commitment that people are able to invest. You want your people to feel they can choose between options, selecting one that's the best match for them. Success isn't measured by how many people come to your church's program but by how many people stretch their faith by engaging heart, soul, body, and strength in striving to make a difference for Jesus. There is a big difference between these two measurements. Don't be discouraged if your initiatives start small. Remember that in Ezekiel 47, the water flowing from the temple began with a trickle but eventually became a raging river saturating everything in its path.

What small victory can you experience and celebrate?

It's important to define success as a series of small victories. Find one thing and do it well. Don't try to tackle everything, lest you end up going everywhere and nowhere at the same time.

Suppose your congregation has walked through the heart-wrenching agony of one of your church families losing a child through opioid addiction or texting while driving, and now, one year later, the parents have voiced a desire to be used by God to help other families avoid or cope with the same tragedy. They truly own the idea that God "comforts us in all our troubles, so that we can comfort those in any trouble with the comfort we ourselves receive from God" (2 Cor. 1:4).

You can already celebrate many victories in this story, from God's faithfulness in comforting this grieving family to his compassion in giving them such big hearts that they now want to comfort others. Next up for them is to form a leadership team for this ministry (when it happens, you can celebrate that as a small victory) and to hold their first meeting (another small victory). If the group receives favor in the local media, which leads to new people being drawn to it, that's another victory to celebrate. If someone in the group puts their faith in Christ, that's yet another victory. Every time you can identify God's favor, celebrate it! Whatever you brag on, you tend to see more of it happen.

Where do you see invitations and receptivity?

Too many churches are well prepared for 1994. If only 1994 would come again! Prediction: it won't. Yes, it's important to recognize how God has opened doors and showered blessing in the past. But don't assume he'll do exactly the same again, especially if your neighborhood has transitioned or the makeup of your congregation has changed. One thing is certain: the culture around you has shifted dramatically. Our culture is a constantly moving target, and we need to be constantly on the search for fresh, new wineskins from which to pour the timeless gospel message to emerging generations.

That killer Vacation Bible School program from 1994 will likely need a new face or format to reach gen Z. The Living Christmas Tree choir may have drawn huge crowds in the '80s, but maybe another way to creatively share the glory and awe of Christmas is needed for today.

People today, as in every era, are seeking to satisfy the needs of their soul. For some it's a need for purpose and divine direction in life, and for others it's a need to make new friends, get help with relationships, or find hope in a challenging circumstance. All of these are invitations to relationship, which then provides a bridge for your church to share what the God of the universe has done for you.

How can you partner with other community-based organizations?

Your impact will almost always be smaller if you work alone. In this book, you've seen example after example of how Liquid Church has networked with all kinds of other organizations in our community, from informal groups to nonprofits to governmental agencies, without compromising our message.

Take the free market described in chapter 8. Sure, we could have prayed, created the giveaway, put up a few signs, and encouraged our people to help spread the word. But we're convinced God multiplied the impact by first having us develop a relationship with the mayor, meet with the social service people he suggested, and say to them, "We'd love to help with what you're doing already. Can you introduce us to some low-income families who could really benefit from our free market?"

It's important to keep your church simple and not try to reinvent the wheel with every ministry. We have no plans to start a soup kitchen or homeless ministry, because we already know people who are killing it in those areas. Rather we offer to come alongside those ministries and provide money, muscle, and volunteer power to amplify the good work they're already doing on a larger scale.

How can you change the culture of your church?

Suppose you've read this book, and you shook your head at each point. "But you don't understand," you kept responding. "My church is full of great people. We have a rich heritage of serving this community, but we are totally stuck in museum mode. There's just no heart or ability to get involved with a trickle of God's momentum in our city."

Sounds like the culture of your church needs to undergo a fundamental transformation. I want to affirm that transformation is possible and that a ministry mentor can help you walk through revitalizing your church. You won't have to change your address! What you need is beyond the scope of this book, but I can suggest a few starting points to leaders, pastors, or heads of ministry.

- *Meet God afresh.* If you're not passionate about touching your city, others won't be either. If you don't believe God can use your church, no one else will. You need a promise from God's Word to stand on. This might lead you to go on a spiritual retreat to become more passionate, as Elijah was in 1 Kings 18:30–39. Notice how Elijah stepped out in bold faith, repeatedly pouring water over his earthly altar to saturate it. The result? God sent fire from heaven to set it ablaze!

- *Preach about the river.* People want to understand the why. Reinforce the biblical foundations for being a change agent in your city, town, suburb, or village. Yes, be practical with the what and the how, but always include and start with the why.
- *Build appropriate dissatisfaction with what you're doing—or not doing—at present.* Just before they crossed the Red Sea, the Israelites were longing for the horrible status quo of slavery when the Egyptian army was bearing down on them. But a sense of do-or-die desperation—and God's miraculous provision!—propelled them to a brand-new beginning. Lasting change is usually triggered by a holy dissatisfaction, a conviction that things cannot remain as they are and that God has a better future in store for his people.
- *Celebrate each win, no matter how small.* Most struggling congregations have a low corporate self-esteem. It shows up when people are unwilling to step up. It's voiced when people excuse themselves by saying, "We're just a small church" or "I'm only a layperson." As you praise God for each tiny gain, you will build hope and faith for bigger wins.
- *Recruit allies.* Don't try to change the whole church at once. Sow seeds with your opinion leaders. Get allies on board, and you'll not only minimize resistance with others but also bring them along.
- *Equip lay leaders with an outward focus.* Build reproducing teams of volunteers, especially with the young adults among you. If fewer than 50 percent of the people present for worship on a typical weekend are engaged in some way, it's time to evaluate your approach to ministry. Does your church really practice the idea that a pastor's purpose is to equip the saints for the work of ministry (Eph. 4:11–12)?
- *Align church resources to face east.* How much of your church's ministry right now is about the care and maintenance of your existing programs? If more than 75 percent of your church's time, talent, and treasure is internally focused, then it's time to

restructure.[3] Make sure your budget and your staff give increasing priority to the evangelistic river flowing outward, not to the typical default of internal maintenance.

- *Find balance.* At the same time, don't position all your staff and teams in doing ministry; you need to create ways to support the ministers. Remember the old Home Depot slogan "You can do it; we can help"? That should be the posture of the pastor and staff toward the people. Do the members of your congregation have 100 percent confidence that you believe God has a ministry for each of them and that you 100 percent support the unleashing of their gifts? The greatest way to sabotage frontline workers is to make them feel alone and unsupported. Another way to sabotage them is to be a bottleneck.

WHAT GOD WANTS FROM ME . . . AND FROM YOU

What does ministry success look like? Lives changed by Christ. In one of our campuses, we have a twenty-foot wall graphic of a Latino man named Carlos coming up out of the waters of baptism, pumping both fists in the air like he just scored a winning Super Bowl touchdown. His T-shirt says, "Alive!" and there's a look of pure joy on his face. Carlos was saved on Easter, and he and his daughter were baptized together and now serve on our church's media team. That's what success looks like on our scorecard—lives changed and families saved by the love of Jesus. People taking next steps in obedience to their Savior. People who want to be involved in serving and helping others grow in their faith.

We exist to bless those outside our walls, to serve our neighbors, especially those who have given up on church but not on God, and especially people on the margins. We want to shower God's compassion on those closest to his heart. When that happens, it is God's definition of success.

Liz is a single mom raising a son named Bo who has cerebral palsy. They got involved with Liquid Church, and one winter Liz's home had ceiling damage. She mentioned it in passing to one of the volunteers who loves on her son through our special needs ministry.

That volunteer helped mobilize two of our small groups, and one weekend they invested more than two hundred hours renovating Liz's house. They put up a new ceiling and repaired the leak in the roof that had caused the ceiling problems. They also installed insulation, painted a bedroom, powerwashed the house, fixed the deck, and did landscaping outside. The coolest part is that Bo got to help! They went out of their way to involve him wherever possible.

That's the church of Jesus at its best. The compassion of Christ had so penetrated the hearts of these men that it overflowed in love and service to others, especially a family in need. This was not an official church outreach organized by leaders. This happened organically, when two small groups heard about a need and said, "We can do something about this!"

I wonder what kind of ripple effect happened with the gospel when family, friends, and neighbors heard about the care and support she received? News like that has a way of spilling out all over.

"Do for one what you wish you could do for everyone."

That kind of generous heart is what God uses to unleash the love of Christ into a raging river of compassion. It's hearts that bond together to meet the practical needs of the most vulnerable. It's hearts so healed and transformed by what God has done for them that they sacrifice their Saturdays to serve a single mom and her child with special needs. As my friend Andy Stanley says, "Do for one what you wish you could do for everyone."[4]

THE UNSTOPPABLE RIVER FROM YOUR CHURCH

Do you want to see God grow trickles into currents and ultimately an unstoppable river? The bottleneck is not God. The bottleneck is not lack of a transformational message. The bottleneck is not a shortage of people to love. Nor is the bottleneck a lack of spiritual thirst.

People in your community are far more ready than you realize to talk about spiritual matters. They may be skeptical or cynical about the idea of church, but when you serve, act with compassion, and show generosity, at some point they'll begin to ask questions about the Savior of the world, the one whose living water can refresh their soul as it has yours.

That's how a tidal wave begins. As you saturate your community with the gospel, you bring God's heavenly reality to earth, and it changes the landscape of your city.

The huge reservoir near our campus has more than enough water for every home around it, but that's only a drop in the bucket compared with God's immeasurable resources. All the people in those homes need water; they can't survive without it. Even more, they desperately need Jesus' living water for their souls.

Today is the day. How will you lead your church to boldly launch into God's great river?

Dive Deeper

I hope the conclusion of this book is the start of your journey. Remember, Jesus is always inviting his disciples to venture out into deeper water (Luke 5:4). How is he calling you deeper?

 ANKLE DEEP In this chapter, I described Acts 1:8 as Jesus' saturation strategy. Of the places or groups that God has enabled your church to touch, which is your Jerusalem (local influence), your Judea (surrounding area), your Samaria (regional enemies), your ends of the earth (global territories)? Which offers the best opportunity at the moment for greater saturation?

KNEE DEEP What is the next new, specific action you'll take as a result of reading this book? Can you frame it as a goal to be achieved within the next six months? It can be small, but make it measurable. Who besides you at your church will own it, so you can work together and hold each other accountable? If you've been unpacking this as a team, work to develop an actionable timeline together.

WAIST DEEP This book describes several "all hands on deck" calls to our entire church to meet needs beyond our congregation. If God is leading you to a similar "all in" mission, what will it be? When? How? What do you believe God wants to do through you? I invite you to make your prayer for it my favorite benediction: "Now to him who is able to do immeasurably more than all we ask or imagine, according to his power that is at work within us, to him be glory in the church and in Christ Jesus throughout all generations, for ever and ever! Amen" (Eph. 3:20–21).

ACKNOWLEDGMENTS

I wrote this book at the strong encouragement of my coauthor, Warren Bird, who is a trusted friend and mentor and more recently a board member at Liquid Church. I am deeply grateful for Warren's influence in my life, his passion for the local church, and his humble heart for advancing Christ's kingdom. But this book wouldn't have happened without the additional help and insight of hundreds of people.

It was quite an adventure to relive the dozens of stories shared in these pages (all told by permission), each involving one or more persons special to me. Let me start by underscoring my thanks to the Lord, who has patiently redeemed and transformed my life and is still doing so! God lavishly blessed me with my precious wife, Colleen, my beautiful soulmate who helped start Liquid with me all those years ago and continues to influence our church to this very day. I've loved sharing this incredible God-adventure with her and our amazing children, Chase and Del—all of whom I thank for their encouragement, patience, and willingness to allow some of our family stories to be immortalized in print and onstage.

From my heart, I thank every member of Liquid's staff (both past and present) for your love for Jesus and your heart to sacrificially serve his people. None of this would have been possible without the shared leadership of my courageous brothers Dave Brooks and Mike Leahy, whose families have been part of Liquid's story from the very beginning. Pastors Hyo Sil Siegel and Karen Shannon are gifted leaders who've been a joy to lock arms with in this journey; your fingerprints are all over Liquid's ministry. I'm also grateful for my executive assistant, Jannet Morgan, who helped organize not only this book project but *mi vida loca* too. Jannet has positively influenced Liquid's staff culture behind the scenes, infusing it with celebration, a spirit of laughter, and fun. I feel blessed to partner with my talented friend Greg Crippen, whose graphic design visually brought many of this book's ideas to life. Without all of you, there might not be much story to tell!

Thanks also to the many ministry mentors who have shaped my life, especially those named in this book who helped inspire the dream of bringing living water to our thirsty generation. My special appreciation to the pioneers who started Liquid, including the elders and gracious congregation of Millington Baptist Church, and to the heroes of the faith in the merged congregations at Mountainside and Garwood.

Many people have read portions of our manuscript and provided helpful input. We appreciate how each of you sharpened our thinking and improved ideas, including those who allowed us to tell stories about yourself or your family. At the risk of accidentally omitting someone, I want to thank the following friends who contributed to one of the drafts in some way (in alphabetical order): Robert Barba, Lauren Bercarich, Rich Birch, Michelle Bird, Dave Brooks, Jonathan Brozozog, Elizabeth Chang, Patrick Collins, Sara Crippen, Bob Cushman, Helen Cushman, LaTasha Estelle, Kristin Flynn, Wayne Francis, Esther Goetz, Amy J. Gregory, Kep James, Mark Johnston, Brad Leach, Colleen Lucas, J. Skipp Machmer, Craig Massey, Kayra D. Montañez, Jannet Morgan, Marv Nelson, Ron Ovitt, Suzanne Pearson, Peter Pendell, Jeff Piepho, Janet Saulter-Hemmer, Monika Sawicki, Suzi Soares, Karen Shannon, Jinu Thomas, Nithin Thompson, Ron Walborn, and Rebecca Wheeler.

By now, those who are part of the Liquid Church congregation will have seen many names they know. I wish I could print everyone's name here, because this book is their story—*your* story—of a living God who is saturating our lives with the life of his Son, which is spilling over to each of our families, friends, neighbors, and work colleagues.

Warren Bird, my coauthor, whose hand has been in every paragraph (including this one), affirms his appreciation for all the people named in these acknowledgments, many of whom he got to meet and interview. He also thanks his wonderful and supportive wife, Michelle, and the many ministry mentors in his own life, including Robert Cowles, Carl George, Dale Galloway, Bob Cushman, Dave Travis, and Dan Busby, plus the wonderful small group at his church, who have prayed for and cheered him on.

Warren especially wants to thank Esther Thompson, his executive assistant, for her diligence and care with the endnotes and many other details of the book.

ECFA (the Evangelical Council for Financial Accountability) not only has accredited Liquid Church as one of its members but is Warren's employer, whom he thanks for their tremendous flexibility and support. What a gift of encouragement the staff there represents!

Together, we want to give a special shout-out to the team at Zondervan, who worked through multiple drafts of the front cover plus many tweaks of the table of contents, offering help and encouragement at each step of the way. Ryan Pazdur, Nathan Kroeze, Brian Phipps, Amy Bigler, and others—together, we've made an amazing team!

Finally, to you the reader, please know that we have prayed for you continually through the writing process, that our words would enlarge your vision of God's dream for your life and ministry. We believe God wants to lead you out into deeper waters, and that he wants to see trickles turn into currents and finally into raging rivers that saturate your city and beyond with the gospel of Jesus Christ.

If God has used this book to inspire your leadership or help your ministry in some way, we'd love to hear about it. Just turn to "Meet the Authors" for our contact information and let us know how God has used this book to impact your world.

Oh, and would you do us a quick favor? We'd appreciate it if you took a few minutes to write a review of this book online. Just one or two sentences about something you found helpful or inspiring and your thumbs-up will help motivate others to check it out. Thanks, friends!

NOTES

INTRODUCTION

1. Sarah Calise, "A Foothold on History," National Baseball Hall of Fame, *https:// baseballhall.org/discover-more/stories/short-stops/foothold-on-history*.

2. For 2018, Liquid Church was number 43 on the *Outreach* magazine list of fastest growing churches at *https://outreachmagazine.com/outreach-100-list .html*. It also appeared in the list in 2016 (no. 55). It was also mentioned in a 2016 *Outreach* magazine cover story, "The Changing Face of the American Megachurch" by Warren Bird.

3. The next chapter will offer some research about how the United States, the Northeast, and New Jersey in particular need more vibrant, life-giving churches and ways for the gospel to splash out into our communities. For now, if you'd like to see a religious profile of your state, go to this link for New Jersey, and then select your own state: *www.pewforum.org/religious-landscape -study/state/new-jersey/*.

4. Charles Grandison Finney, *Memoirs of Reverend Charles G. Finney Written by Himself* (New York: A. S. Barnes, 1876).

5. George Barna and David Kinnaman, *Churchless: Understanding Today's Unchurched and How to Connect with Them* (Wheaton: Tyndale, 2014), 41.

6. One of the best (and most readable) commentaries about the true percentage of unchurched adults by a respected academic is the chapter titled "Involvement" in Mark Chaves, *American Religion: Contemporary Trends* (Princeton, NJ: Princeton Univ. Press, 2011), 43–54. He discusses frequency of attendance and how attendance trends have changed over the last fifty years.

CHAPTER 1: I DARE YOU TO DIVE DEEPER

1. One measure is the regional decline in the number of people who identify themselves as Christian. According to Pew research, the Northeast has experienced a dramatic decline, the largest of any region (as measured between

2007 and 2015). Another measure is the ratio of fast-growing or larger churches to the size of the region, such as the annual lists created by *Outreach* magazine at *http://outreachmagazine.com*. The Northeast (New Jersey, Pennsylvania, New York, Massachusetts, Connecticut, Rhode Island, Vermont, New Hampshire, and Maine) is 18 percent of the total US population, but on *Outreach's* lists it's an unusually good year if even 5–10 percent of the largest or fastest growing churches are there. A third measure is the number of Protestants. Nationally, the average is 51 percent, but when analyzed by region, the Northeast has the fewest at 32 percent. Pew Research Center, "America's Changing Religious Landscape" (May 12, 2015), chap. 4, *www.pewforum.org/2015/05/12/chapter-4 -the-shifting-religious-identity-of-demographic-groups/*. To see the religious makeup of your state, county, or city, see *www.usreligioncensus.org/*.

2. Pew Research Center, "America's Changing Religious Landscape." See also Jack Jenkins, "'Nones' Now as Big as Evangelicals, Catholics in the US," March 21, 2019, *https://religionnews.com/2019/03/21/nones-now-as-big-as -evangelicals-catholics-in-the-us/*.

3. Daniel Cox and Robert P. Jones, "America's Changing Religious Identity," Public Religion Research Institute (PRRI) (September 6, 2017), *www.prri.org/ research/american-religious-landscape-christian-religiously-unaffiliated/*.

4. James Hudnut-Beumler and Mark Silk, *The Future of Mainline Protestantism in America* (New York: Columbia Univ. Press, 2018).

5. Total baptism tally between Liquid's launch on Easter Sunday 2007 and June 2019.

6. Erik van Sebille, Eric Oliver, and Jaci Brown, "Can You Surf the East Australian Current, Finding Nemo–Style?" *The Conversation* (June 5, 2014), *https://theconversation.com/can-you-surf-the-east-australian-current-finding-nemo -style-27392*.

7. Elmer Towns and Douglas Porter, *The Ten Greatest Revivals Ever* (Ann Arbor, MI: Servant, 2000), 2–3.

8. Robert D. Putnam and David E. Campbell, *American Grace* (New York: Simon and Schuster, 2010). See the chapter titled "Religion and Good Neighborliness."

CHAPTER 2: THE ACCIDENTAL BIRTH
OF LIQUID CHURCH

1. For US church attendance, see "Fast Facts about American Religion," Hartford Institute for Religion Research, *http://hartfordinstitute.org/research/ fastfacts/fast_facts.html#attend*. For Canadian church attendance, which is lower than that of the US, see Warren Bird et al, "Canadian Church Study," *www.leadnet.org/Canada*. See also Pew Research Center, "America's Changing Religious Landscape" (May 12, 2015), chap. 4, *www.pewforum.org/2015/05/12/ chapter-4-the-shifting-religious-identity-of-demographic-groups/*.

2. Lifeway Research, "Americans Open to Outreach from Churches" (March 23, 2009), *https://lifewayresearch.com/2009/03/23/americans-open-to-outreach-from-churches/*.

3. Bob Smietana, "Poll: You're Probably Inviting Friends to Church," *Christianity Today* (July 13, 2018), *www.christianitytoday.com/news/2018/july/inviting-friends-church-lifeway-research.html*.

4. Tim Lucas, *You Married the Wrong Person: The Relationship Secret Every Couple Needs to Know* (Liquid Church, 2015).

5. John Leland, "Christians Say Hello. Gay Activists Say Hmmm," *New York Times* (June 6, 2005), *www.nytimes.com/2005/06/06/nyregion/christians-say-hello-gay-activists-say-hmmm.html*.

CHAPTER 3: OUR SATURATION STRATEGY

1. H. H. Mitchell, "The Chemical Composition of the Adult Human Body and Its Bearing on the Biochemistry of Growth," *Journal of Biological Chemistry* 158 (May 1, 1945): 628, *www.jbc.org/content/158/3/625.short*.

2. "How Much Water Is There On, In, and Above the Earth?" US Geological Survey (USGS), *https://water.usgs.gov/edu/earthhowmuch.html*.

3. Some of the following insights come from the article "What Is Living Water?" *Our Rabbi Jesus* (September 6, 2015), *http://ourrabbijesus.com/articles/living-water/*.

4. "Do not forget to show hospitality to strangers, for by so doing some people have shown hospitality to angels without knowing it" (Heb. 13:2).

5. For details, see chapter 1, note 1.

6. BHAG stands for Big Hairy Audacious Goal, an idea conceptualized in the book *Built to Last: Successful Habits of Visionary Companies* by James Collins and Jerry Porras (Harper Business, 2011). According to Collins and Porras, a BHAG is a long-term goal that changes the very nature of an organization's existence. The audacious, faith-stretching goal may seem questionable to people outside the organization but is internally viewed as achievable.

7. Tim Keller, "To Transform a City: How Do You Know If You're Reaching a City?" *Christianity Today* 32, no. 1 (Winter 2011), *www.christianitytoday.com/pastors/2011/winter/tim-keller-transform-city.html*.

8. Malcolm Gladwell, *The Tipping Point: How Little Things Can Make a Big Difference* (New York: Back Bay, 2002).

9. Wikipedia, "Pork Roll," *https://en.wikipedia.org/wiki/Pork_roll*.

CHAPTER 4: LOVE THE OVERLOOKED: SPECIAL NEEDS

1. Autism New Jersey, "Autism Prevalence Rate," *www.autismnj.org/understanding-autism/prevalance-rates/*.

2. David Briggs, "Study: U.S. Churches Exclude Children with Autism, ADD/ADHD," ARDA: Association of Religion Data Archives (July 9, 2018), citing

a study by the National Survey of Children's Health, *http://blogs.thearda.com/trend/featured/study-u-s-churches-exclude-children-with-autism-addadhd/*.

3. Centers for Disease Control and Prevention, "CDC's Work on Developmental Disabilities," *www.cdc.gov/ncbddd/developmentaldisabilities/about.html*.

4. Jesus' thirty-seven recorded miracles are found in this list: *www.thoughtco.com/miracles-of-jesus-700158*. Of them, twenty-five (68 percent) involve people with special needs. The twelve in the list that don't seem to qualify include miracles like changing water into wine, calming a storm, feeding large crowds, and raising the dead.

5. National Down Syndrome Society, "Down Syndrome," *www.ndss.org/about-down-syndrome/down-syndrome/*.

6. Vicki Hyman, "N.J. Teen Makes Huge Impact on ABC's 'Speechless'—without Saying a Word," NJ.com, March 26, 2017, *www.nj.com/entertainment/tv/index.ssf/2017/03/speechless_jj_actor_micah_fowler.html*.

7. Skye Jethani, "Special Needs Boy Removed from Worship," *Christianity Today*, *www.christianitytoday.com/pastors/2011/june-online-only/special-needs-boy-removed-from-worship.html*.

8. Amy Becker, "The Ministry of the Disabled: How Christians with Intellectual Disabilities Are Serving Churches (Not Just Being Served by Them)," *Christianity Today* (April 20, 2018), *www.christianitytoday.com/ct/2018/may/ministry-of-disabled.html*.

9. Andrew Whitehead, quoted in Michael Staton, "Researcher Finds Chronic Health Conditions Are a Stumbling Block to Church Worship for Children," *Newsstand* (July 9, 2018), *http://newsstand.clemson.edu/mediarelations/researcher-finds-chronic-health-conditions-are-a-stumbling-block-to-church-worship-for-children/*.

10. Allison Klein, "Lucas Was Just Named 2018 Gerber Baby. He Has Down Syndrome," *Washington Post* (February 7, 2018), *www.washingtonpost.com/news/inspired-life/wp/2018/02/07/lucas-was-just-named-2018-gerber-baby-he-has-down-syndrome/?utm_term=.9ed3949a0155*.

11. Tim Tebow Foundation, *www.timtebowfoundation.org*.

12. To learn more and to find contact information, see *www.liquidchurch.com/specialneeds*.

13. Erik W. Carter, *Including People with Disabilities in Faith Communities* (Baltimore: Brookes, 2007), 2.

14. Ibid., 8.

15. To learn how Christians with special needs are serving their churches, read *Christianity Today*'s inspiring cover story "The Ministry of the Disabled" (April 20, 2018), *www.christianitytoday.com/ct/2018/may/ministry-of-disabled.html*.

CHAPTER 5: IGNITE THE IMAGINATION: CREATIVE COMMUNICATION

1. America's current population may own a Bible, but a surprisingly low number read it or know what it teaches, as this survey shows: "Americans Are Fond of the Bible, Don't Actually Read It," *https://lifewayresearch.com/2017/04/25/lifeway-research-americans-are-fond-of-the-bible-dont-actually-read-it/*. Furthermore, the percent of people who view the Bible as God's Word is decreasing, as Gallup documents: "Record Few Americans Believe Bible Is Literal Word of God," *https://news.gallup.com/poll/210704/record-few-americans-believe-bible-literal-word-god.aspx*. Contrast this to eras in American history when the Bible was the primary textbook, such as the McGuffey Reader for grades 1–6; an estimated 120 million copies were sold between 1836 and 1960: "William Holmes McGuffey and His Readers," *www.nps.gov/jeff/learn/historyculture/upload/mcguffey.pdf*. The Museum of the Bible has a display on the Bible's role in American culture and its influence on everything from literature to media to public morality: *www.museumofthebible.org/press/back ground/floor-2-impact-of-the-bible-bible-in-the-world*. Two recent general assessments of religious change in the United States are: Robert D. Putnam and David E. Campbell, *American Grace: How Religion Divides and Unites Us* (New York: Simon & Schuster, 2010); Claude S. Fischer and Michael Hout, *Century of Difference: How America Changed in the Last One Hundred Years* (New York: Russell Sage Foundation, 2006).

2. Lydia Saad, "Sermon Content Is What Appeals Most to Churchgoers," Gallup (April 14, 2017), *https://news.gallup.com/poll/208529/sermon-content-appeals -churchgoers.aspx*.

3. Carey Nieuwhof, "7 Disruptive Church Trends That Will Rule 2018," *https:// careynieuwhof.com/7-disruptive-church-trends-that-will-rule-2018/*.

4. For a sketch of the tithingman at work, see *www.newenglandhistoricalsociety .com/puritan-tithingman-powerful-men-new-england/*.

5. Doug Oss and Mark Batterson, "Right-Brain Preaching: Capturing the Imagination of Your Listeners," *Enrichment, http://enrichmentjournal.ag.org/ 200801/200801_116_RightBrainPreach.cfm*, emphasis added.

6. Christian Jarrett, "Why the Left-Brain Right-Brain Myth Will Probably Never Die," *Psychology Today* (June 27, 2012), *www.psychologytoday.com/us/ blog/brain-myths/201206/why-the-left-brain-right-brain-myth-will-probably -never-die*, and Robert H. Shmerling, "Right Brain / Left Brain, Right?" Harvard Health Publishing (August 25, 2017), *www.health.harvard.edu/blog/ right-brainleft-brain-right-2017082512222*.

7. Hilary Brueck, "There's No Such Thing As 'Auditory' or 'Visual' Learners," *Business Insider* (February 20, 2018), *www.businessinsider.com/auditory-visual -kinesthetic-learning-styles-arent-real-2018-2*.

8. Joe Fryer, "Inside the Last Blockbuster Video Store in America," NBC News (July 17, 2018), *www.nbcnews.com/news/us-news/inside-last-blockbuster-video-store-america-n892246*.

9. Oss and Batterson, "Right-Brain Preaching."

10. "*Hotwash* is a term picked up in recent years by the Emergency Preparedness Community" and involves "the immediate 'after-action' discussions and evaluations of an agency's . . . performance following an exercise, training session, or major event." Wikipedia, "Hotwash," *https://en.wikipedia.org/wiki/Hotwash*.

CHAPTER 6: QUENCH THEIR THIRST: COMPASSIONATE CAUSE

1. United Nations, "The Millennium Development Goals Report" (2012), 54, *https://d26p6gt0m19hor.cloudfront.net/whywater/English2012.pdf*.

2. World Health Organization, "Drinking-Water" (February 7, 2018), *www.who.int/en/news-room/fact-sheets/detail/drinking-water*.

3. "Some 842,000 people are estimated to die each year from diarrhea as a result of unsafe drinking-water, sanitation, and hand hygiene" (ibid.). Deaths by violence include suicide, homicide, and war; suicide is 56 percent of that total, and the remaining 44 percent (out of 1.4 million total deaths by violence) is 616,000 deaths per year (World Health Organization, "10 Facts about Violence Prevention" [updated May 2017], *www.who.int/features/factfiles/violence/en/*). See also Max Roser, Mohamed Nagdy, and Hannah Ritchie, "Terrorism" (updated January 2018), *https://ourworldindata.org/terrorism*.

4. UNICEF Rwanda, "Press Release: Launch of National Water Supply and Sanitation Policies and Strategies on the Occasion of World Water Day 2017" (March 22, 2017), *www.unicef.org/rwanda/media_19672.html*.

5. See Living Water International, *www.water.cc*. I'm so passionate about what this nonprofit group stands for that I'm on their board of reference *(www.water.cc/leadership)*. Their purpose mission statement is, "Living Water exists to demonstrate the love of God by helping communities acquire desperately needed clean water, and experience 'living water'—the gospel of Jesus Christ—which alone satisfies the deepest thirst." The organization has completed nearly twenty thousand water projects in more than seventeen developing countries across Latin America and the Caribbean, Africa, and Asia as part of their ongoing commitment to provide water, for life, in Jesus' name. Living Water's goal is to see holistic behavior change by supporting the local church and equipping local people to serve their own communities.

6. As of April 2019, Liquid Church has helped fund and complete 284 clean water wells (30 with charity: water and 254 with Living Water International) in nine nations.

7. WHO/UNICEF Joint Monitoring Programme for Water Supply and Sanitation, "JMP 2015 Annual Report," 9, *https://d26p6gt0m19hor.cloudfront.net/whywater/JMP-2015-Annual-Report.pdf*.

Notes ■ 277

8. UNICEF Rwanda, "Water, Sanitation and Hygiene," *www.unicef.org/rwanda/wes_8300.html.*
9. WHO/UNICEF, "JMP 2015 Annual Report," 9.
10. Wikipedia, "Jerrycan," *https://en.wikipedia.org/wiki/Jerrycan.*
11. charity: water, *www.charitywater.org.*
12. See note 5 for this chapter.
13. Brian Hobbs, "Adoption Option Takes Off: Broken Arrow Church Emphasizes Adoption, Foster Care," *Baptist Messenger* (November 27, 2012), *www.baptistmessenger.com/adoption-option-takes-off-broken-arrow-church-emphasizes-adoption-foster-care/.*
14. One starting point is to go to the Evangelical Council for Financial Accountability *(ECFA.org)*, which vets Christ-centered ministries for financial integrity. Its "find member" tab enables you to search for ministries by location, type, and other factors and then to see a profile, including a financial summary and giving opportunities, of each organization. By the way, Liquid Church is ECFA certified.

CHAPTER 7: UNITE THE GENERATIONS: MINISTRY MERGERS

1. Santa Maria della Concezione dei Cappuccini (Our Lady of the Conception of the Capuchins) was commissioned in 1626 by Pope Urban VIII, whose brother, Antonio Barberini, was a Capuchin friar. View photos of the crypt at *https://en.wikipedia.org/wiki/Capuchin_Crypt.*
2. See the denomination-by-denomination list in *How to Break Growth Barriers* by Carl George and Warren Bird (Grand Rapids: Revell, 2017), 149–50.
3. Jim Tomberlin and Warren Bird, *Better Together: Making Church Mergers Work* (San Francisco: Jossey-Bass, 2012).
4. Ed Stetzer and Warren Bird, *Viral Churches: Helping Church Planters Become Movement Makers* (San Francisco: Jossey-Bass, 2010), 1, 101.
5. Kara Powell, Jake Mulder, and Brad Griffin, *Growing Young: Six Essential Strategies to Help Young People Discover and Love Your Church* (Grand Rapids: Baker, 2016).
6. William Vanderbloemen and Warren Bird, *Next: Pastoral Succession That Works* (Grand Rapids: Baker, 2014), 9.
7. For more on the restart initiative of New Life Community Church (Chicago, Illinois), see *https://newlifecommunity.church/restart/.*
8. Lee Kricher, *For a New Generation: A Practical Guide for Revitalizing Your Church* (Grand Rapids: Zondervan, 2016).

CHAPTER 8: INSPIRE GENEROSITY: GUILT-FREE GIVING

1. "Pastor Tim Lucas on CNN's TJ Holmes Show—Reverse Offering" (September 28, 2011), *www.youtube.com/watch?v=W9rfMGaVAV4.*
2. Wikipedia, "Hurricane Irene," *https://en.wikipedia.org/wiki/Hurricane_Irene.*

3. Greg Laurie, "Money and Motives," *www.oneplace.com/ministries/a-new -beginning/read/articles/money-and-motives-9220.html*.
4. New York City Relief, *www.NewYorkCityRelief.org*.

CHAPTER 9: DEVELOP UNTAPPED TALENT: LEADERSHIP CULTURE

1. For an entire chapter with numerous examples of ICNU conversations, see *Hero Maker: Five Essential Practices for Leaders to Multiply Leaders* by Dave Ferguson and Warren Bird (Grand Rapids: Zondervan, 2018).
2. See the Leadership Network report "Inside Job: Large Church HR Directors Offer Unique Perspective on Their Work" by Warren Bird, free download at *http://leadnet.org/salary/*.
3. For further description of their system, see "How Church of the Highlands Gets 33% of Their Attenders to Volunteer" by the Rocket Company (March 6, 2013), *https://therocketcompany.com/how-church-of-the-highlands-gets-33-of-their -attenders-to-serve/*.
4. See the profile of Mark Johnston in *Teams That Thrive: Five Disciplines of Collaborative Church Leadership* by Ryan Hartwig and Warren Bird (Downers Grove, IL: InterVarsity Press, 2015), 249–50.

CHAPTER 11: HOW DO YOU SATURATE *YOUR* CITY?

1. Tim Keller, "To Transform a City: How Do You Know If You're Reaching a City?" *Christianity Today* 32, no. 1 (Winter 2011), *www.christianitytoday.com/ pastors/2011/winter/tim-keller-transform-city.html*.
2. Ed Stetzer, *Christians in the Age of Outrage: How to Bring Our Best When the World Is at Its Worst* (Wheaton: Tyndale Momentum, 2018), 8–11, 28.
3. Tim Keller, "To Transform a City: How Do You Know If You're Reaching a City?" *Christianity Today* 32, no. 1 (Winter 2011), *www.christianitytoday.com/ pastors/2011/winter/tim-keller-transform-city.html*.
4. Don Everts and Doug Schaupp, *I Once Was Lost: What Postmodern Skeptics Taught Us about Their Path to Jesus* (Downers Grove, IL: InterVarsity, 2008), 31.
5. Mark Chaves, *American Religion: Contemporary Trends* (Oxford Univ. Press, 2011), 13.
6. Pew Research Center, "Where Americans Find Meaning in Life" (November 20, 2018), *www.pewforum.org/2018/11/20/where-americans-find -meaning-in-life/*.
7. Joseph Pine and James Gilmore, *Experience Economy*, updated ed. (Boston: Harvard Business Review Press, 2011).
8. Want to learn more about feeding and clothing the homeless? Our friends at New York City Relief lead the way with an army of compassion that weekly brings the hope of Jesus to the hurting on the streets. Visit *https:// newyorkcityrelief.org/*.

9. See the Pew Research Center religious landscape study "Attendance at Religious Services" for an interactive table about church attendance by age, gender, and other factors at *http://www.pewforum.org/religious-landscape-study/attendance-at-religious-services/*.

10. "Why Americans Go (and Don't Go) to Religious Services," Pew Research Center, August 1, 2018, *http://www.pewforum.org/2018/08/01/why-americans-go-to-religious-services/*.

11. Griffin Paul Jackson, "The Top Reasons Young People Drop Out of Church," *Christianity Today* (January 15, 2019), *www.christianitytoday.com/news/2019/january/church-drop-out-college-young-adults-hiatus-lifeway-survey.html*.

CHAPTER 12: LAUNCH POINTS IN THE RIVER: SUGGESTIONS FOR LEADERS

1. SUEZ / Hoboken Water Services, "Your Water Quality Information: Consumer Confidence Report" (June 2018), *www.mysuezwater.com/sites/default/files/HobokenCCR2017.pdf*.

2. The average US resident uses about ninety gallons of water per day at home, according to the US Geological Survey. See the USGS Water Science School, "Water Questions and Answers: How Much Water Does the Average Person Use at Home per Day?" (updated December 2, 2016), *https://water.usgs.gov/edu/qa-home-percapita.html*.

3. For a great set of ministry ratios with commentary and tips, see *What Every Pastor Should Know: 101 Indispensable Rules of Thumb for Leading Your Church* by Gary McIntosh and Charles Arn (Grand Rapids: Baker, 2013).

4. Andy Stanley, "One, Not Everyone" (Alpharetta, GA: North Point Resources), *https://store.northpoint.org/products/one-not-everyone*.

SCRIPTURE INDEX

MEET THE AUTHORS

Tim Lucas is the founder and lead pastor of Liquid Church, named one of America's 100 Fastest Growing Churches by *Outreach* magazine (2018). Tim started Liquid "on accident" with a dozen twentysomething friends meeting in the basement of a 150-year-old church. Since launching in 2007, Liquid has experienced rapid growth and thousands of changed lives. The innovative church has grown to seven locations across New Jersey, with five thousand people in Sunday attendance and more than 2,400 baptisms to date. The vision of Liquid is to saturate the state with the gospel of Jesus Christ and reach the next generation for Jesus.

A dynamic communicator, Tim is a sought-after conference speaker known for connecting God's Word to modern life with humor, heart, and creativity. He leads the Northeast Pastors Coaching Network to equip and coach pastors, ministry leaders, church planters, replanters, and churches of every shape and size. He is also the author of *You Married the Wrong Person: The Relationship Secret Every Couple Needs to Know.*

Liquid's innovative approaches to outreach have been spotlighted on CNN, FOX News, the *New York Times*, and *The Today Show.* Tim is a graduate of Wheaton College (Illinois). He and his wife, Colleen, raise their two children just outside of New York City.

Follow him on Instagram and @pastortimlucas.

Warren Bird, an award-winning writer and researcher, is vice president for research and equipping at the Evangelical Council for

Financial Accountability *(ECFA.org)*. His background includes pastoring, seminary teaching, and a thirteen-year run as research director at Leadership Network.

Warren has authored or coauthored thirty books, including *Hero Maker* (Dave Ferguson as lead author), *How to Break Growth Barriers* (Carl George as lead author), and *Unleashing the Word* (Max McLean as lead author).

Warren is a graduate of Wheaton College (BA, MA), Alliance Theological Seminary (MDiv), and Fordham University (PhD). He and his college-sweetheart wife, Michelle, live in metro New York City.

Follow him on Twitter @warrenbird and at Linkedin.com/in/wbkd.

FREE RESOURCES FROM
Liquid Church

We warmly invite you to use and share any resources you find at the church website, LiquidChurch.com, or on the Liquid Church mobile app for your smartphone. On both you'll find everything from a decade's worth of teaching videos to the latest outreach ideas that we are exploring. All are free.

Please visit LiquidChurch.com/books to access additional resources for this book, including:

- Chapter-by-chapter videos to amplify your understanding of each ministry current with real-life examples.
- Small-group discussion guides.
- Downloadable PDFs to help pastors and ministry leaders who want to communicate these ideas to their congregation, inspire leaders, or train staff.
- Link to Liquid Church's latest annual report.
- Other bonus material relevant to the book.

Exploring the idea of a merger? Visit LiquidChurch.com/HelpForChurches to view a sixteen-minute documentary of our church revitalization story.

Interested in visiting Liquid Church? We welcome visits from pastors, church planters, ministry leaders, and volunteer teams who'd like a "backstage tour" to learn more. Just email backstage@liquidchurch.com to request a visit.

Interested in ministry coaching? Liquid Church hosts the Northeast Pastors Coaching Network, a year-long monthly mentoring process led by Pastor Tim Lucas and the Liquid team. The Coaching Network equips lead/senior pastors, ministry leaders, church planters, and replanters to reach the next generation for Christ. Visit LiquidChurch.com/Coaching to learn more.

For any reprint or foreign translation permissions, see the front of this book for contact information for Zondervan.